Low Income Youth in Urban Areas

A CRITICAL REVIEW OF THE LITERATURE

Bernard Goldstein

Low Income Youth in Urban Areas

A Critical Review of the Literature

Bernard Goldstein
Rutgers, The State University

with the assistance of

Barbara Steinberg and Harry C. Bredemeier

HOLT, RINEHART AND WINSTON, INC.

New York   Chicago   San Francisco   Atlanta   Dallas
Montreal   Toronto   London

To Louis Wirth
Who Cared

Copyright © 1967 by Holt, Rinehart and Winston, Inc.
All rights reserved
Library of Congress Catalog Card Number: 67-11814
2627503
Printed in the United States of America
2 3 4 5 6 7 8 9

Preface

A number of influences have converged to focus more attention on the urban poor in the 1960s than at any time since the 1930s. The Civil Rights movement, with its demands for political, economic, and social equality have led legislators, educators, and social scientists to puzzle over the interrelationships of jobs to education, education to housing, housing to jobs. Concern with the relatively high rate of unemployment among young urban Negroes leads inevitably to the same tangle of factors. Chagrin at the high rate of rejection of young people from low-income families by the Selective Service leads to the question of education and its relation to family status, attitudes, and values. The very affluence of American society in the 1960s serves to call attention to those who have seemed destined to remain in the backwaters rather than to move into the mainstream of American life.

Not all poverty is urban. But the inner sectors of the larger, older cities populated to an increasing extent by Negroes (and Puerto Ricans) have come to be defined as significant incubation points for the ills associated with poverty. And education is seen as the major stumbling block to, as well as the major vehicle for, integrating into American life those groups stigmatized by being poor.

Whatever the source of interest in the poor, and whatever form it takes, differences immediately become apparent in discussions of the causes of and the solutions for poverty. Is unemployment basically a result of inadequate demands for goods and services, or the lack of appropriate skills in a segment of the labor force? Do people lack skills because they are not motivated to learn, or because no one has been willing to develop teaching methods and materials to meet their particular needs? Do people appear to lack motivation because they are alienated, or because they have internalized a set of values in which material gain is not salient? If there is a "lower class culture" or a "culture of poverty" that serves to isolate a segment of the society from the broader culture, should we respect that culture in the name of pluralism, or seek to change it in the name of the greater social welfare? If we wish to change the culture, should we develop strategies for changing people, or for changing the institutions that shape people? If people with low levels of skill

iii

have poor self-images that inhibit self-employment, is it more effective to raise skills as a means of improving the self-image, or improve the self-image as a means of creating the confidence with which to acquire greater skills?

The raising of such questions has produced a great range of answers, all too often based on a minimum of evidence. The growing interest of social scientists and others in the poor has pointed up serious theoretical and substantive problems. Such terms as "working class," "lower class," and "the poor," which served well enough when the social system as a whole was the unit of analysis, prove ambiguous when attention is turned to the supposed referents of these categories. "Lower class" behavior and values lose their concreteness when one attempts to untangle the influence of class from the influences of race, religion, and ethnicity. Terms such as "culturally disadvantaged" or "educationally deprived" seem less apt and scientifically neutral when the poor are present and refuse to have such designations thrust upon them.

These problems became apparent as we searched the literature for what was known about urban youth, with particular reference to those who are loosely defined as "lower class" or "poor." We discovered that no one had done for "our" poor what Oscar Lewis had done for those of Mexico.[1] Nor had anyone done for the Northern, urban Negro of the postwar era what Drake and Cayton had done for those of like life chances almost a generation ago.[2] Community studies have tended either to exclude Negroes from consideration or to focus on power and decision making, areas of community life in which the urban poor are conspicuously underrepresented. As a consequence, it became necessary to piece together research conducted for various purposes under various frames of reference, utilizing a multiplicity of methods, in an effort to determine what we know for certain, what we think we know, and what we do not know about youth from low-income families in urban areas.

This review of the literature is presented in the faith that knowledge can lead to more effective programs, strategies, and tactics. It is hoped that it will prove useful to a variety of audiences. The Economic Opportunity Act of 1964 has set the stage for the development of programs to alleviate or eliminate poverty in hundreds of communities. An awareness of the data concerning life styles of urban youth from low-income families should provide useful guidelines to policy makers, program directors, and project personnel. The increasing availability of federal funds for improvement of on-going programs and for experimentation with new ones in both vocational and general education provides the opportunity for significant developments in this basic area. The material presented here is pertinent, both as a contribution to the education of teachers, and as a source from which educators may broaden their grasp of the totality of the life of this population. Finally, by pointing up areas in which data are lacking or inadequate, the review may help to focus the

[1] Oscar Lewis, *Five Families: Mexican Case Studies in the Culture of Poverty.* New York: Basic Books Inc., 1959; *The Children of Sanchez.* New York: Random House, Inc., 1961.

[2] St. Clair Drake and Horace R. Cayton, *Black Metropolis: A Study of Negro Life in a Northern City.* New York: Harper & Row, Publishers, 1962.

attention of researchers on some problems worthy of immediate investigation.

The organization of the material is relatively simple. In the first four chapters of Part One, we have followed a roughly chronological order, discussing urban low-income youth first in the context of the family into which they are born, then in relation to their education, next in terms of their transition to the world of work, and, finally, in the process of the formation of their own families. The last three chapters are relatively independent, dealing with religion, government and the law, and leisure-time activities. Part Two, Appendix, contains the annotated references of the sources used in the above-mentioned chapters.

Any review of the literature involves decisions concerning the boundaries of what is to be included, and inevitably not all of the decisions are consciously made. This review grew out of a search of the social-science literature for data about urban youth, data drawn from research utilizing class and race or ethnicity as significant variables. Since the senior personnel involved all suffer from a sociological bias, it may well be that readers from other disciplines or fields of practice will feel that some part of their literature is not adequately represented. We began by searching through the major abstracting publications and followed leads to published and unpublished materials as best we could. Literature published before 1950, or dealing primarily with adults, was included only when it seemed particularly relevant. Speculative pieces or general commentaries not directly based on research were included on similar pragmatic grounds. On the other hand, no effort was made to peruse the psychoanalytic literature. Finally, given the core of our interest, sometimes arbitrary decisions had to be made about how far to trace psychological, economic, or social factors that might have related in some indirect way to the issue under surveillance.

We think we have here a representative picture of what is known and speculated about the growing-up experiences of lower-class urban youth, with all the ambiguities, contradictions, and gaps in that knowledge. It is our hope that the presentation of that picture will have a sobering effect on ill-conceived approaches to the problems of the poor, as well as a catalytic effect on those concerned with the collection of basic data and the formulation of basic knowledge.

New Brunswick, N.J.   B. G.
May 1967

Acknowledgments

Much of the bibliographic work was done by Mrs. Barbara Steinberg and Mrs. Selma Rudnick. Mrs. Steinberg also prepared first drafts of a number of the chapters. The final drafts of Chapter 1, "Family of Orientation," and Chapter 4, "Family of Procreation," were prepared by Professor Harry C. Bredemeier.

All drafts of the manuscript were typed with alacrity, accuracy, and good humor by Mrs. Belle Sicurella.

This book was undertaken as part of a Cooperative Research Project (No. 2071) supported by the Office of Education of the United States Department of Health, Education, and Welfare.

Contents

Preface iii
Acknowledgments vi

PART ONE: CRITICAL REVIEW 1

Chapter 1 Family of Orientation 3
Chapter 2 Education 31
Chapter 3 Work 62
Chapter 4 Family of Procreation 82
Chapter 5 Religion 100
Chapter 6 Government and Law 109
Chapter 7 Leisure-Time Activities 120

PART TWO: APPENDIX 133

Introduction 135
Annotated References for Chapter 1 136
Annotated References for Chapter 2 160
Annotated References for Chapter 3 211
Annotated References for Chapter 4 231
Annotated References for Chapter 5 242
Annotated References for Chapter 6 250
Annotated References for Chapter 7 263

INDEXES 273

Part One

CRITICAL REVIEW

Chapter One

FAMILY OF ORIENTATION

Although it is the intent of the authors to report primarily on the state of descriptive knowledge of lower-class life, an interesting anomaly appears when one approaches the lower-class child's family of orientation. There is a notable absence from the research literature of descriptions of their families from the *children's* point of view, which is the point of view that would be consistent with the rest of this book. That is to say, what knowledge there is—and we shall see below how adequate that is—is not knowledge about the experiences of lower-class children in their families. It is, rather, knowledge about how lower-class parents treat their children, often interpreted by the researcher in terms of its theoretical impact on the child, but not described as the child experiences it.

For this reason, much of the material in the present chapter might, with at least equal appropriateness, have been taken up in the context of the lower-class family of procreation. We have chosen to slice reality in the present way, however, in order to highlight what is known and can be inferred about the quality of growing experiences in the lower class, even though that process from the child's point of view needs still to be reported. In the chapter on the family of procreation (Chap. 4), we shall stop short at the point of child-rearing practices, preferring to discuss them here on the ground that their primary impact is, after all, on the children.

It is in their families of orientation that, obviously enough but crucially, low-income children, like all others, receive their initial orientation to the world. More accurately, it is their families of orientation that determine which orientations children will develop, either by providing those orientations directly, or by not doing so, and thus allowing nonfamilial agencies to determine them.

In order to assess the state of our knowledge in this respect, it is necessary to do two things before considering what is known and not known about the actual structure and operation of working-class families. The first is to determine what it is *relevant* to know—that is, to determine just what children are dependent on their families for, during their developmental periods. The second is to determine what difference it makes for the outcome of those dependencies whether the family of orientation is structured, or operates, in one way or another. Only then is it useful to survey the actual descriptions of working-class families that may be found in the literature.

For the first requirement—that of deciding what it is relevant to know —we will adopt the frameworks of Erik Erikson,[1] Talcott Parsons,[2] and J. McV. Hunt,[3] who have developed in systematic form models of the socialization process, in terms of which we can attempt to picture the socialization experiences of working-class children. We shall first present those models in synoptic form; and then consider for each stage of development (1) the environmental conditions theoretically considered crucial for successful passage through that stage, and (2) the research literature shedding light on the degree to which lower-class children are likely to have those conditions provided to them by their families of orientation. We shall not, however, attempt to report on the research literature dealing with the relationship between child-rearing practices and children's reactions, regardless of class, this having been done as well as it can be by Hoffman and Hoffman.[4]

Stages of Development
and Their Critical Requirements

Hunt's emphasis is primarily on cognitive development, while Parsons' and Erikson's emphases are on more general psychoemotional development.

Erikson[5] distinguishes five major stages of development through adolescence: infancy (the first year), early childhood (the second and third years), "play age" (fourth and fifth years), "school age" (sixth through twelfth years), and "adolescence" (presumably, thirteenth through perhaps the eighteenth years).

Hunt deals with finer distinctions in the early years, distinguishing between (1) the first four and a half or five months, (2) the second four and a half or five months, (3) the period between nine months and eighteen months, (4) the period from age one and a half to age four, (5) that

[1] Erik H. Erikson, "Identity and the Life Cycle," in George S. Klein, ed., *Psychological Issues*. New York: International University Press, Inc., 1959.

[2] Talcott Parsons and Robert Bales, *Family, Socialization and Interaction Process*. New York: The Free Press of Glencoe, 1955.

[3] J. McV. Hunt, *Intelligence and Experience*. New York: The Ronald Press Co., 1961.

[4] Martin L. Hoffman and Lois W. Hoffman, eds., *Review of Child Development Research*. New York: Russell Sage Foundation, 1964.

[5] Unless otherwise noted, all references to Erikson, Parsons, and Hunt are to the three works cited above.

from age four to age seven or eight, (6) that from age seven or eight to eleven or twelve, (7) adolescence.

Parsons, in his turn, distinguishes five major stages, without specifying the ages associated with each: the familiar oral, anal, Oedipal, latency, and adolescent stages.

In view of the uncertainty of and variability in all such delineations of discrete periods, we shall, for present purposes, synthesize the Parsons-Hunt-Erikson distinctions by noting the following stages and substages:

1. Infancy (oral) (first year)
   a. First half year
   b. Second half year
2. Early childhood ("anal")
   a. Third half year
   b. Fourth half year through third year
3. Nursery school and early elementary school (Hunt's fourth through seventh year period) (Parsons' Oedipal and latency periods) (Erikson's "play age")
4. Major elementary-school period—grades three through six; ages eight through eleven (Hunt's sixth stage) (Parsons' latency period) (Erikson's "school age")

As far as cognitive development is concerned, the importance of the child's environment in the early years has been impressively shown by Bloom,[6] who analyzed a series of longitudinal studies of individual development in an effort to discover patterns of growth. Concerning intelligence, he concluded that

> . . . in terms of intelligence measured at age 17, at least 20% is developed by age one, 50% by about age 4; 80% by about age 8; and 92% by age 13. . . . We would expect variations in environment to have relatively little effect on the I.Q. after age 8, but we would expect such variations to have marked effect on the I.Q. before that age, with the greatest effect likely to take place between the ages of about 1 to 5. [p. 68]

What it is about the environments that affect children's development we shall now consider, as well as the evidence that exists concerning class differences in environments in the important respects.

Infancy

Nearly all writers seem to agree on the importance during this period of a warmly supportive environment. Erikson labels this the critical point at which the basic character trait of "trust *vs.* mistrust" is acquired. It is

---

[6] Benjamin Bloom, *Stability and Change in Human Characteristics.* New York: John Wiley & Sons, Inc., 1964.

a "receptive" period or an "incorporative" period, in which, if all goes well, a basic sense of trust is developed that undergirds the child through the rest of his life.

Erikson is by no means a simple-minded determinist here. In fact, he cautions (about all stages, not only this one), "what the child acquires . . . is a certain *ratio* between the positive and negative which, if the balance is toward the positive will help him to meet later crises with a better *chance* for unimpaired total development." [p. 61]

Like Hunt, Erikson also distinguishes between two substages of this stage—a "passive" and an "active" incorporative stage. During the first of these, the infant is receptive to whatever stimuli happen to come his way— taste, touch, sound, sight. During the second, he actively reaches out— bites, listens, looks, reaches.

This distinction is quite close to Hunt's, who writes that

> . . . during the first 4½ or 5 months of a child's life, what appears to be critical [for his *cognitive* development] is *variation* in stimulation for the various receptor modalities. . . . During the second 4½ to 5 months . . . it would appear to be critical for the child to have available a *variety* of relatively *familiar* situations which he can recognize, in which he has developed an interest, and on which he can act in a fashion that either prolongs or reproduces that phenomena that would interest him. [p. 274]

Hunt speculates, in this connection, that herein lies the *cognitive* significance of a one-to-one relationship with an attention-paying mother; but he goes on to wonder whether by the same token, several *different* (but constant) mother figures may not even further widen the child's "range of curious interest in human behaviors." [p. 274]

In short, Erikson says that the child's identity at this stage amounts to the formula "I am what I am given"; and Hunt says that the fundamental units of the child's intelligence are determined by the variety of familiar stimuli he is given. To be in a family that generously, and variously, *gives to* the infant would seem, then, to be critical for this period.

Parsons' analysis supports this, but he adds the further suggestion that at this stage a certain "demand" on the part of the supportive mother is also important—the "demand" that the infant respond to her—reciprocate her smiles and caresses. Parsons' suggestion makes it possible, then, to add to Erikson's hypothesis that "under-support" will lead to a basic sense of mistrust, the further possibility that there may be such a thing as "over-support," in the sense of giving too much in perhaps too "indifferent" or "offhand" a way, without engaging the infant in a transaction that causes him to play a role in return.

On the emotional side, then, we might tentatively hypothesize that an "optimum" amount of support from his environment produces the sense of trust of which Erikson speaks; that a "deficit" of support produces Erikson's mistrust; but that a "surfeit" produces "dependency." On the cognitive side (and still more speculatively) we might hazard that an optimum amount of variety of stimulation produces the curiosity appetite of which Hunt speaks; that a deficit produces lethargy and boredom; and that a surfeit produces a defensive closing in, or a tendency to tune out the outside world.

Turning to the research literature, one finds that there are no systematic descriptions, let alone measurements, of varying family practices as they affect the individual during this presumably important stage of development.

What exists, to begin with, is Bronfenbrenner's[7] masterful survey and reanalysis of fifteen studies of child-rearing practices conducted in various parts of the country between 1932 and 1957. For that period, we shall rely entirely on his report.

As reported by Bronfenbrenner, a major focus of the studies during the period of infancy was on feeding, weaning, and toilet-training practices. The major conclusion is that middle-class mothers rather faithfully follow the changing fashions in child-care recommendations by "experts." During the period before World War II, these seemed to emphasize what Parsons would call "denial of reciprocity" and the firm input of "demands" on the infant. As Bronfenbrenner quotes Wolfenstein,[8]

> Weaning and introduction of solid foods are to be accomplished with great firmness, never yielding for a moment to the baby's resistance. . . . bowel training . . . must be carried out with great determination as early as possible. . . . The main danger which the baby presented at this time was that of dominating the parents. [pp. 409–410]

Consistent with such advice, earlier studies showed that middle-class mothers in fact were less likely to offer the breast at all, were more likely to offer it on a fixed schedule when they did offer it, were more likely to wean the infant early, and were likely to begin and complete bowel and bladder training at earlier ages than lower-class mothers.

After World War II, however, the advice from experts changed:

> The child became remarkably harmless. . . . When not engaged in exploratory undertakings, the baby needs care and attention; and giving these when he demands them, far from making him a tyrant,

[7] Urie Bronfenbrenner, "Socialization and Social Class Through Time and Space," in E. E. Maccoby, T. M. Newcomb, and E. L. Hartley, eds., *Readings in Social Psychology,* third ed. New York: Holt, Rinehart and Winston, Inc., 1958, pp. 400–425.

[8] Martha Wolfenstein, "Trends in Infant Care," *American Journal of Orthopsychiatry:* 23 (January 1953), 120–130.

will make him less demanding later on. . . . mildness is advocated in all areas; thumbsucking and masturbation are not to be interfered with; weaning and toilet training are to be accomplished later and more gently. [p. 410]

And, sure enough, the later studies reviewed by Bronfenbrenner show that middle-class mothers were *more* likely to be supportive and permissive in the feeding and training respects enumerated above than lower-class mothers. About 1950, however, the expert advice swung again toward some misgivings about all-out "permissiveness"; and the studies made after that period suggest a tendency for middle-class mothers to be less "relaxed" than formerly, although still a little more so than lower-class mothers. Boek, Sussman, and Yankauer (1958) found only a slightly greater tendency for Class I and Class II mothers to be breast-feeding their three-to-six-month-old infants, and found also that the higher the class level the shorter the length of time breast-feeding was continued.

It needs to be emphasized, however, that what we know from these studies are facts about breast-feeding, and the ages of weaning and toilet training. These facts suggest that, during the fifties, lower-class children were less likely than middle-class children to have the kinds of experiences theoretically supposed to generate a sense of trust in the responsiveness and generosity of the world. But we do not know anything about the general tone or atmosphere or quality of mother-child relationships, factors that might well be more indicative of "support" than the sheer frequency or timing of feeding. That is, what kind of affectional interaction goes on *during* feeding, bathing, coddling, holding, diaper changing, and so on?

Moreover, of course, we know nothing about the nature of the stimuli and their variety, familiarity, and controllability suggested by Hunt as critical for cognitive development.

One isolated bit of information about this age period that may contain a clue to future behavior has been reported by Williams and Scott (1953). They studied the families of 104 four-to-eighteen-month-old Negro babies, half of them middle class and half, working class. They found that the working-class mothers were significantly more "permissive" (breast-fed longer, used flexible feeding and sleeping schedules, minimized discipline, and placed fewer restrictions on movements); and such practices tended to produce babies who performed better on standardized motor tasks.

Early Childhood

The second and third years of the child's life are a period of active exploration and tests of his own will and autonomy. Erikson epitomizes the period by suggesting that here the child's identity is given by the formula

"I am what I will." The *literal* "anal" crisis, notes Erikson, is but a dramatic example of a more general and pervasive "crisis" of the child's learning to what extent he is his own boss and can consequently tenaciously "hold on" and forcefully "let go" (of toys, people, clothes, and the like, as well as feces) as he chooses; and to what extent *he* is the helpless slave of more powerful others.

What Parsons calls "denial of reciprocity" (that is, refusal by the socializing agent to accept the socializee's definition of the situation) would seem to be the crucial input from the child's family at this stage, as well as the "demands" made on the child. An optimum amount of "denial" or "demands," the theory goes, results in what Erikson calls a "sense of autonomy," which to him is the lasting product of a successful negotiation of this second stage. An excessive amount, however, may lead to Erikson's alternative outcome, a sense of "shame and doubt" as to the rightness of one's own wishes and desires. And, it might be added in a continuation of that logic, an insufficient amount of denial, or of requirements to make progress, might be expected to lead to a lasting[9] kind of willfulness or self-centeredness.

(Erikson mentions both of these outcomes, but sees both as alternative outcomes of the *one* "socialization error" of *too much* restriction. [p. 68])

Hunt focuses on the intellectual significance of the opportunities provided or not provided for the child during the earlier part of this age (nine to eighteen months) to exercise autonomy. In his words, during this period,

> . . . as means become separated from ends and as the child begins to explore various means to achieve his ends, it is probably critical for the child to have an opportunity to try out his new-found motor skills and to observe the effects of his variations in effort. [He needs, for example] . . . an opportunity to throw things and watch their trajectory, an opportunity for manipulative practice play with a wide variety of materials, and an opportunity to climb and walk freely. It is through such manipulations and motor activities that the child apparently develops the beginnings of his conceptions of space, time, and causality. [p. 275]

During the later part of this early childhood period, the child "is diverting a major share of his time to playful imitation, [and therefore] having a variety of models to imitate which supply the basis for later intellectual skills would appear to be important." [p. 275] The "models" Hunt has in mind here are older persons who talk with and to the child, ask and answer questions, count things for him, manipulate things and show him how to do

---

[9] Like Erikson, we use such terms as "lasting" and "permanent" in these paragraphs in only a relative sense—with the phrase "if nothing happens later on to compensate for the deficit or surfeit," always to be understood.

so, correct his mistakes, and who, withal, communicate enthusiasm for all those intellectual activities.

In comparing the functionality for child development of different family systems, then, what we need to look for at this stage are the structures and processes that either do or do not in various degrees permit and encourage the two-to-four year old to assert himself, to explore at will, to talk with older people, to manipulate his material environment, and to receive corrective feedback to his many errors.

Here, as Bronfenbrenner remarks, a severe difficulty emerges in the effort to interpret the research literature, a difficulty that plagues the analysis of differential experiences at all later age periods also. It is that different researchers interviewed mothers of children of different ages; and it is often not clear at what age of the child any reported practice was followed. We cannot, then, be sure that the class differences reported in relevant behavior areas are characteristic of the particular age we are concerned with. We report them in the context of their *theoretical* relevance in order to highlight the areas in which more refined research is needed.

According to Bronfenbrenner's analysis, lower-class mothers are significantly more likely than middle-class mothers to thwart their children's exploratory and self-assertive actions. They are, specifically, more likely to inhibit children's sexual explorations, and less likely to tolerate displays of aggression either toward siblings or toward parents. They are also less likely to tolerate behaviors such as thumb sucking, or eating with fingers.

But about the other dimensions of experience presumably important at this age, we know virtually nothing—the opportunities to talk with older people, to manipulate the material environment, to receive corrective feedback, and so on.

What further indications we have are consistent with the general impression that the families of lower-class children provide considerably less opportunity for the development of a "sense of autonomy." Rainwater, Coleman, and Handel (1959), for example, describe the working-class mother as perceiving her child as a "source of pleasure," with which she is very involved, but as not perceiving him as an individual. The middle-class mother, on the other hand, is less involved in her children, but does see them as separate, complex persons.

Deutsch's (1963) data indicate a similar paucity of opportunities for cognitive development. He reports a "poverty of perceptual experience" in the lower-class child's home that slows his rate of maturation. He writes,

> In order for a child to handle multiple attributes of words and to associate words with their proper referents, a great deal of exposure to language is presupposed. Such exposure involves training, experimenting with identifying objects and having corrective feedback, listening

to a variety of verbal material, and just observing adult language usage. Exposure of children to this type of experience is one of the great strengths of the middle class home, and concomitantly represents a weakness in the lower class home. [pp. 173–174]

However, Pavenstedt (1965) reports a comparative study of upper- and "very low lower" class families that more vividly than most studies suggests some important differences between the two. She found that the upper lower-class mothers (all native-born but chiefly of Italian, Greek, and Syrian background, with only a few Negroes) "talked to their children from an early age. In fact, they projected adult comprehension and responses onto the infants, sometimes even the newborn. . . . all the children [of thirty families] were feeding themselves by the time they were two and dressing themselves before they were three." [p. 5]

She also reports that "the concept that children needed to be trained, to be taught to obey and conform was universal; fear of delinquent behavior was widespread." [p. 6] These parents, too, administered "spankings . . . at a surprisingly early age." [ibid.]

By contrast, in the "very low lower" families,

> The outstanding characteristic . . . was that activities were impulse-determined; consistency was totally absent. The mother might stay in bed until noon while the children were kept in bed as well or ran around unsupervised. Another time she might decide to get them up and give them breakfast at 6, have them washed and dressed and the apartment picked up by 8:30. Or the children might get their breakfast from the neighbors. . . . These mothers always dressed their children . . . None of the children owned anything; a recent gift might be taken away by another sibling without anyone's intervening. The parents often failed to discriminate between the children: A parent, incensed by the behavior of one child, was seen dealing a blow to another child who was close by. Communications by words hardly existed . . . [p. 94]

Along the same lines Wortis and others (1963), who studied 250 lower-class Negro women with two-and-one-half-year-old children, and re-studied forty-seven of them when the children were five, draws a picture of extremely disorganized homes, with "permissiveness" to such a degree that it was closer to indifference. They conclude,

> The inadequate incomes, crowded homes, lack of consistent familial ties, the mother's depression and helplessness in her own situation, were as important as her child-rearing practices in influencing the child's development and preparing him for an adult role. It was for us a sobering experience to watch a large group of newborn infants, plastic human beings of unknown potential, and observe over a five-

year period their social preparation to enter the class of the least-skilled, least-educated, and most-rejected in our society. [p. 307]

White's (1957) study of seventy-four mothers and their two-and-one-half- to five-and-one-half-year-old children is relevant here also. Thirty-six of the families were middle class; thirty-eight, working class; the latter, however, had distinctively higher status than some of the lower-class families described in other reports discussed in this chapter. (Most of the mothers had at least some secondary education; a little less than half of the fathers had had some college; and the cut-off point of income was "under $5,000.") This may be related to the fact that White found few differences in child-rearing practices—virtually none with respect to "oral behavior and feeding regimen," age of bowel training (although working-class mothers were inclined to be more severe), demonstrativeness, or of "fighting back" behavior. There were significant differences in the tendencies for middle-class mothers to be willing to drop the subject if the child refused to do what he was told, to respond to the child's crying, and to permit aggressiveness toward the parents. As far as resulting child behavior is concerned, no differences were found in tests of ability to delay gratification, personality ratings, or aggression in doll play. An interesting difference was found, however,

> . . . on the second visit, four months later, when the children were rated on their change in psychological health. . . . The middle class children were more frequently rated better or same, while the working class children were worse or same. The difference was highly significant. [p. 709]

In general, the fact is that we do not have a clear and detailed picture of life for two and three year olds in any of the social classes. We do have the general impressions of several writers and the reports of others about the child centeredness of contemporary middle-class families, and about middle-class sensitivity to psychological "rules" of child rearing. Contrasting these aspects with both the harassing crowdedness and alleged authoritarianism of working-class and lower-class homes, we emerge with a vague hunch that the conditions necessary for a sense of autonomy are rather more likely to be found in middle-class than in working-class families. Moreover, the existing literature permits us to imagine that the opportunities for lower-class two and three year olds to "throw things and watch their trajectory," to manipulate a wide variety of toys and objects, and to get "corrective feedback" from their talking are, relatively, small. But hunch and imagination are about all we have.

The Age of Nursery School, Kindergarten, and First and Second Grades

Hunt calls this the "intuitive phase" of the "sensori-motor stage" and observes that here the child is "continually in the process of bringing his intuitions in correspondence with reality." Here

> . . . having ample opportunity for corrective discussions would appear to be crucial. If this be true, children reared in families where parents take the pains to understand the child's questions, to explain the reasons for actions, and to discuss with him the nature of things should show more rapid rate of intellectual development than children whose parents ask for unquestionable obedience and for children to be only seen and not heard. [p. 279]

Erikson, as we have noted, divides the developmental periods somewhat differently at this and the next stage, which makes direct comparison and analysis slightly awkward. His third stage (the "play age") includes only the fourth and fifth years of the child's life (what we have loosely called the age of nursery school and kindergarten); and his fourth stage ("school age") includes the last two of the years (the sixth and seventh) that we are including in the stage now being discussed.

The fourth and fifth years of life, says Erikson, are those in which the "identification formula" is "I am what I imagine I will be." It is also, in another formulation, the age of the "intrusive mode," in which the child intrudes himself into space by walking (now in an assured manner) and into other people by physical attack, by aggressive talk, by a consuming curiosity, and by sexual fascination. In still another formulation it is the time of "making," in the sense of "being on the make," enjoying competition, insisting on goal attainment, deriving pleasure from conquest.

It is also the time of the Oedipal crisis and of crucial sex-role identification. Whereas in the former stage, the chief drive was to keep out younger siblings (for example) from his affairs, and a frequent emotion was jealousy, now the desire is to *displace* people who are already there; and a frequent emotion is rivalry, or "anticipatory rivalry."

It is, in short, a time of testing the limits of *"initiative";* and the danger (for boys—as usual in these discussions, there is less explicit attention paid to the fate of girls), according to Erikson, is that the inevitable failure in the rivalry with a father will, if made too crushing or humiliating, result not in a "lasting" sense of the propriety and possibility of initiative, but to a pervasive sense of guilt. Put otherwise, at this stage a *conscience* is developed—"that great governor of initiative" [p. 80]; and it may become *over*established, resulting in deep feelings of the lack of a right to exercise initiative, to assert one's self, or to the feeling that one's spontaneous desires must not be expressed.

In the vein of the logical speculation begun above, we may hazard the thought that an "optimum" amount of permission to assert the self at this stage results in Erikson's "initiative"; that a deficit (or a surfeit of "denial") results in "guilt" and self-suppression; and that a deficit of denial results in a conscienceless amorality, at the extreme "psychopathy."

In short, assuming that by age four the child has learned the world can be trusted to give him what he needs because he "matters" to it, assuming he has learned there are satisfactory boundaries around what is him and his that are respected by outsiders, assuming he has developed "cell assemblies" [Hunt, p. 85] or "schemata" [Hunt, p. 112] in his brain representing a variety of sensory experiences and manipulative actions—assuming all this, he is now ready to explore the world and his relations to it more aggressively. He is now about to discover the limits of his own initiative, the "reasons" the world is the way it is, and the kind of person he is supposed to become.[10]

During the child's fourth and fifth years, then, he needs for both his cognitive and his psychic-emotional development a family of orientation that encourages his expressions of initiative without allowing his delusions of grandeur to get out of hand, and that responds sympathetically but correctively to his physical, manual, and verbal explorations. He also needs appealing and "copyable" models of sex-role identification.

On the cognitive side, there are two studies that bear on the consequences of different family environments and on the class relationship of differing environments. One is that of Hess, Shipman, and Jackson (1965) who studied 163 Negro mothers and their four-year-old children in an effort to discover how the teaching styles of the mother shape the learning styles and the information-processing strategies of their children. The investigators first taught the forty upper-middle class, forty-two upper-lower class, forty lower-lower class, and forty-one welfare mothers certain tasks; and then had the mothers teach their children. The tasks consisted of sorting and classifying objects in various ways, and in carrying out a joint cooperative task with the children.

Detailed analyses were then made of the mothers' verbal and nonverbal behaviors in teaching and working with their children; and of the children's degree of success in learning the tasks. Not many differences were found among the three lower classes; but sharp differences were found be-

---

[10] Assuming he does *not* enter this stage with those happy residues from past stages, he is still about to make those discoveries—but, unless his environment now compensates for its past deficits, what he "discovers" is not likely to be functional for him.

tween the middle-class mothers (and their children's success) on the one hand, and the lower-class mothers and children on the other.

The middle-class mothers were found to use many more words in talking to their children, to use longer and more complex sentences, and to use more abstract words. In addition, as the authors write in their conclusion, lower-class mothers were significantly more likely to provide

> . . . a cognitive environment in which behavior is controlled by status rules rather than by attention to the individual characteristics of a specific situation, and one in which behavior is . . . [impulsive rather than] mediated by verbal cues or by teaching that relates events to one another and the present to the future.

In short, they conclude, "the meaning of deprivation is a deprivation of meaning." [p. 886]

Another relevant study is one conducted by Wolf (1964). Wolf's subjects were fifth graders and their mothers, but since the variables he investigated are presumably variables that characterize family environments over long periods, we report the study here because of its direct relevance to the issues we are discussing. Wolf selected sixty fifth graders on a stratified random basis (seventeen with fathers from "high" occupational levels, twenty from "middle," and twenty-three from "low"), from over a thousand fifth graders in a school system near Chicago. He took their IQ scores from school records, and interviewed their mothers in order to derive ratings of the familial "press for achievement motivation," "press for language development," and "provision for general learning."

He discovered high positive correlations between various combinations of the environmental measures and IQ scores; but only very low correlations between class level and IQ. Wolf noted that "lower lower" class children were distinctly underrepresented in his sample; but it is still worth noting that he also found no relationship between class and his measures of environmental processes.

Evidence from other studies is somewhat more consistent with the Hess, Shipman, and Jackson (1965) findings concerning class differences in the tendency for parents to communicate extensively with their children. The lower-class child seems more likely than the middle-class child to find his parents "closed," "inaccessible to . . . [his] communication," and likely to explode in anger at his efforts to "intrude." (Maas, 1951) Presumably, all of the suggestions discussed in the preceding section regarding the authoritarianism and obedience demands of the working and lower classes operate to inhibit further the children of those classes at this stage.

In addition, there is evidence that working-class mothers are "much more severe" in sex training and "modesty" training than middle-class mothers, less tolerant of aggression toward the parents, more likely to use physical punishment and ego-damaging ridicule to control the child, less likely to use reason and praise as positive controlling devices. [Bronfenbrenner, p. 413]

McKinley (1964) provides data along the same lines. He had approximately 260 adolescent boys (eleventh and twelfth grades) complete questionnaires, interviewed sixteen fathers of thirteen- through nineteen-year-old boys, and reanalyzed interviews with 360 mothers of kindergarten-aged children. On the basis of these data he reports tendencies for lower-class parents to be more likely than middle-class parents to use "relatively severe" techniques of discipline and to use physical sanctions; and for fathers to evidence more hostility toward their sons. (The data [p. 148] also suggest, however, that hostility toward sons and tendencies to use severe discipline vary at least as much with the fathers' satisfaction with their work as with the social classes.)

Peil (1963), in a study of Negro and white mothers of first graders in three Catholic schools in Chicago, found that Negro mothers were both more ambitious for their children's success in school and more punitive in disciplining their children. Peil states that the white parents were from the lowest income area in the near-southwest side of Chicago, which was still all white, and that the Negro parents lived in a "roughly comparable" area; but the facts that the Negro parents were sending their children to parochial schools and that 63 percent of all the mothers had completed high school make it uncertain just what social class is represented here.

Nor are the child's efforts to exercise initiative so likely, at least in the very lower class, to be guided into productive channels.

> Another area in which the lower-class child lacks pre-school orientation is the well-inculcated expectation of reward for performance, especially for successful task performance. The lack of such expectations, of course, reduces motivation for beginning a task and, therefore, also makes less likely the self-reinforcement of activity through the gaining of feelings of competence. In . . . impoverished broken homes there is very little of the type of interaction seen so commonly in middle-class homes, in which the parent sets a task for the child, observes its performance, and in some way rewards its completion. Neither, for most tasks, is there the disapproval which the middle-class child incurs when he does not perform properly or when he leaves something unfinished. [Deutsch (1963), p. 172]

Pavenstedt's (1965) comparative study referred to above, is illuminating here also. Speaking of her stable working-class families, she writes, "as their children came of school age, parents showed more concern that they conform to the teacher's expectations than about learning per se." About the disorganized families, she reports, "We have seen children dashing into the apartment crying from some injury, run past mother to their bed and continue to scream there. The mothers seldom inquired about their injuries or attempted to comfort them—ridicule was as likely to be the response." [p. 11]

With respect to sex-role identification and the "Oedipal crisis" at this stage, there is little direct evidence. Miller[11] gives an interesting account of lower-class boys of five and six playing "the dozens," ("playing house") a practice consisting of two male antagonists making derogatory remarks about one another's mothers. [For example: *One Boy:* "I hear you b – – – your mother last night." *Other Boy: "Your* mother's a Greyhound Bus!" (That is, as Miller explains, "everybody gets on.")]

Miller suggests that the ubiquity of this game in lower-class areas is related to the absence of "stern and concerned" fathers in many households, and to the fact that there tends to be a strong emotional bond between mothers and sons. This latter tendency is supported by McKinley (1964), who reports a greater tendency for lower-class boys than for middle- or upper-class boys to say that they get more of their emotional support from their mothers than from their fathers. [p. 109] Miller speaks of "a tendency for females to equate the roles of 'husband' and 'son,' and in some measure to adopt similar sexual expectations of both" (and, similarly, for males to equate the roles of "wife" and "daughter").

Given a close and sexually tinged bond, then, and given the power of the incest taboo, playing "the dozens" is to be understood, Miller suggests, as providing "a vehicle for open discussion of a topic of widespread private concern, thus to some extent mitigating the aura of deep and secret stigma surrounding this issue. . . . [In addition it provides] the opportunity to engage in collective public fantasies about mother-son intimacy [and thus] could serve as a mechanism for dissipating the force of pressures toward incest."

The theoretically expected sex-role identification problems of some lower-class boys who lack adequate male models has received no research, so far as we can ascertain. Nor does there seem to be any research focused on the comparable development of girls.

As far as the development of "conscience" is concerned, we are no better off. Berelson and Steiner[12] include in their "inventory of scientific findings" the following generalizations on the subject:

[11] Walter B. Miller, *City Gangs,* Chap. 6. To be published in 1967 by John Wiley & Sons, Inc., New York. Quotations here are taken with permission from Miller, from an unpublished manuscript. Pagination is not yet available.
[12] Bernard Berelson and Gary A. Steiner, *Human Behavior: An Inventory of Scientific Findings.* New York: Harcourt, Brace & World, Inc., 1964.

C13. The more the control of the child is love-oriented, rather than based on physical punishment, the more effective is the parents' control over desired behavior and the stronger the development of the child's guilt feelings for improper behavior.

C14. The earlier the socialization, the stronger the guilt feelings.

C15. The less the parental warmth and identification or the more the parental punishment, the slower the development of conscience. [p. 77]

If these are sound generalizations, and if the empirical generalizations discussed above about lower-class authoritarianism and/or indifference are valid, it would seem that lower-class children are more likely to develop either overrepressive or underrepressive consciences than are their middle-class peers.

There is much evidence that this is so, although most of it points, in spite of the alleged punitiveness of lower-class parental discipline, to a tendency for lower-class children to have underdeveloped, rather than overdeveloped, consciences. It may be that the erraticness of discipline prevents its seeming harshness from resulting in a strict superego; and, as we shall see, there is also a lesser tendency for lower-class parents to "absorb" their children's identifications, which would have the same result.

Haller and Thomas (1962) administered a "System Personality Factor Test" to 440 seventeen-year-old males in a culturally homogeneous Michigan county. Although all of the correlations between SES (socioeconomic status) and personality adjustment on various dimensions were low, the authors report that low SES respondents were, to a statistically significant degree, more likely to lack internal standards, will control, and character stability, as compared to high SES boys.

Miller and Swanson[13] similarly found middle-class adolescents to be characterized by the acceptance of responsibility for their own conduct, by a desire for mastery of self by rational means as a prelude to mastering the world, and by the feeling that control and sacrifice are worthy of effort because they are for one's own good. In contrast, the working-class individual, the authors generalize, often holds the world rather than himself responsible for his misfortunes and is consequently more direct in his expression of aggression.

Davis (n.d.) adds that the lower-class child "is allowed to fight when he is angry, and to laugh when he is triumphant. . . . Physical aggression is regarded as normal . . . and he learns to take a blow and to give one." In the same vein, Lipset (1963) asserts, concerning the lower-class person, that "From early childhood he has sought immediate gratifications rather than engage in activities which might have long term rewards" [p. 114];

[13] Daniel R. Miller, Guy E. Swanson, et al., *Inner Conflict and Defense.* New York: Holt, Rinehart and Winston, Inc., 1960.

and LeShan (1952), correlatively, reports that in the lower classes there are quick sequences of tension and relief, while in higher classes there are longer tension-relief sequences.

On the other hand, Straus (1962) found no correlation between SES and scores on a deferred gratification scale, although he cautions that this may be due to the fact that lower-class boys were underrepresented in his sample of 338 junior and senior class boys in four high schools in Wisconsin.

Evidence relevant to the foregoing generalizations of Berelson and Steiner exists in limited form. The necessary ingredient of close identification with parents for superego development seems to be more characteristic of middle-class life than of lower-class. Himmelweit (1955) found that among third-grade boys in London, middle-class children felt more accepted than did lower-class children, felt they could discuss things with their parents, and felt that parents shared their interests. As Arnold Green[14] put it a long time ago, "To the extent that a child's personality has been absorbed [through a learned dependence on his parents' love], . . . a disapproving glance may produce more terror than a twenty-minute lashing. . . . [in a lower-class boy who has only his hide at stake. Such a boy may be more likely to] develop guilt feelings to help prevent himself from getting into further trouble." [p. 39]

Of further relevance to this issue of class differences in youths' development of self-control and superego formation is Rainwater's (1956) study of twenty-five eighth graders of both sexes in lower- and middle-class schools. On the basis of responses to the Szondi test, Rainwater concluded that, in his sample, middle-class adolescents were more dependent on people and more likely to work through people to derive gratification. The lower-class adolescent seemed to have less acceptance of a dependency need, and to be more oriented toward manipulation of objects for purely egocentric satisfactions without regard to the human nature of the objects.

Downing and others (1965) strongly suggest that such a tendency "not to regard" the human nature of objects (if it proves to be a tendency beyond Rainwater's twenty-five cases) does not mean an *unawareness* of human sensitivities. Working with a group of seventh-grade boys and girls, mostly Negro, in a depressed area of New York City, they found on the basis of Rorschach tests that, compared to a group of white upper-middle-class youngsters, these boys and girls were "more responsive to social stimulation and more sensitive to the details of social situations. . . . The teachers reported that they were more interested in people than in abstractions. The teachers felt that these youngsters were keenly sensitive to the feelings, motivations, and thoughts of those around them, especially their parents or guardians, teachers, and classmates." [p. 201]

[14] Arnold W. Green, "The Middle Class Male Child and Neurosis," *American Sociological Review*: 2 (February 1946), 31–41.

Downing and her associates also report, however, observations that confirm those reviewed above concerning the lack of self-control of lower-class youngsters. On the Rosenzweig Picture-Frustration Test,

> Compared with the normative group, the present population is markedly and significantly more Extrapunitive, considerably less Intrapunitive, and somewhat less Impunitive. . . . [W]hen they are frustrated they are more likely to hit out in an aggressive fashion than to blame themselves or to try to explain the situation away. . . . The most striking conclusion one can draw from these results is that the total pattern of the present population more nearly approximates the normative pattern for the 8 year-old group than it does the normative group of 12 to 13 year-olds. [pp. 141–142]

The general tendency for lower-class children's life situation to retard their moral development receives further support from Kohlberg's[15] finding that, although all children seem to pass through the same stages of moral judgment, "middle class children seemed to move faster and farther." [p. 406]

Perhaps the Berelson-Steiner[16] summary description of lower-class child-rearing practices is the best way of describing the state of our knowledge at present including its contradictions:

> . . . lower class infants and children are subject to less parental supervision but more parental authority, to more physical punishment and less use of reasoning as a disciplinary measure, to less control of sexual and other impulses, to more freedom to express aggression (except against the parent) and to engage in violence, to earlier sex-typing of behavior (i.e., to what males and females are supposed to be and do), to less development of conscience, to less stress toward achievement, to less equalitarian treatment vis-à-vis the parents, and to less permissive upbringing than are their middle class contemporaries. [p. 480]

The Later Age of Elementary School

During his sixth and seventh years, the child is, according to Hunt, continuing to bring "his intuition into correspondence with reality" and continuing to need "corrective discussions" and active concern with "the nature of things." For Erikson, however, these are the beginnings of the next stage of psychic emotional development, which lasts throught the twelfth year.

---

[15] Lawrence Kohlberg, "Development of Moral Character and Moral Ideology," in Martin L. Hoffman and Lois W. Hoffman, op. cit., p. 406. This is a review article, in which Kohlberg cites some of his own unpublished research.

[16] See footnote 12.

Beginning at age six, the child's identification formula is "I am what I learn" and his experiences from then through age twelve, says Erikson, determine whether he will develop a "lasting" sense of "industry," or a sense of "inferiority."

> . . . Children at this age *do* like to be mildly but firmly coerced into the adventure of finding out that one can learn to accomplish things which one would never have thought of by oneself, things which owe their attractiveness to the very fact that they are *not* the product of play and fantasy but the product of reality, practicality, and logic; things which thus provide a token sense of participation in the real world of adults. [p. 84]

Erikson's comments on the kinds of things the child needs from his environment during this period are restricted to the kind of *teachers* he needs. Interpolating, however, we suggest that what the child primarily needs from his family of orientation during this period is a consistent and strong reinforcement of the notion that his school learning is important, that his successes are genuinely praiseworthy, and that his obstacles are worth serious consideration.

Although they depart from one another in terms of the exact demarcation of critical ages in this context, Erikson and Hunt converge on the opinion that cognitive development is the crucial kind of development taking place between age six and twelve. Hunt, however, further specifies a critical period between eight and twelve (a "period of concrete operations" in Piaget's notation). During this phase, "opportunities to cope with a variety of objects, gadgets, and materials would appear to be important for intellectual development." [p. 281]

Construction toys, chemistry sets, nature-study trips—such "inputs," Hunt suggests, are important for the development of the intellectual concept of causality; and so are experiences in which the child is required, and helped, by older persons to think through the logical steps of an "explanation."

Given, we conclude, a family of orientation that emphasizes the importance of the child's elementary school performance and that encourages at home his involvement with intellectual mastery, the child will develop a sense of industrious involvement with competence. Given *under*emphasis on such orientations, the child may develop a sense of something like "omnipotence," in the sense of expecting things to come easily and failing to develop the capacity for concentrated effort; or perhaps be driven to find some compensatory way of identifying himself with the "real world" of adulthood. Given *over*emphasis, he may develop a sense of inferiority and incompetence as a result of his repeated failures.

The poor fare no better with respect to meeting these needs than they do with others, although here, too, the reports are both contradictory and scanty. Rainwater, Coleman, and Handel (1959) describe the working-man's wife as seeing school as a necessary evil, with her interest in associated activities such as the PTA being concerned with the immediate situation of the child. She does not expect her child to feel at home in school; it is merely another indication that it is hard for her to feel a part of society. In general, the working-class woman is so preoccupied with the stability of her basic human relations that she does not have "the freedom to commit energy to impersonal tasks such as school learning." [p. 109] She cannot identify with the school situation and, although some desire their children to be socially mobile and look to education to accomplish this, most are satisfied with working-class life and do not see any need for change. Brooks and others (1962) found, in this connection, that children's absences from school were related both to parental attitudes toward school, and to social class, although they did *not* find the expected relationship between class and parental attitudes.

On the other hand, Riessman (1962) cites Sears and others to the effect that deprived parents are more concerned that their children do well in elementary school than are middle-class parents. Whatever the incidence in the lower class of parental concern, Kahl (1953) has shown rather impressively that the difference between lower-class youngsters with sufficient intelligence to attend college who choose to do so and those who do not so choose is a difference between parents who trained their sons from grammar school on to take school seriously and parents who did not.

Bell (1964) studied 202 lower-class Negro mothers of children in nursery school or kindergarten to discover their educational aspirations for their children, particularly their long-range aspirations for college education. If those long-range aspirations affected their behavior toward their kindergarten children, Bell's findings may be germane here. The principle suggestion was that there are significant differences *within* the lower class, according to a mother's level of education and size of family. He found that "low status" mothers (zero to eight years of education and seven or more children) had lower aspirations than "high status" mothers (nine or more years of education and six or fewer children).

The nonschool opportunities to develop a "sense of industry," in Erikson's phrase, are also, apparently, less well supplied to lower-class than to middle-class youngsters by their families of orientation. Middle-class parents are consistently more likely, Bronfenbrenner's survey shows, to expect children to help around the house by age five, to help with younger siblings, to begin to cook and help with dishes if they are girls, and to pick up and take care of their toys.

One of Bronfenbrenner's findings from his survey should be reported here, in view of its apparent relevance to this age group, even though, theoretically, its developmental relevance would appear to be more closely related to the "initiative" issue of the preceding age.[17] This is the finding that middle-class mothers seem to have placed more restrictions on their children's freedom of movement than lower-class mothers before World War II, and fewer restrictions after that period. The restrictions referred to here concern such things as confining the child to the home yard or block or neighborhood, preventing him from going to movies alone or with other children or from going "downtown," requiring him to go to bed at a certain time, checking on his whereabouts, and so on.

Blood's (1961) study of family control over children's television viewing indicate that in this area, middle-class parents continue to be more selective and restrictive than lower-class parents.

Relatedly, Kohn and Carroll (1960) indicate that middle-class mothers want their "ten or eleven year-old" children to develop their own standards of conduct, and consider desirable behavior to consist of the child's acting according to his own principles; whereas working-class parents value conformity to proscriptive rules more highly. (These, it should be noted, are statements of values, not descriptions of parental behavior.)

Along similar lines, Kohn (1959a) found working-class parents stressing "obedience to parents" as the most important value, with middle-class parents considering this less important than self-control and considerateness of others. In another paper (1959b) Kohn reports his finding that middle-class parents are more likely than working-class parents to resort to physical punishment of their children when the latter seem to reveal an *intent* to violate standards the parents think should be internalized. Working-class parents, on the other hand, are triggered into physical punishment more often by the immediately descriptive consequences of their children's wild play or fights with siblings. Kohn also found that working-class mothers are much less likely to punish their sons for defiantly refusing to do what they are told to than are middle-class mothers, but *more* likely to punish their daughters for such behavior.

In general, as Bronfenbrenner has shown, physical punishment is the disciplinary technique lower-class youngsters are more likely to experience, while that of middle-class youngsters is "reasoning" and a temporary withdrawal of parental love.

There is some evidence of expected results from the pathogenic experiences that lower-class youngsters have in their families of orientation. Sewell and Haller (1959) found that the lower-class fourth-to-eighth graders had

---

[17] Environmental "inputs" to the developing child, which are specified as crucial for given stages, are not to be understood as having their importance *confined* to that period. They continue to be important at all stages of development, and it is even likely that deficits or surfeits at one period can be compensated for at later periods, although the limits of this are not at all known.

significantly lower scores on thirty items from the California Test of Personality. These they factor analyzed into four factors accounting for 90 percent of the variance: "concern over achievement," "concern over social status," "rejection of family," and "numerous symptoms." Burchinal, Gardner, and Hawkes (1958) similarly found greater indications of personality maladjustment among lower-class children, as measured by their fathers' occupational and educational levels and by their mothers' educational levels, especially in the case of children's "inferiority feelings."

The achievement motivation of youth, which we take to be akin to Erikson's "sense of industry," in different social classes has received considerable attention from social scientists. Rosen (1956) stratified the male population of two high schools in New Haven by Hollingshead's Index of Social Position, and drew a random sample of five from Class I, twenty-five from Class II, and thirty each from Classes III, IV, and V. He administered a projective test developed by McClelland to measure achievement motivation; and, to measure achievement values, a questionnaire based on Florence Kluckhohn's profiles of cultural orientation. (Belief in the possibility of actively manipulating the environment vs. passively adjusting to it; present vs. future orientation; and familistic vs. individualistic orientation.) He found highly significant class differences in achievement motivation, the means from Class I to Class V being 8.40, 8.68, 4.97, 3.40, and 1.87. Less dramatic but still significant were differences in achievement values, the class means from Class I to Class V being 4.6, 4.1, 3.8, 3.0, and 2.5.

Moles (1965a) calls attention to McClelland's finding that

> . . . when mothers stress the son's looking after himself before they stress the mastery of tasks, the boy's need for achievement is lower than when achievement is stressed first. . . . [E]arly mastery training promotes high need for achievement only when it does not signify generalized restrictiveness, authoritarianism, or "rejection" by parents. Thus, if a boy is expected to 'make decisions by himself' at an early age, this may mean that the parents help him to become self-reliant and masterful or that they push him to take care of himself and not be a burden to the family. When it is the latter, he will not develop a high need for achievement because the parents are not interested in his mastering tasks, only in his being out of the way. [p. 6]

Moles then suggests that several aspects of lower-class family life may lead precisely to this emphasis on self-reliance rather than mastery; namely, great preoccupation of the (often alone) mother with making ends meet, large numbers of children to care for, absence of household routines, displacement of children to streets because of overcrowding.

The different outcomes of their family experiences for lower- and higher-class boys are also observed in the report of Rosenberg (1965), who studied the values, in the sense of criteria of self-assessment, of over 5000 boys in New York State. Higher-class boys, he found, are more likely to say it is important to be well-respected, looked up to by others, intelligent, a person with a good mind, a logical, reasonable type of person, imaginative, and original. Lower-class boys, on the other hand, are more likely to emphasize being good at working with their hands, at fighting and wrestling, being tough, not afraid of a fight, suspicious, and cynical. (Girls, Rosenberg found, have remarkably similar values across class lines.)

Douvan's (1956) study of over 300 high school seniors in a midwestern community, using the McClelland test of achievement motivation, found that lower-class students' scores on the achievement motivation test were higher if they had been previously stimulated to try hard on an ability test by the offer of material reward. The offer of a material reward made no difference for the achievement motivation scores of middle-class students, suggesting that the latters' "need-achievement" is a part of their character structure, while the formers' is dependent on situational exigencies. (The further implicit suggestion is plain, that the absence of functional family-of-orientation experiences *can* be compensated for by such formal agencies as the school system.)

The "sense of industry" that Erikson identifies as the crucial successful outcome of the developmental task of six-to-twelve-year-old children—a "latency" period in which, apparently, only sexuality is latent—would seem to be related to educational attainments and aspirations. There is some evidence that family-of-orientation experiences vitally affect outcomes in this area.

The survey of 2800 families by Morgan and others shows clearly, to begin with, that the education of the head of a family is "far more important than any of the other variables" in determining the education actually attained by children.[18] This is confirmed by Turner's (1962) survey of over 2000 nonethnic high school seniors in Los Angeles, in which parental education was found to be highly associated with a high level of ambition.

A hint of the mechanisms behind such associations has been provided in several of the studies mentioned above. Additional suggestions are contained in Stendler's (1951) finding that lower-class mothers are less likely than middle-class mothers to prepare their children for the first grade by the teaching of the alphabet or nursery rhymes, or to be concerned with their children's report cards. At the other end of the educational ladder, Brooks' (1964) study of almost 300 mothers (273 of them Negro) who were receiving public assistance and at least one of whose children had dropped out of high school shows a similar picture of inability to influence adolescents' educational careers. Three fifths of the mothers had talked at

[18] James N. Morgan and others, *Income and Welfare in the United States.* New York: McGraw-Hill, Inc., 1962.

some time to their child's last teacher, but in only a tenth of these cases was the conversation about the child's learning problems or about finding ways in which he could do better. Nearly all the mothers were disturbed or angry when their children left school, but half of them felt unable even to try to do anything about it, and had not talked with the child about the decision before it was made.

In another article Moles (1965b) reports evidence consistent with the Hess, Shipman, and Jackson (1965) finding of no differences *among* three levels of low-income families; this is inconsistent with the Pavenstadt findings of differences among different levels. The Moles findings, moreover, reaffirm some of the notions reported above concerning the *desires* and *efforts* of lower-class mothers to encourage children's school success, and contradict such reports as Rainwater's and others mentioned above. Moles found that 93 percent of his 800 fifth- and sixth-grade children (all low income and over half on welfare) said their mothers thought they should finish college; 51 percent said their mothers helped them most of the time with their homework; 80 percent perceived their mothers as expecting better school work than the children felt it possible to do. From the mothers' side, 67 percent said they would be dissatisfied with low-prestige manual occupation for their children; 70 percent said they read stories to their preschool children at least once a week.

On another dimension, too, some doubt is cast on the existence of class differences in values or attitudes about school. Brooks, *et al.* (1962) found that certain parental attitudes were strongly related to the regularity of school attendance by public elementary-school students; but that there was no relationship between those attitudes and class level. On the other hand, there *was* a significant relationship between attendance and certain class characteristics; namely, parents' level of education, gross family income, and occupation of father.

When coupled with the Hess, Shipman, and Jackson study, these data suggest a picture of lower-class parents who do their best to urge and perhaps pressure their children to succeed academically, but who are unable to provide the concrete experiences that would enable their children to do well. Consistent with the Hess, Shipman, and Jackson findings also is Moles' report that 76 percent of the mothers in his sample agreed that obedience and respect for authority are the most important virtues children should learn. The Hess, Shipman, and Jackson conclusion was that the cognitive environment they observed their lower-class mothers providing was one that

> . . . produces a child who relates to authority rather than to rationale, who, although often compliant, is not reflective in his behavior and for whom the consequences of an act are largely considered in terms

of immediate punishment or reward rather than future effects and long range goals. [p. 886]

The concern of lower-class mothers with their children's obedience, and at the same time their feelings of inadequacy in dealing with them are revealed in the findings of Kantor *et al.* (1958). The authors administered an attitude questionnaire to 815 mothers of third-grade public school children, and reported that the lower-class mothers were more likely to agree that obedience to their parents is the most important thing children can learn; but also more likely to agree that parents cannot influence some children, that standards of discipline and conformity are hard to establish, and that the sexual interests and problems of children are difficult to handle.

What most of these studies show, then, is that a "sense of industry," like a sense of trust, of autonomy, and initiative, and like the cognitive sequences essential for adequate development are significantly influenced by experiences in families of orientation; and that children from lower-class families of orientation, even though their aspirations may be high, have experiences that handicap them significantly in those respects.

One factor, however, must be considered before drawing oversimplified generalizations from these findings, and this will be further developed in the next chapter. It is that the formal educational structure *can,* in some cases, compensate for those handicaps.

Adolescence

Erikson identifies the crucial aspect of the adolescent period as a "search for identity," with the chief danger being "identity diffusion." The search for identity is a search for a stable, satisfying synthesis of all the adolescent's earlier identifications and challenges. It is a search for assurance that "one's ability to maintain inner sameness and continuity (one's ego in the psychological sense) is matched by the sameness and continuity of one's meaning for others." [p. 89]

Identity diffusion is epitomized for Erikson by the exclamation of Biff, in Miller's *Death of a Salesman,* to his mother, "I just can't take hold, Mom, I can't take hold of some kind of a life." [p. 91] It is a threat, Erikson feels, that "is unavoidable at a time of life when the body changes its proportions radically, when genital maturity floods body and imagination."

Most of the bizarre aspects of the adolescent youth culture, from its fads and rigid conformities to its occasional destructiveness and self-destructiveness, are interpreted by Erikson as strenuous efforts by adolescents to guard against a sense of identity-diffusion by finding *some* "hold of *some* kind of life."

Although Erikson is not explicit on this, it would seem that the environment most conducive to the adolescent's simultaneous sense of continuity and differentness is one that would readily provide him with responsible, challenging, and "important" roles to play, and would do so in a manner that clearly symbolized for him and for all his "others" that *this* young person is now moving into a new stage. Paul Goodman[19] has probably come as close as anyone to developing this thesis.

This, of course, is saying no more than what sociologists and others have been saying for a long time; namely, that the growing "stretch-out" in complex societies between the time of physical maturation on the one hand and the achievement of social maturity on the other produces a period in which "identity diffusion" is, for many adolescents, more probable than "identity clarity." Since this is a large scale sociocultural phenomenon, adolescents' families of orientation are as inextricably caught in it as the adolescents themselves; and it is not clear precisely what patterns of family structure and processes are most functional for helping the adolescent to cope with his problem.

Whatever the situational structures that facilitate or impede adolescents' coping with an "identity crisis," the degree to which they come upon the crisis with, so to speak, a backlog of successes or failures from previous crises will certainly affect their chances. For this reason, the findings of Mitchell (1957) are probably relevant here. Administering the California Test of Personality to all fifth and seventh graders in a midwestern community, he found that at both grade levels a significantly higher proportion of low-status children (classified by Warner's Index of Status Characteristics) showed evidence of economic worries; feelings of rejection or persecution, and consequent aggressive tendencies; feelings of insecurity; psychosomatic complaints or nervous symptoms; unfulfilled desires for increased independence; unfulfilled desires for new experiences; troublesome anxiety reactions.

In considering the strictly intellectual growth of the adolescent, Hunt is, similarly not so detailed and explicit with respect to the kinds of environmental "inputs" the adolescent needs. The crucial intellectual development at the beginning of adolescence is the individual's emancipation from "concrete operations" and his ability to "operate with operations." His thought processes, in other words, (assuming successful transition through the earlier stages) cease to be confined to the classification, ordering, and manipulation of concrete *things;* and become involved with the manipulation of abstract propositions according to logical principles. As one aspect of this development, Hunt notes that "With the new-found dominance of his thought processes, the adolescent can see that the way the world is run

[19] Paul Goodman, *Growing Up Absurd.* New York: Vintage Press, Inc., 1962. See especially Chaps. 1 and 2.

is only one out of a great variety of possible ways that the world might be run. He takes delight in conceiving of alternative ways to run the world that might be better." [p. 231]

As far as concerns the inputs necessary to stimulate and nourish this development, Hunt suggests only that environmental demands for, and opportunities to engage in, verbal and other symbolic logical manipulation of propositions are essential. Again, then, apart from encouragement and support for the adolescent's school participation in such exercise, it is not clear precisely what functions the family of orientation can perform (with the obvious exception of those probably rare families in which the practice of controlled verbal argument and logical analysis is part of the family culture).

There is surprisingly little actual research on adolescents and their *family* relationships; and, as we have indicated before, it is not always clear to what extent the relations that are reported between adolescent attitudes or personality variables and family environment are to be understood as suggesting a causal relationship holding for that period in time, or one reflecting the results of family environments at earlier critical stages. Obviously, many of the studies reported above had adolescents as their subjects. As explained earlier, we have dealt with their findings in the context of the developmental period at which their behavioral or characterological focus was *theoretically* relevant.

Perhaps the studies most closely relevant to the particular developmental tasks of adolescence are those dealing with general feelings of self-acceptance and self-esteem, and (in view of Hunt's suggestions) with abstract logical and intellectual interests. Even here, the data are sparse, and yield an unclear picture.

Of possible relevance to the 'identity-diffusion" problem described by Erikson is the early finding of Havighurst and Robinson (1946), who had an unspecified number of children and adolescents write brief essays on "The person I would like to be like." They found a general developmental trend, with young children writing of parents, middle children turning to glamorous ideals, and late adolescents describing a composite of desirable adult characteristics. Their finding of relevance here is that lower-class children lag behind middle-class children in leaving the "glamor" model.

Carroll (1945) found exactly the same distinction between lower-class and middle-class Negro adolescents in her study of 300 such teenagers in Baltimore.

As far as studies of adolescent general self-esteem are concerned, the remarkable fact is that there are very few that report on class differences.

Rosenberg (1965) derived a seven-point Gutman scale from such items as "I feel that I have a number of good qualities," and "I certainly feel useless at times," administered to over 5000 New York State high school students. Classifying students into upper-, middle-, and low-class groups on the basis of fathers' occupations and incomes, he found that low-status boys were significantly more likely to have low self-esteem. The class differences for girls were in the same direction, but not significantly different. Rosenberg also shows that part of the dynamics of adolescents' self-esteem is related to the closeness of father-son relationships; and that it is the fact that lower-class boys are less likely to have such close relationships that seem to mediate their low self-esteem. (There are virtually no class differences among girls with respect to closeness of relations with fathers.)

There are a few studies of general personality adjustment. Sewell and Haller (1959) found a small positive relationship between social status and scores on the California Test of Personality; and Haller and Thomas (1962) found low positive correlations between class and total adjustment scores, using the "Sixteen Personality Factor Test."

Chapter Two

EDUCATION

It should come as no surprise to the informed reader that, by every conceivable measure, children of low-income families do not do as well in school as children from more affluent ones. The evidence has been presented in full and dramatic detail for the essentially white populations such as those in Elmtown or River City;[1] for the essentially Negro population of Harlem;[2] for the mixed population of Big City and New York City;[3] and for cities in general, by Conant.[4] Dreger and Miller (1960), in a review of psychological studies comparing Negroes and whites published in the main between 1943 and 1958, state that Negroes score lower on both traditional and so-called culture-free or culture-fair tests of intellectual functions. Goldberg (1963) suggests as a special problem for research the question "What accounts for the consistently lower academic status of children from disadvantaged ethnic groups, especially the Negroes, than of children from lower class white families living in the Northern cities?" We propose to look first at some of the research aimed directly at the issue of the school achievement of children from low-income families.[5]

In a survey of AFDC recipients conducted in 1961, Mugge (1964) found that while 96.3 percent of child recipients age six to seventeen were

[1] August B. Hollingshead, *Elmtown's Youth*. New York: John Wiley & Sons, Inc., 1949; Robert J. Havighurst and others, *Growing Up in River City*. New York: John Wiley & Sons, Inc., 1962.

[2] Harlem Youth Opportunities Unlimited, Inc., *Youth in the Ghetto*. New York: HARYOU, Inc., 1964.

[3] Patricia Cayo Sexton, *Education and Income*. New York: The Viking Press, Inc., 1961; Eleanor B. Sheldon and Raymond A. Glazier, *Pupils and Schools in New York City: A Fact Book*. New York: Russell Sage Foundation, 1965.

[4] James B. Conant, *Slums and Suburbs*. New York: McGraw-Hill, Inc., 1961.

[5] For an excellent British study focusing on the problems of education in low-income urban areas, with findings consistent with those of the American studies, see John Barron Mays, *Education and the Urban Child*. Liverpool, England: Liverpool University Press, 1962.

attending school, more than one out of eight seventeen-year-old recipients were not in school for reasons other than physical or mental incapacity. The AFDC children tended to be in the appropriate grade for their age during the first four school ages, but by age seventeen they were almost a full grade behind their non-AFDC age peers. At most ages above nine, the proportion of AFDC children retarded is more than twice that of comparable age groups in the general population. At the same time, while there is a proportion of AFDC who are advanced, by age fourteen this proportion is only half that of the general population.

The relationship between class, race, intelligence, and achievement was explored by Kennedy, Van De Riet, and White (1963) among Negro children in five southeastern states. The sample showed a significantly lower mean IQ than that found among the white schoolchildren used to establish test norms, and a negative relationship between IQ and age. Further, "the Binet IQ was highly correlated with socioeconomic level, the upper socioeconomic level having a mean of 105 and the lower socioeconomic level a mean of 79." [p. 109] On the achievement level, this group was approximately two months behind the standardization sample at the second-grade level, but was one grade and two months behind by the sixth grade. Achievement level was also positively correlated with socioeconomic level. The authors note, however, that social status did not explain a major amount of the variance.

Based on a study of 543 urban public school children stratified by race, grade level, and social class, Deutsch and Brown (1964) found that fifth grade IQ scores did not differ significantly from first-grade scores. However, at each status level, Negro children scored lower than white children, and this difference increased for each higher status level. The authors concluded that the influence of race becomes increasingly crucial as social-class level increases.

Wilson (1963b) examined the effects of social stratification and residential segregation in fourteen elementary schools of one district in California and concluded that race, school atmosphere, and social stratification have independent but similar consequences. In the schools where children from working-class homes were predominant, positions of leadership were held by students with low educational aspirations. Rejection of the norms of school achievement was supported by the peer group. In an earlier report based on the same study, Wilson (1959) noted that working-class children in schools where middle-class children were predominant did better than their counterparts in "working-class" schools. Similarly, children from professional- and middle-class families did not achieve as well as expected in schools with a higher proportion of working-class children.

Shifting our focus to the secondary school level, one of the earliest examinations of the relation between socioeconomic status and achievement is that by Coleman (1940). Using data from a national sampling of unstated quality, consisting of over 4700 respondents from grades seven, eight, and nine, he found that children from the higher status group had a significantly higher median IQ, were better readers, scored better in geography and history, and ranked higher in problem solving. In a study of 705 students in these same grades in six schools, Abrahamson (1952) found that upper- and lower-middle-class students received more than their share of high grades. In three of the schools, such students won all eighteen academic awards. Similar findings are reported by Schultz (1958) from a study of 100 Negro ninth-grade pupils in two Florida schools. Students whose parents had more education and higher socioeconomic status were more likely to be high achievers. Finally, Heimann and Schenk (1954) found significant differences related to social-class level in both school marks and measured mental ability among 144 sophomores in four Wisconsin high schools.

Somewhat mixed findings are reported by Curry (1962) in a study of achievement among sixth-grade children. The effect of socioeconomic status appeared greater as intellectual ability decreased. Thus, it seemed not to have affected the scholastic achievement of high-ability students, but it did affect language achievement in the middle intellectual-ability group, and achievement in reading, language, and total achievement for the low socioeconomic-status group.

Though the instances are few, there are contrary findings. As noted earlier, Goldberg claimed that as a general rule, Negro children from low-income families achieved less well in schools than did comparable white children. Antonovsky and Lerner (1959) did not find this to be the case in Elmira, New York. On the basis of a class-matched sample of Negro and white students from lower socioeconomic status, they found that, despite greater handicaps, Negroes did as well academically as whites, dropped out of school less frequently, and enrolled more often in the college-preparatory course.

There is a further caution that should be noted. While Dreger and Miller (1960) noted the consistent lower performance of Negro children on tests of intellectual functions, they also noted that Negroes average well within the normal IQ range for whites. And while Goldberg (1963) explored the sources of lower achievement by children of low-income families, she also made another significant point:

> Despite consistent differences in demonstrated intellectual and academic ability . . . there is a great deal of overlapping. In all studies there are some in the one group who resemble the other group far more than their own. And in all comparisons of lower- and middle-class children there is a sizable though smaller proportion of the former who score high on tests, do well in school, plan on advanced education and have a high degree of similarity to the school perform-

ance of middle-class children. Conversely, there are middle-class children whose motivation and performance are poor, indeed. [p. 81]

We have reviewed a variety of studies that seek to relate social origins to differences in school performance. Even if there is general agreement concerning a positive relationship between social origins and school performance, there remain a number of major issues that need to be explored. These may be put in the form of questions.

To what extent are there differences in the preschool experience of children, related to social origins, that result in children coming to school with significantly different levels of preparation?

To what extent do schools define children on the basis of their social origins, and thus provide significantly different experiences?

To what extent are there social-class differences in expectations and aspirations that cause the school experience to be differentially defined?

What They Bring with Them

When the child arrives at school, he comes at a particular stage of psychological and physiological development, and with certain values and expectations. What happens to him consequently is a function of his interaction with the school and the interplay of influences from home, community, and school. We do not propose to attempt to untangle this web of influence, nor to hazard guesses about the relative importance of vectors of influence. It is important, however, to get some sense of the state in which the child arrives at school.

Such a summary has been attempted by Deutsch (1963) on the basis of considerable research with lower-class, socially impoverished youngsters. He has characterized these children as coming from an unstable family without a successful male model. They live under marginal social and economic conditions, which include: a lack of privacy; limited opportunities to explore the outside world; a lack of esthetically pleasing surroundings; and a scarcity of books, toys, puzzles, pencils and paper, and a lack of guidance and encouragement in their use. The major consequence, according to Deutsch, is stimulus deprivation—a restriction in variety of stimulus and a less systematic ordering of stimulation sequences. This means, in terms of school-related abilities, the lower-class child arrives with a variety of significant skill handicaps, which include:

1. Deficiency in the equipment necessary to learn to read,
2. Greater distance from maturation ceiling,
3. Poor auditory discrimination,[6]

[6] This point is elaborated in Cynthia P. Deutsch, "Auditory Discrimination and Learning: Social Factors," *Merrill-Palmer Quarterly*: 10 (July 1962), 277–296.

4. Insufficient experience with correction of enunciation, pronunciation, and grammar,
5. Less developed memory function,
6. Greater difficulty in handling items related to time judgments,
7. Less opportunity to use adults as sources of information, correction, and the reality testing involved in problem solving and the acquisition of new knowledge,
8. Inadequate exposure to language use and manipulation,[7]
9. Deficit in syntactical organization and subject continuity,
10. Insufficient understanding and knowledge of the physical, geographical, and geometric characteristics of the world.

The way in which social-class background has its impact on the ability to learn to read has been pointed up by Milner (1951). Forty-two first-grade students from three elementary schools were tested and interviewed, and data were also collected from thirty-three of forty-two sets of parents or parent substitutes. Milner found a positive relationship between reading readiness and certain patterns of parent-child interaction, and between those patterns and social status. She concludes,

> Specifically, the lower-class child of this study seems to lack chiefly two things upon entering school as compared with the middle-class child of this study: a warm positive family atmosphere or adult-relationship pattern which is more and more being recognized as a motivational prerequisite for any kind of adult-controlled learning, not only of the verbal skills; an extensive opportunity to interact verbally with adults of high personal value to the child and who possess adequate speech patterns. [p. 111]

Discussions of the school behavior and achievement of children from low-income families have emphasized the negative or dysfunctional values brought from home. Thus, for example, Toby (1957) has argued that both middle- and lower-class children react negatively to school initially, but the lower-class child does not have the support from peers and family that helps impress the middle-class child with the importance of schooling. Davis (1948) has elaborated on this point in the following way:

> Whereas the middle-class child learns a socially adaptive fear of receiving poor grades in school, of being aggressive toward the teacher, of fighting, of cursing, and of having early sex relations, the slum child learns to fear quite different social acts. His gang teaches him to fear being taken in by the teacher, of being a softie with her. To study homework seriously is literally a disgrace. Instead of boasting

[7] For further detail, see Martin Deutsch, "The Role of Social Class in Language Development and Cognition," *American Journal of Orthopsychiatry*: 35 (January 1965), 78–88.

of good marks in school, one conceals them, if he ever receives any. The lower-class individual fears *not* to be thought a street-fighter; it is a suspicious and dangerous social trait. He fears *not to curse*. If he cannot claim early sex relations, his virility is seriously questioned. [p. 30]

Finally, Goldberg (1963) has written,

> Perhaps the most significant area of difference between lower- and middle-class school populations relate to their differences in motivation toward school and their perception of the purposes and meaning of schooling. . . . Miller and Swanson contrasted the values of the two groups as follows: The middle-class family members believe that their economic position can be improved through effort and sacrifice. They are willing to postpone gratification for greater future reward. They need to maintain a reputation for honesty, responsibility and respectability. They must accumulate money and social graces, develop abstract thinking ability needed for advancement in their work . . .

> These diverse *Weltanschauungen* find direct expression in school behavior. The middle-class child is "good" because from the earliest years he is taught to control expressions of anger and to inhibit direct aggression. He responds to appeals to internalized standards of right and wrong since he has learned that one cannot transgress against social demands if one wants to "get ahead." The lower-class child has been brought up on direct expression of aggression in the home and in the street. Since control of such behavior is seen to have little relevance to social position or job maintenance, there is no need to teach the child the skills of control. [p. 80]

But none of the above descriptions or analyses is based on the observation or study of children in school. Toby does not specify the age of the subjects of his remarks. Davis bases his on studies of child-rearing practices. It is quite apparent that while Goldberg starts out to say something about children from low-income families, she ends up by inferring qualities based on their family background. This is not to deny that it is reasonable to expect that differences in the family into which children are socialized will produce different kinds of children. We are pointing out, however, that statements concerning the values or aspirations of working-class children tend to be based either on examination of working-class adults, or on children in junior high school or higher grades. There is little evidence concerning the values and aspirations with which children enter kindergarten or first grade. Thus it is not possible to say whether the values found subsequently are those that were there originally or are a product of interaction between child, school, family, and community.

To this point, we have focused on the early grades in an effort to sift out some findings about personal attributes which, it may be said, are brought to the school situation and affect the impact of the educational experience. There is another body of data, from "Project Talent," that is relevant when viewed from a particular perspective. It concerns "general academic aptitude," which may be viewed as one component in the student's personal make-up; and it relates to high school students. It is relevant if we think of these data as telling us something about what youngsters "bring" to high school, though at this educational stage it is impossible to sift out the sources of this component.

In 1960, a staff headed by John C. Flanagan of the University of Pittsburgh administered a two-day battery of tests and questionnaires to 440,000 secondary school students in 1353 high schools, carefully selected to be representative of American secondary schools. On the basis of a "measure of general academic aptitude," a representative subsample of all students was divided into deciles. Males in the lowest five deciles were twice as likely as males in the top two deciles to come from families possessing (according to the respondents) only "the necessities or less"; and although over half of those in the lowest five deciles came from blue-collar families, less than a third of those in the top decile did so. Contrariwise, about 57 percent of the top decile students came from white-collar families, but only 15 percent of the bottom decile students did.

Further, between 53 and 60 percent of those in the bottom five deciles had fathers who had not graduated from high school, while only about a third of those in the top two deciles had such relatively uneducated fathers. Two fifths of those in the top two deciles had fathers with some college education, but only between a fourth and a third of those in the bottom five deciles had such educated fathers.[8]

Part of the analysis of the Project Talent data consisted of classifying schools into relatively homogeneous groups. One such group consisted of twenty-seven schools serving predominantly low-income students, and a second, of fifty-five schools serving predominantly middle-income students, both in the large cities of New York, Philadelphia, Detroit, Chicago, and Los Angeles.

The means and standard deviations of selected test scores in the two types of schools are shown in Table 1.[9]

According to these data, there is virtually no overlap of the middle two thirds of the two populations (the mean plus and minus a standard

[8] John C. Flanagan and others, *The American High School Student*. Pittsburgh, Pa.: (Project Talent) University of Pittsburgh, 1964.
[9] From unpublished computer printout of Matrix IA, kindly loaned by Project Talent to the Rutgers University Urban Studies Center.

TABLE 1.   MEANS AND STANDARD DEVIATIONS OF SELECTED TEST SCORES OF STUDENTS IN LOW- AND MIDDLE-INCOME SCHOOLS IN FIVE LARGE CITIES

TEST, GRADE, AND SEX	MIDDLE INCOME		LOW INCOME	
	Means	Standard Deviation	Means	Standard Deviation
General information test—twelfth-grade boys	157.24	17.12	117.46	24.35
General information test—twelfth-grade girls	127.23	16.15	97.22	18.15
English test—tenth-grade boys and girls	78.12	7.06	66.56	6.98
English test—twelfth-grade boys and girls	84.82	5.21	76.34	5.80
Mathematics I—twelfth-grade boys and girls	8.84	1.46	6.07	1.50
Mathematics II—twelfth-grade boys and girls	11.47	2.43	7.80	2.21
Reading comprehension—twelfth-grade boys and girls	33.72	4.27	25.15	5.58
Creativity—twelfth-grade boys and girls	9.40	1.54	6.46	1.95
Abstract reasoning—twelfth-grade boys and girls	9.51	0.93	7.66	1.22
Science information—twelfth-grade boys	10.94	1.88	6.23	3.62
Mechanical information—twelfth-grade boys	12.33	1.17	8.55	2.38

Source: Project Talent Matrix IA.

deviation), with low-income students consistently below middle-income students in the same school system.

The Quality and Quantity of Education

Although concern with differential treatment of children in school because of social origin has only recently become a public issue, relevant evidence has been available for some time. Warner, Havighurst, and Loeb (1944) in the early 1940s discussed in general terms how school systems responded to community values to select from the population those who could use its resources as a mechanism for social mobility. Hollingshead (1949) subsequently described the process in much more explicit detail.

It has generally been recognized that state responsibility for education means that the quality and quantity of education received by children is in part a function of the relative wealth of the state and its willingness to support education. Moreover, the same principle holds within a state— the level of education for a given community varies with the local tax base, the tax rate, and the formula for state aid. Morgan and others have shown that, proportionately, low-income families benefit more per dollar of income from public education than other families. They note, however, that

> . . . the spending units with lower incomes generally live in areas where the public school expenditures per pupil are also lower. Hence the degree to which education equalizes opportunity is something less

than it might be. . . . children of the highest income families attend schools where expenditures per child are 6 percent above average, and children in the lowest income families go to schools where the expenditure per child is 13 percent below average.[10]

Sexton (1961) has detailed the difference that social origin makes in the kind of school attended, at least for one metropolis. On almost every conceivable measure, schools in low-income areas compare unfavorably with those in better areas. They tend to be older, have far less in the way of both educational and recreational facilities, and despite the greater need, are less likely to have remedial programs. Finally, a greater proportion of the teaching time is provided by substitutes (who may be certified) in schools serving low-income areas. Cloward and Jones (1963) claim that children from low-income areas also receive less instruction than other children:

> One force making for lower levels of academic achievement among impoverished youth is the fact that they receive less instructional time. . . . Because of the greater turnover of teachers in slum schools, their relative inexperience, and the geographic mobility of low-income families, slum youth receive less actual instructional time than do school children in middle-class neighborhoods. [p. 191]

Children from low-income families receive less instruction in another sense—they tend to be absent more and to leave school sooner than other children. Sexton noted in her study that children from low-income areas change school more often, leave (for a variety of reasons) more often, lose more time because of illness, and in general have a lower attendance rate. The findings of studies of school dropouts, from the early effort of Eckert and Marshall (1938) and Karpinos (1943) and Karpinos and Sommers (1942), to those of Bertrand (1962), Bowman and Matthews (1960), David and others (1961), the Health and Welfare Association of Alleghany County (1962), Livingston (1958), and Thomas (1954), for example, can be summed up in the words of Davie (1953): "the lower one goes in the social structure, the greater the proportion of children who are not attending school." Palmore (1963) has suggested that among lower-class children, drop-out rates are significantly higher among those from the lower-class neighborhoods. Dillon (1949), however, in a study of all students leaving school in the year 1944–1945 in a number of cities found the children not significantly different from the rest of the population with reference to stability of home (unbroken family) and economic condition. It should also be noted that many of the above authors found other factors,

[10] James N. Morgan, M. H. David, W. J. Cohen, and H. E. Brazer, *Income and Welfare in the United States.* New York: McGraw-Hill, Inc., 1962, pp. 305–306.

such as education and aspiration of father, intelligence level, and involvement in extracurricular activities were related to survival in school.

Nam and Folger (1965), in their analysis of demographic and social factors related to school retention, found that "the relative importance of factors associated with entrance into, and continuation in, school varies along points of the education continuum." [p. 461] Thus, for example, ethnic differences and urban-rural residence are relatively important at the beginning of the school career, and much less important at higher levels of education. Ability, they find, is the most important factor related to graduation from high school and college. "Socioeconomic status has a small to moderate independent effect at all points along the continuum, but its strongest effect is probably at college entrance." [p. 461]

There is some evidence to suggest that teachers perceive and treat children from low-income families differently from other children. Riessman[11] has been an articulate spokesman for the view that the middle-class orientation of school personnel results in systematic discrimination against the children of the less privileged in the community. In his study of Chicago schoolteachers, Becker (1952) found that three problems were of greatest significance to the teachers: (1) teaching itself, (2) discipline, and (3) the moral acceptability of the student. Teachers reported children from slum areas as the most difficult to teach successfully, the most difficult to control, and the least acceptable in terms of moral values concerning health and cleanliness, sex and aggression, ambition and work, and the relations of pupil to teacher. One result, according to Becker (1952) is two major types of careers.

> . . . most movement in the system is a result of dissatisfaction with the social-class composition of these [lower-class] school populations. Movement in the system, then, tends to be out from the "slums" to the "better" neighborhoods, primarily in terms of characteristics of the pupils. Since there are few or no requests for transfers to "slum" schools, the need for teachers is filled by the assignment to such schools of teachers beginning careers in the Chicago system. Thus, the new teacher typically begins her career in the least desirable kind of school. [p. 472]

The other type of career involves adjustment to the "slum" school situation. The teacher learns appropriate teaching and disciplinary techniques, revises her expectations about how much material can be taught, and learns to be satisfied with a smaller accomplishment.

The way teachers feel about students has, as one might expect, implications for the children's feelings about themselves and their behavior.

[11] Frank Riessman, *The Culturally Deprived Child.* New York: Harper & Row, Publishers, 1962.

Davidson and Lang (1960), in a study of fourth, fifth, and sixth graders, report a positive correlation between (1) children's perception of their teacher's feelings toward them and their perception of themselves, (2) favorable perception of teachers' feelings and good academic achievement, and (3) favorable perception of teachers' feelings and desirable classroom behavior. Most relevant here is the finding that each of the above three variables is related to social class. The two factors of social class position and achievement are independent in their effect upon the way a child perceives a teacher's feelings toward him. The authors conclude,

> The interrelation found between children's perception of teachers' feelings, school achievement, behavior and socioeconomic status are particularly significant since the majority of children in the public schools throughout the country come from families of low social class status. It is therefore likely that a lower class child, especially if he is not doing well in school, will have a negative perception of his teachers' feelings toward him. These negative perceptions will in turn tend to lower his efforts to achieve in school and/or increase the probability that he will misbehave. His poor school achievement will aggravate the negative attitudes of his teachers toward him, which in turn will affect his self-confidence, and so on. [p. 114]

Supporting this kind of contention, Abrahamson (1952) in a study of grades seven through nine in six communities, found that students of higher social class were more often chosen by teachers to do "favor-running errands" while lower-class students received more than their share of punishment.

There are contrary findings, however. Based on a study of the interaction of third-grade teachers in nineteen classrooms in two schools, Hoehn (1963) concluded that there is a relationship between teacher behavior, measured both quantitatively and qualitatively, and student achievement, but not between teacher behavior and student social status. According to Hoehn, teachers tend to concentrate, in quantitative terms, on low achievers, though in terms of the quality of their behavior, they "favored" pupils of high achievement. DeGroat and Thompson (1949) based a study on a sample of 133 elementary school pupils, finding that a small proportion of pupils received most of the approval and disapproval, according to the pupils themselves. Those receiving the approval showed higher test intelligence, higher achievement, and a higher level of adjustment than their less-favored classmates. Apparently, however, there was no examination of the effect of social class. Wallin and Waldo (1964) in their study of eighth graders, found neither class nor race differences in the feelings of respondents that they enjoyed the "favorable regard"—acceptance, sympathy, understanding, and fair treatment of their teachers. And while the teachers perceived higher-class children more favorably than lower-class children of both races on a dimension of general adjustment, the findings were mixed on two other measures.

Additional contrary data are reported by Fox, Lippitt, and Schmuck (1964) from a quite different type of study. They were engaged in a comparative analysis of learning cultures in some thirty classrooms in seven different school systems. One finding was that social class and "utilization of intelligence" (a measure of ability against achievement) were related for girls but not for boys. The authors also conclude:

> In contrast to the relative importance of satisfaction with the teacher [in utilization of intelligence], the data also indicate that familial social class is a minor factor in influencing pupil utilization in our population. Although social class and utilization are associated, the impact of social class is diminished as the effects of other social influences are held constant. Particularly for the boys, familial social class and parental support are less important than the factors of peer group status and satisfaction with the teacher in influencing utilization. [pp. 130–131]

The studies just reviewed are all based on fairly limited observations. The Project Talent study mentioned earlier provides data on a much larger sample of schools, and contains findings that are often inconsistent with the preceding generalizations.[12]

Four "types" of schools, in addition to the large city schools referred to above, were distinguished, with a further distinction made between "low-income" and "middle-or-higher" income schools within each type: five schools in low-cost housing and low-income areas of cities between 250,000 and 1½ million population, and twenty-one schools in those cities in moderate and high-cost housing areas; forty-seven urban Northeastern low-income schools, and forty-seven urban Northeastern "middle income" schools; twenty-four urban Southeastern low-income schools, and forty-five urban Southeastern middle-income schools; eleven urban Western low-income schools, and eighty-three urban Western middle-income schools.

These permit five comparisons between low-income and middle-income schools in as many different regions or city sizes. According to these data, in only one area are per-pupil expenditures less for low-income students than for others: in the urban Northeast (excluding cities of 250,000 or more), the figures are 362 dollars and 461 dollars, respectively. In all other areas, the difference is no larger than 33 dollars. (In cities of 250,000 to 1½ million, the difference is 13 dollars and in cities of over 1½ million, it is 3 dollars. Even in the urban Southeast, it is only 24 dollars.)

Starting salaries are also approximately equal in low and high income-

---

[12] The following section is also based on the unpublished Matrix IA loaned by Project Talent to the Urban Studies Center.

area schools in all five comparisons; and, as another index of school "treat-ments," in all but one of the five comparisons, low-income schools have *more* books in the library than do higher-income schools.

In the five largest cities (New York, Los Angeles, Chicago, Philadel-phia, Detroit), the low-income school buildings are distinctly older than the higher-income buildings (an average of approximately thirty-seven years compared to twenty years); but in the urban Northeast, urban South-east, and urban West, low-income schools are, on the average, distinctly newer. In cities of 250,000 to 1½ million, the average age of buildings is identical.

In the case of all five comparisons, low-income students are *less* likely to be on double schedules than are higher-income students; and average class sizes of low- and higher-income schools are almost exactly the same in all five ecological areas.

In large and "medium large" cities, low-income students do have teachers who are, on the average, less experienced. The average teacher in large-city, high-income schools has taught for about thirteen years; his low-income-school counterpart, for a little over six years. In medium-large cities, the respective figures are about thirteen and ten; and in the other areas, experience is about the same.

One question that is rarely raised about these various school charac-teristics is what educational difference they make, even where there are differences between low- and middle-income schools. The Project Talent data permit an approach to this problem by providing correlation coeffi-cients between various school characteristics and student achievements on standardized tests. We report here the findings with respect to scores on the English test, for the twenty-seven low-income and the fifty-five middle-income schools of the five largest cities.

Consistent with some of the assumptions made in the literature re-viewed above, per-pupil expenditures make more of a difference for English achievement among low-income students than among middle-income stu-dents. The correlation coefficients (r) are 0.456 and 0.065, respectively. Having experienced teachers is also, apparently, more important for the for-mer than for the latter, although, as noted above, the former in fact tend to have the less-experienced ones. The correlation between teachers' experience and students' English achievement is 0.547 among low-income students, and 0.158 among middle-income students.

Certain other common-sense assumptions, however, are inconsistent with these data. Low-income students, for example, do *better* (in English achievement) the *larger* the class sizes ($r = 0.546$); the *larger* the senior class ($r = 0.712$); the *fewer* the study halls provided ($r = -0.478$); the *fewer* the books in the library ($r = -0.117$); the *lower* the starting sal-aries of teachers ($r = -0.134$); the *more* students on double schedules

($r = 0.162$); the *higher* the drop-out rate ($r = 0.203$); and the *lower* the participation of parents in PTA ($r = -0.323$).

In nearly all those cases, the findings for higher-income students either are the reverse, or are that the variable makes no difference: high-income students do better the *smaller* the class size ($r = -0.314$); the *more* study halls are provided ($r = 0.304$); the *more* books in the library ($r = 0.397$); the *higher* the starting salaries for teachers ($r = 0.363$); the *lower* the drop-out rate ($r = -0.439$); and the *greater* the participation of parents in PTA ($r = 0.388$).

We do not suggest that these correlations are to be taken seriously as indications of what does and does not make for academic achievement among low- and middle-income students; only that, manifestly, we have not begun to understand the factors that do so.

In exploring ways in which youth of low-income families might encounter an educational experience different from that of other youth, we have focused primarily on the formal aspects of the educational system. But there is another area in which social-class origins may exert an influence—the area of friendship patterns, student government, and extracurricular activities. Schmuck, for example, found that

> . . . peer-group liking structure and pupil involvement in the group help to fashion a pupil's cognition of himself in relation to the peer group; that this recognition of self in relation to others is associated with a pupil's attitudes toward self and school; and that a pupil's personal conception of his place in the peer group is related also to his utilization of abilities.[13]

Thus, if social class were a significant factor in this aspect of school life, it might help to explain some ways in which social class influences school behavior.

A preliminary issue is to determine whether children are aware of class and at what age or grade level this awareness is manifested. This was attempted by Stendler (1949), with grades one, four, six, and eight of one school system. She reports that fourth graders show a beginning awareness of class symbols, while eighth graders are beginning to distinguish between economic and noneconomic symbols of status. Upper-middle-class children were most conscious of class symbols at all grades. First-grade children show the least tendency to choose in-school friends along class lines, with fourth and sixth graders increasing this tendency. With reference to out-of-school friends, Stendler reports that among sixth and eighth graders, there is little

---

[13] Richard Schmuck, "Some Relationships of Peer Liking Patterns in the Classroom to Pupil Attitudes and Achievement," *The School Review,* 71 (Autumn 1963), 337–359.

social interaction between upper-middle and working-class youth. Thus it would appear, for this community at least, that social origin is a powerful influence on friendship patterns at the equivalent of the junior high school level.

In a study of 380 children in grades five, six, ten, and eleven, Neugarten (1946) found that by the fifth grade, class differences in friendship and reputation were well-established. The lower-class child generally found himself rejected by both peers and teachers. The strength of such patterns is shown by Cook (1956) as the result of an experiment aimed at influencing social interaction among forty-four tenth-grade students. Initial sociograms and questionnaires showed lower-class children tended to be underchosen and upper-class children overchosen. In negative ratings, the lower-class children were named with great frequency by upper and middle levels as "not liked, dirty, smelly, fights a lot, and dumb." Following the individual counselling and group-management intervention, the picture changed somewhat in terms of leadership structure and group interaction, but the direction of choice was still upward, reflecting the power of social stratification.

Somewhat more complex findings are reported by Oppenheim (1953) as a result of a study of English school boys in the third year. Class differences were found with reference to characteristics considered desirable in the selection of friends, on the basis of a structured questionnaire. However, on the basis of sociometric tests, there appeared to be no relationship between actual cliques and what would have been expected because of the differences in values. Further, when required to offer characteristics of a "good friend" in response to an open-ended question, the boys provided a list almost completely different from that in the structured questionnaire, with no significant class differences. Thus, the author concludes, that while class differences were found with reference to values considered important by American parents, popularity and friendship patterns were not bound up with the socioeconomic status of families.

Putting aside the above contrary evidence, and assuming that social class does lead to invidious comparisons in which low-income youth are defined as less desirable, the question is, What consequence does this have for them? The obvious answer would be that such negative evaluations would lead to a negative self-image, lower levels of aspiration and achievement, and so on. As we have seen, there is some evidence that teachers may have such an effect. But little research appears to have been done concerning the effect of social evaluations by peers including social class as a variable. A study along such lines was conducted by Buswell (1953) using two groups of children, one tested in both kindergarten and first grade, the other examined in fifth and sixth grades. Using sociometric data, she sorted out one group well-liked by others, a second composed of children not well-liked. The liked-not and liked groups differed significantly on measures of achievement at both grade levels, a finding similar to that of Ryan and Davie with reference to senior high school students.[14] Turning to the factors associated with social acceptability, Buswell concluded that,

> . . . it was rather definitely shown that achievement as such is related to social acceptability, that it is the intellectual factor associated with this achievement which is the basic component in the relationship, and that socioeconomic status as such has little relationship to social acceptability. [p. 47]

However, if we accept the findings mentioned earlier, it may be that socioeconomic status as such *had not as yet* become a salient factor in social acceptability.

A tendency for extracurricular activity to be more characteristic of higher socioeconomic status was shown by Coleman (1940) and by Smith (1945). Smith also reported a positive relationship between such activity and the scores on tests of social adjustment and vocabulary. Abrahamson (1952), mentioned earlier, reported that students of higher social-class background tended to participate more in extracurricular activities, to receive high social-acceptance scores, and to hold most of the student-government offices. Baeumler (1965) found no difference in membership or attendance rates among high school students, but did find that children of middle-class families were more likely to hold offices than children from working-class families.

Though the above findings tend to be consistent, the earlier studies may be dated and the statistical analyses are often modest. In an interesting study, Udry (1960) tested the general applicability of the role of social class with a sample of secondary school pupils in a rapidly growing suburb. In terms of our concern here, he found no significant relationship between social class and same-sex friendship groups. He suggests that in a relatively new community, with a changing student body and teaching staff, class position may not be clearly defined and preconceptions based on class may not have taken hold. Comparing high school students categorized as "low prominence" and "high prominence" on the basis of the number and type of mentions in the student newspaper, Jones (1958) found that social status exerted only a small influence.[15]

[14] F. J. Ryan and James S. Davie, "Social Acceptance, Academic Achievement and Aptitude among High School Students," *Journal of Educational Research*: 52 (November 1956), 101–106.

[15] For a thoughtful comparison of the influence of social class on students at the secondary school level in the United States and Britain, see F. Musgrove, *Youth and the Social Order*. Bloomington, Ind.: Indiana University Press, 1964.

Aspirations

One of the major explanations for the lower level of school achievement among youth from low-income families white and Negro, has been that of aspirations. Partly because of their family background, partly because of the way they are treated in school, it is said, large numbers of these youths do not value education as highly, nor do they aspire to as much education as youths from more fortunate backgrounds. Some support for such a contention is found in the conclusion of Wylie (1963) that more modest self-estimates of school-work ability occur in girls rather than boys, Negroes rather than whites, and low-status rather than higher-status children. There are contrary findings, however. Brookover, Paterson, and Thomas (1962) examined the relationship between self-concept of ability and school achievement among junior high students. They found a significant relationship between these two factors. While there was also a positive relationship between the family socioeconomic status and self-concept of ability, this factor did not materially affect the correlation between self-concept of ability and school achievement.

Though not, strictly speaking, a component of aspirations, how young people feel about school in general is probably related to achievement. Unfortunately, while numerous vivid quotations reflecting the feelings of some youth are available, there are few systematic comparisons of students from different socioeconomic backgrounds. One source is the Purdue Opinion Poll, as reported by Remmers and Radler (1957). The results in Table 2 may be viewed as reflecting attitudes to some aspects of schooling. It is clear that there are no sharp differences between the groups, with one exception. Less than half the low-income group think teachers are underpaid, while almost two thirds of the high-income group think they are. This may reflect the different perspectives from which they assess teachers' pay, or a relative evaluation of the performance of teachers. Similarly, the lesser willingness of low-income students to permit teachers to be critical may reflect a lesser opinion of teachers or a lesser tolerance for free speech.

There is another set of items, shown in Table 3, that is somewhat relevant. While the differences are not large, they are consistent. Students from higher-income families are willing to take more responsibility, to have more to say in the running of the school. It might be argued that this result indicates that students from low-income families do not see themselves as much a part of the school as a system. The consistently higher proportion of "undecided" responses among students from low-income families might also be taken as a measure of alienation.

TABLE 2. ATTITUDES TO SOME ASPECTS OF SCHOOLING

	INCOME[a]	
	Low	*High*
Are or are not your high school teachers as friendly and sympathetic as you would like them to be?		
Are	50%	51%
Are not	40	39
Undecided	10	10
In discussing controversial topics, do your teachers usually present all sides of the question fairly, or do they tend to present a prejudiced viewpoint?		
Present all sides	60	61
Prejudiced	21	25
Undecided	19	14
Should or should not high school teachers be free to criticize our government or our economic system?		
Should	61	70
Should not	22	19
Undecided	17	11
Are public school teachers underpaid or are they not?		
Think public school teachers are underpaid	46	63
Would you or would you not like to be a high school teacher?		
Would	18	18
Would not	74	75
Undecided	8	7

Source: Remmers and Radler (1957), pp. 132–134.

[a] For the first two items, the terms "Low Income" and "High Income" are used. For the last three, "Low Socio-Economic Status" and "High Socio-Economic Status" are used. No definition is given of these terms.

A study more directly related to the problem was conducted by Coster (1958) by means of a questionnaire administered to 3000 students in nine high schools in Indiana. He found no difference between students of different income levels on items pertaining to attitudes toward school, school programs, and the value of education. However, there were differences on items pertaining to social life, being liked by other pupils, opinions about

TABLE 3. WHAT DO YOU THINK A STUDENT GOVERNMENT SHOULD BE ALLOWED TO DO?

		FAMILY INCOME[a]		
		Low	Med.	High
Plan assemblies and convocations	Yes	67%	74%	80%
	No	14	13	11
	Undecided	19	13	10
Make rules about conduct in school	Yes	61	70	72
	No	24	21	18
	Undecided	11	6	6
Hold a court and try students who break rules	Yes	43	44	50
	No	43	46	43
	Undecided	10	7	6
Have power to fine or otherwise punish students who break rules	Yes	34	33	37
	No	53	55	54
	Undecided	10	9	7
Poll students on ways to improve school	Yes	77	88	86
	No	9	4	7
	Undecided	12	5	5
Meet with teachers and principals to advise them on how students feel about school matters affecting them	Yes	81	89	90
	No	10	4	7
	Undecided	7	5	3

Source: Remmers and Radler (1957), pp. 138–139.
[a] There is no indication of the cutting points for these categories.

other pupils, feelings of parental interest in school work, and personal interest of teachers—findings compatible with many reported earlier.[16]

Turning now to the issue of educational aspirations among Negro youth as compared to white, the evidence is far from conclusive. In a study

[16] For a vivid description of how working-class British youth feel about school, see M. P. Carter, *Home, School and Work.* New York: The Macmillan Company, 1962.

of twenty-five white and twenty-five Negro elementary school pupils matched for socio-economic status and test intelligence, Boyd (1952) found the Negro children had a significantly higher level of aspiration. One component of the aspiration measure concerned academic performance in high school. Antonovsky and Lerner (1959), in their study of Elmira high schools referred to earlier, concluded that the Negro students showed a more positive and constructive attitude toward school than the corresponding white group. They viewed education as the avenue to achievement. Collecting data from 873 Negro and white students in grades nine and twelve of four large Kansas City high schools, Gist and Bennett (1963) found that Negro educational aspirations exceeded those of white students. While there was no difference as to the kind of future education desired, whites more than Negroes tended to decide against a future education.

Holloway and Berreman (1959) examined educational plans and aspirations of 313 Negro and white male pupils of grades six, seven, and eight in three urban elementary schools, with regard to both race and class, though the proportion of middle-class Negro students was small. They found no difference in educational aspirations by race when class was held constant. The educational aspirations of all race-class categories were predominantly high. The educational aspirations of the Negro middle-class students were as high as their plans, and while both Negro and white lower-class students scaled down their educational aspirations as compared to their plans, Negroes did so no more than whites. None of the above studies was conducted in the metropolitan areas where the educational problem is most acute.

Gottlieb (1964) has compared aspirations and expectations of white and Negro students by social class and by region. Generally speaking, for both Southern and Northern white students, the lower the class background, the lower the mobility aspirations. Among Negro youth, however, more than 80 percent at each class level expressed a desire for college, with Negro males from Southern segregated schools more likely to do so than those from Northern schools. At the same time, and pointing up the hazard of dealing with measures of "aspiration," Negro youth from each social class and type of school were less likely than comparable whites to select occupational fields requiring graduate or professional training.

Gottlieb found the usual pattern, among white respondents, of a declining discrepancy between college-going aspirations and expectations at each higher-status level. Among Negro students, however, at least 20 percent of those aspiring to college did not actually expect to go, at each status level.

> Negro students at the southern segregated schools are more likely than those in the northern schools to match expectations with aspira-

tions. The greatest discrepancy is found among Negro youth in the northern interracial high schools. [p. 936]

Some of the problems in comparing Negro and white students with reference to values or goals or aspirations can be found in the study by the Lotts (1963) of high school seniors in Kentucky. Because of wide differences in background and intelligence, they found it necessary to select a matched-pair subsample for more careful analysis. In the total sample, white students scored significantly higher on need for social recognition and on need for love and recognition while Negro students scored significantly higher on need for academic recognition. Among those who claimed to be college bound, these same differences were found. But only the Negro-white difference on need for academic recognition persisted for the matched-pair subsample. Also, while the white students scored significantly higher on a measure of achievement motivation, the difference, though in the same direction, was not significant within the matched-pair subsample.

Going directly to the issue of the relationship between social status and educational aspirations, Sewell, Haller, and Strauss (1957) collected data from a one-sixth sample of all high school seniors in Wisconsin in 1947–1948. With intelligence held constant, there was an association between status and aspiration, as measured by responses to questions concerning education the student planned to obtain after graduation.

Similar findings are reported by Elder (1962) on the basis of data from a large-scale study of junior and senior high school students in North Carolina and Ohio.

> Within each age and sex group among high and low achieving adolescents we find that mean motivation scores generally increase from the lower stratum to the upper middle class and from less than a tenth grade education for mother and father to some college or more. [pp. 48–49]

Another kind of behavioral test of the relationship between ability, status, and aspirations has been provided by Pohlman (1956), who examined the relevance of these factors in the choice of a secondary school by a sample of white adolescents in St. Louis. He anticipated that, regardless of ability, children whose parents held the lowest status would not go on to secondary school at all, that those from slightly higher-status families would choose a trade or technical school, and that increasing status would lead in turn to parochial general, public general, private parochial, and other private academic high schools. The data supported this contention in a general way, with ability being more important than status only in one situation—girls choosing between technical and general high school.

Caro (1963) reports that in his sample of 144 male juniors in four

St. Paul high schools, some 90 percent of the middle-class students indicated that if free to do whatever they wanted after high school, they would go to college. Only about 20 percent of lower-class youth responded in this vein.

This widespread orientation to college was also demonstrated by Krippner (1965), who found that better than three quarters of the *low-achieving* upper-middle-class junior high school students in his sample planned to go to college.

Krauss (1964) administered questionnaires to seniors in four San Francisco Bay area high schools and found that 64 percent from middle-class homes planned to attend college, while only 41 percent from working-class homes planned to do so.[17]

If the desire to go to college can be taken as a crude measure of aspirations, then the analysis of Jaffe and Adams (1964) of the attitudes of parents and children as reflected in opinion polls just prior to World War II and around 1960 is of some interest. They found that the intentions of parents, between 1939 and 1959, rose more rapidly than did those of high school students. However, class differences in the intentions of high school students remained about constant. About two thirds of the children of professional and managerial families planned to go to college in 1939 and 1959, as compared to about two fifths of children of manual workers.

If, as has been suggested, there are class differences in motivation, achievement, and aspirations, with middle-class youth having greater educational motivation and aspiration, and higher levels of achievement in high school, then the obvious question arises about the mechanisms involved by which social-class position becomes translated into relevant attitudes, values, and behaviors. Several have been suggested: social origin plays a role in friendship patterns which, in turn, influence values and achievement; parental or family values that differ by class are transmitted to the offsprings in a variety of ways; or some combination of these processes is at work. There are a number of studies that explore these alternatives.

Haller and Butterworth (1960) studied peer-pair relations among seventeen-year-old boys in one Michigan county and decided the evidence concerning the influence of interaction with peers on aspirations, while in the proper direction, was inconclusive. On the other hand, Bell (1963), on the basis of data from male students in one high school, concluded that there was a positive association between aspiration levels and students' interaction in higher-status groups.

Alexander and Campbell (1964) explored the influence of peer rela-

[17] Similar findings, comparing working-class and middle-class youth in British grammar schools, are reported by Eva Bene, "Some Differences Between Middle-Class and Working-Class Grammar School Boys in Their Attitudes Toward Education," *British Journal of Sociology*: 10 (June 1959), 148–152.

tions on educational aspirations and attainments without becoming involved in the issue of influence of class in the formation of peer associations. They concluded that

> . . . a student at a given status level is more likely to *expect* to attend college, to have a strong desire to go to college when he *does* expect to go, to *want* to go when he *does not* expect to, and actually to attend when his best friend does rather than does not plan to go to college; these relationships are stronger when the choice is reciprocated. [p. 575]

McDill and Coleman (1963) explored the relationships between status in adolescent social systems, college intentions, and academic orientations, using a freshman-to-senior panel of high school students, and found the relationships quite complex. Students with high status in adolescent social systems were more likely to change to both a positive orientation to attending college and a negative orientation toward academic achievement than those of low status. For those outside the leading crowd, not part of a group that takes college for granted, college plans more often stem from and lead to achievement orientation. The authors offer the following explanation for the apparently contradictory values of the high-status group:

> A general orientation widely held and widely admired by teen-agers may account for the paradoxical combination of college plans and a negative evaluation of achievement: an orientation toward "sophisticated," "adult" activities. For a teen-ager in a generally middle class environment, college holds promise of such activities—campus social life, freedom from parental control, a shift to new friends, and all the other social attributes of college. But being a brilliant student promises none of these. Rather it is associated with childhood, with good grades and gold stars dispensed by teachers. . . .
>
> Whatever the association that adults see between college and intellectualism, adolescents who are at the center of their high school social system see the two as quite distinct entities: college promises adult status, but scholastic achievement carries the connotation of acquiescence and subordination to adults. [p. 918]

Turning now to the role of the family, Siemans (1965) found, in a study of Canadian high school youth, that educational-aspiration levels increased with increasing strength of father's and mother's encouragement for continuing education. However, this relationship disappeared when the results were analyzed by class, suggesting that encouragement was a function of other status characteristics.

Cohen (1965) found that parents of upwardly mobile working-class boys had a favorable abstract evaluation of a college education and (1) deliberately encouraged going to college from an early point in the boy's life, (2) showed a concern for school performance, and (3) aspired to middle-class jobs for their son. She suggests two types of parental motivation—a *vocational* orientation that emphasizes the desirability of jobs requiring a college education, and a *status* orientation that emphasizes the college degree as an entrée to middle-class status. Behavioral pressure for good performance at the high school level was not related to mobility, as Elder (1962) also found. "We concluded that parental pressure is more crucial during the early years when attitudes toward school are being formed." [p. 425] On the other hand, Bordua (1960), in a study of students in the ninth through the twelfth grade, found that parental stress was positively related to college plans, even with class (as measured by father's occupation) controlled.

In addition to examining the usual factors—social class, parental education, religion, and so on, usually correlates of academic motivation and achievement, Elder (1962) looked at the effects of parental training and educational goals. He found adolescent academic motivation to be positively related to the involvement of the mother and father in independence training in both middle and lower classes. A similar relationship held between independence training and achievement, as measured by grade average. As to the class differences that remain, Elder writes,

> The residual social class effect may be partially explained by differences between middle and lower class values. Although parental independence training may stimulate the desire to achieve, the objects and activities in which this motivation is invested and toward which it is directed are likely to be consonant with the values of the child and his parents. The lower class child may, as a result of his parents' training, have a need to achieve, but not in a middle class institution such as the public school. [p 81]

Of the three variables—class, parental education, and paternal independence training—the latter accounted for the greater portion of the variance in academic motivation, with parental education being more important than social class. Finally, independence training, as an indirect way of inculcating a desire to achieve, seemed more effective than direct efforts to force greater academic interest or achievement.

Some efforts have been made to examine simultaneously the influence of both peers and parents on educational aspirations. Krauss (1964), in looking for the sources of aspiration among working-class youth who did go to college, concluded they involved both peer associations and certain conditions within the family. With regard to the family, such factors as evidence of upward strivings, a history of college experience and high occupational status of the father were associated with college aspirations. College-oriented working-class students were likely to have like-minded friends and to have been extremely active in extracurricular activities.

> The similarities between college-oriented working-class and the college-oriented middle-class students are striking in regard to occupational preference, income expectations, belief in the existence of opportunity, interest in national and international affairs, interest in classical or serious music, and the number of books recently read. In political preference and attitude toward labor, the college-oriented working-class students are more "conservative" than other working-class youths, but less so than college-oriented middle-class youths. In their attitudes toward the role of government, college-oriented working-class students were somewhat closer to the college-oriented middle-class youngsters than to other working-class students. [p. 876]

Kahl (1953) likewise points to the father's status and aspirations as explaining differential aspirations among working-class boys with the ability to go to college.[18]

In a further analysis of data already referred to, McDill and Coleman (1965) assayed the relative weight of family and peer influences in the college plans of high school students. In the freshman year both family background (that is, father's education) and respondent's status in the high school social structure are significantly related to college intentions, with family background accounting for more than twice as much of the variation in college plans. By the senior year, however, the pattern is reversed. Regardless of family background, the proportion of high-status students planning to attend college increases over the four years while the proportion of low-status students planning to attend decreases. A third factor, parental desire for the respondent to go to college, is even more potent than parental status in the freshman year—it has an effect more than twice as great as the effect of the other two factors—but by the senior year its effect too has decreased rather sharply. There are, however, two sources of difficulty in this study. One may well wonder how salient school status would be in the freshman year, and there is no discussion of the extent to which social class enters into the determination of a student's status in the high school social structure.[19]

[18] Supporting evidence for the idea that college-oriented working-class youth come from what might be called a "submerged middle class" is presented for the British situation by Brian Jackson and Dennis Marden, *Education and the Working Class.* New York: Monthly Review Press, 1962.
[19] See James S. Coleman's *The Adolescent Society.* New York: The Free Press of Glencoe, 1961, pp. 97 ff.

In his study of the social context of ambition, Turner (1964) includes as a consideration the effect of the neighborhood. Thus, he finds that

> The differences in level of ambition between schools in high and low neighborhoods is considerably greater than can be attributed to the differences in individual family background levels. The average level of the neighborhood probably has about as much effect as the level of the individual family background in determining how high the child's ambition will be. [p. 65]

Turner also notes that the determinants of ambition are not the same in all kinds of neighborhoods.

> While the pattern of relationships among background, ambition and I.Q. is similar in the high and low neighborhoods, all the relationships are smaller for men in the low neighborhoods. Ambition is less closely determined by either background or I.Q. and I.Q. is less closely linked with background in the low neighborhoods. [p. 65]

Turner finds a relationship between socioeconomic background and ambition, values and peer-preference patterns, but one that is relatively weak. He finds what he calls "stratification of destination" to be more important than stratification of origin. The choice of friends is more consistently in favor of those with high ambition than those of high background. This finding is in accord with the contention of Stinchcombe (1964) that the fit between the conception of post-high school status and present academic activity is a better indicator of high school "rebellion" than is social origins. Social class does, of course, affect the future status that students imagine for themselves.

Several authors have sought to relate some of the subjective factors discussed above to the kind of school attended by children. This leads to an analysis of school "cultures" or "climates" and how these influence and are influenced by the type of student body in the schools. Thus, for example, McDill and Coleman (1965) also examined the effect of father's level of education and respondent's status in school on college plans in two different school contexts—where college going is highly prized, and where it is not. Where college attendance is not valued, status in school has a negligible effect on college plans; while father's education, which is not as influential as in other schools, is of some importance. Where college going is highly valued, the pattern is as mentioned earlier, with father's education being important in the freshman year, but status in school becoming increasingly significant. The authors conclude that for youth attending schools in which college is not an important value, belief in college must be internalized early and probably comes from the home. Put another way, working-class youth who come from homes in which college going is not valued, and who attend schools in which college going is not valued, are bereft of the usual sources for generating a belief in the value of higher education.

Wilson (1959) approached the problem from another direction. Assuming that students from different social origins have different aspirations, schools dominated by one or another group should have characteristic aspirational climates. Wilson compared the aspirations of students with similar origins who attended schools marked by varying aspirational norms. He found that a larger proportion of working-class children in middle-class schools wanted a college education than was true for working-class children in working-class schools. Similarly, the working-class schools seemed to depress the aspirational level of middle-class children. There is an interaction between achievement and aspiration—those with higher achievement have higher aspirations. However, the achievement of sons of professionals and white-collar workers was found to be more adversely affected in working-class schools than was their level of aspiration. Caro (1963) also noted that lower-class boys in a school with a predominantly middle-class orientation in some ways showed themselves to be closer in plans and general orientation to the middle-class than were other working-class boys.

A significant study of the relationship between social class, ability, achievement, and school cultures is that reported by Michael (1961), based on a national survey of high school seniors. High schools were classified into five climates based on the proportion of the senior class in the top 40 percent of a family-status ranking. Class I schools contained less than 20 percent of this category in the senior class; Class V schools had a majority of its seniors from the top 40 percent. This measure of educational milieu was highly correlated with objective measures of propensity for college going.

Looking first at the relationship of family background, high school climate, and ability, Michael found that within each high school climate a larger proportion of high-status seniors scored above the median on a measure of aptitude. But for any particular status level, those in the top high school climate scored higher than their counterparts in the lowest. Though the increase in the percentage scoring above the median is proportionately greater for highest-status students, Michael also notes that

> the differences between the high school climates is sufficiently great that even the lowest-socio-educational-status youngsters in the most favorable setting surpass the performance of the highest-socio-educational-status seniors in the least favorable context. [p. 590]

While he concludes that high school climate is as important as family background in developing ability, he notes that an analysis of seniors in the top quartile on aptitude shows family background to be more important for those who show very high aptitude.

For those in the top aptitude quartile, for any given status level, the Type V climate shows a higher proportion planning to go to college. However, the differences within climates are much larger than those between climates. For all climates, family status is somewhat more important than ability in predicting college plans. But ability is more predictive in Type IV and V climates.

> The senior's social class and ability are much more predictive of his educational future in the superior educational milieu than in any other social context. In the fifth high school climate, which shapes proportionately more capable youngsters, ability accounts for the greatest portion of variation in college attendance. Conversely, a senior's social class is more predictive of his educational future in the first climate, the social context which develops fewest talented youths. [p. 595]

The importance of social class in Type I climates is in accord with the findings of McDill and Coleman (1965) noted earlier, concerning the relative importance of father's education in predicting college plans in schools where college going is not highly valued.

Sharp exception to the findings concerning the influence of school climate, especially those of Wilson (1959), has been taken by Wallin and Waldo (1964). In their study of eighth graders they found that, using the same measure as did Wilson—specifically, father's educational level—their results were comparable. When, however, the respondent's perception of father's and/or mother's educational aspirations for the child is used as a more direct measure of family environment, the apparent effect of school climate is markedly reduced.

> . . . we found that parental educational aspirations for children as an index of the similarity of children in home-given values with respect to education attenuated the observed influence of school type on boys when measured by the single question and eliminated it when measured by the more complex criterion. In the case of girls, controlling parental aspirations more or less completely eliminated the apparent influence of school type in both instances. [p. 108]

Another finding of importance was that parents of children attending middle-class schools tended to have higher aspirations for their children (as perceived by the children) than parents of children in lower-class schools. The authors suggest this reflects a greater concern on the part of these parents in the educational situs for their children—a factor not explored in most of the studies that have inquired about the role of school climate.

Conclusions

We began this chapter with evidence from a variety of reliable sources establishing rather firmly the proposition that there is a positive relationship between social class of origin and achievement in school. This may be truer in larger cities than in small ones, for Negroes more than for whites, but the general conclusion is inescapable. And yet, when we subject this relationship to more refined analysis, it becomes evident that social-class position itself is too vague a factor to be of much use.

It is apparent that there are children from low-income families who do well in school, who aspire to college and good jobs, and who in fact attain both. There are low-income parents who have high aspirations for their children, who imbue them with the desire to achieve and who provide the kind of upbringing that encourages independence and initiative. It is likewise evident that such subjective factors are not sufficient to insure upward mobility. The quality of the schools attended, the student culture in those schools, and the behavior of teachers and other personnel are relevant. The school has been viewed as a sorting mechanism, conveying to the students the values of the broader society and, more actively, directing students to the curriculum "appropriate" to their station in life.[20] Yet the Project Talent data raise serious questions about this neat formulation and about the relationship between certain attributes of school systems and educational achievement.

It would appear that much might be learned from a systematic analysis of deviant cases. Are children from low-income families who achieve appropriately in the early grades simply more intelligent, or do they come from homes that are significantly different? One of the few comparisons of successful and unsuccessful school achievers from low-income areas was made by Davidson, Greenberg, and Gerver (1962). They were concerned primarily with cognitive and affective factors, and concluded as follows:

> . . . the hypothetical good achiever from an underprivileged environment emerges as a child who is relatively controlled and cautious, often stereotyped and constructed, but who still retains a degree of originality and creativity. He seems more willing . . . to conform to adult demands, has a more positive view of authority figures and greater self-confidence. In cognitive functioning he excels chiefly in tasks requiring memory, attention and verbal abilities. He is also superior in analytical and organizational abilities and generally in processes that require convergent thinking.
>
> In contrast, the composite picture of the poor achiever is that of

[20] Aaron V. Cicourel and John L. Kitsuse, *The Educational Decision-Makers.* Indianapolis, Ind.: The Bobbs-Merrill Co., Inc., 1963.

a child burdened by anxiety, fearful of the world and authority figures and lacking in self-confidence. He is more apt to be impulsive and labile with relatively poor controlling mechanisms. His defenses against anxiety and feelings of inadequacy may be expressed in excessive talking and uncritically favorable surface attitudes toward self and others. Nevertheless, the poor achiever still seems to have sufficient potential for adaptive behavior which the school could build upon. His cognitive capacities are often quite similar in content, approach and process to those of the good achiever and in fact, he demonstrates greater facility in divergent production. Many of his reactions give evidence of creative capacity which might be directed and controlled. From his behavior in the testing situations and in tasks requiring social comprehension, the poor achiever seems to possess substantial understanding of the world around him, although he seems less able to act upon this understanding than the good achiever. [p. 18]

Another analysis of the deviant case is that of Krauss (1964), which dealt with the issue of the ways in which high-aspiration working-class boys compared with both middle-class boys and low-aspiration working-class boys. Krauss found, as did Jackson and Marsden,[21] that working-class boys who are upwardly mobile resemble middle-class boys in their values and aspirations more than they do their "social class" mates.

A widespread explanation for lower achievement among Negro youth has been that of inadequate aspirations. Yet there is scattered evidence strongly suggesting that Negro students, at given social-class levels, show at least as high educational aspirations as their white peers. Is it that the measures are inadequate, or that aspirations do not have the same consequence for Negro youth as for white youth? Deutsch and his associates have produced data relating lower levels of achievement among low-income whites and Negroes to handicaps brought from the home. Another observer has recorded the striking transformation of Negro students from low-income families from the first grade, marked by eagerness and care of dress, to the fourth grade, where all the problems of behavior and attitude are manifest.[22] What is lacking is a systematic approach that ties together the fate of these children both at home and in school so that it is possible to say with some confidence what combination of factors is responsible for any particular outcome.

A theoretical and methodological problem that must be solved before much longer is the development of a measure of status that is reliable across race lines. As Gottlieb (1964) has demonstrated, when a single standard, whether it be educational or occupational, is used as a measure of status

[21] See footnote 18.
[22] Unpublished reports by Mrs. Elaine Battis, based on classroom observations, made to the Urban Studies Center, 1964.

for both Negroes and whites, we find quite different rates of family disorganization, size, quality of housing, and so on, for families that are being
taken as equal in status. If we know that to have a college education means
one thing in the Negro community and another in the white, and that to
be a teacher means one thing in the Negro community and another in the
white, then some way must be found to calibrate measures of social status
so that "holding class constant' becomes more than a ritual.

In recent years, much effort has been put into specialized remedial
programs in subjects such as reading and mathematics, as well as broader
programs designed, in addition, to develop and support a more positive
image of the self. One of the earliest such programs was the "Higher Horizons" project of New York City. The evaluation of that project, to put it
briefly and brutally, concluded that there was no firm evidence that it had
accomplished anything.[23] If the conclusions are valid, then there is good
reason to wonder about the validity of a number of cherished educational
principles, as well as the purpose of the many projects, still in operation,
based on this model.

[23] Wayne J. Wrightstone and others, *Evaluation of the Higher Horizons Program
for Underprivileged Children*. New York: Bureau of Educational Research, Board of
Education of the City of New York, 1964.

Chapter Three

WORK

In American society, a man is known essentially by his work—what he does and for whom he does it. Despite occasional references to the relationship between education and the good life, the major function of the public school system is to groom young people to move, sooner or later, into the labor force. Our purpose in this chapter is to examine the available data concerning various aspects of the shift from school to work, and the ways in which it varies for young people from families differentially located in the socioeconomic status system.

Educational Preparation

In the previous chapter, it was pointed out that children of low-income families were more likely to drop out of school, less likely to take the academic curriculum, and, therefore, less likely to go to college than youngsters from higher-income families. S. M. Miller (1964) has estimated that possibly as many as 60 percent of working-class students graduate from high school (although as many as 25 percent of those who drop out may later return) and somewhere between three tenths and one sixth will have some college. Caro (1965) found, on the basis of a follow-up study of seniors in Jackson County, Missouri, that 57 percent of his sample attended college on a full-time basis for at least part of the immediate post-high school period. Negroes attended at the same rate as whites (although they were more likely to go to a junior college), but social class and academic aptitude were strongly related to college attendance, as indicated in Table 4. Approximately one third of those who had been in college had dropped out, and there was a clear positive association between class and dropping out for women, but only a slight tendency in that direction for men.

Given the emphasis placed on high school graduation, it is interesting to consider the findings of Davis and Hess (1963) in their study of the relationship between achievement in high school and success in later life, that is, eight years after the senior high school year. They found the absolute level of high school grades to be the most potent indicator of later success,

TABLE 4. PROPORTION OF MALES AND FEMALES ATTENDING A FULL-TIME COLLEGE, BY SOCIAL CLASS AND ACADEMIC APTITUDE

SOCIAL CLASS	ACADEMIC ACHIEVEMENT		
	High	Medium	Low
Male			
High	95.7	76.5	65.2
Medium	84.8	69.6	44.3
Low	84.2	35.3	14.3
Female			
High	90.4	70.2	70.0
Medium	70.3	39.0	30.9
Low	63.2	30.6	12.1

Source: Caro (1965), p. 40.

particularly for males. Social participation seemed to have slight association with both high school performance and success in young adulthood.

It seems likely that adult performance is more closely related to events and experiences that occur after high school than to high school behavior, especially to experiences in the family, the social class context and, later, in occupational situations. This is especially true of occupational commitment and other identity measures. Occupational commitment, for example, is related to occupational level, to salary, to social activities, and, of course, to expressed satisfaction with work. It is not significantly related to any high school variable. [pp. vii–11]

It is probable that a majority of working-class youth enter the labor force directly from high school. Before examining the consequence of entry at this level of completed education, we will look at the data on the occupational plans and aspirations of working-class and other young people.

Occupational Aspirations and Plans

An effort to organize the knowledge concerning the ways in which youth of different social origins deal with the various considerations involved in finding an appropriate place in the labor force is complicated by the approach most used by guidance people and psychologists working in this area. Research is dominated by the concept of occupational choice as presented by Ginzberg and/or the development of the self-concept as used by Super.[1] Unfortunately, Ginzberg never provides an operational definition of his concept, never deals with the nature of the process of occupational choice. And though he devotes a chapter to working-class boys, his findings are based on seventeen interviews and do not influence his basic theory. Though Super also does not deal with this problem, the Career Pattern Study in which he is engaged should produce relevant material.[2]

Most of the research on occupational choice is based on college students or college-bound high school students. Since these groups include only a small proportion of working-class youth, who may be considered deviant with reference to the majority of their friends, it may well be that the concept of occupational choice—implying a reasonably rational searching out of alternatives and a selection among them—is not generally applicable to working-class youth. The concept of occupational drift may be more meaningful. This describes much more accurately the behavior of the English working-class children studied by Carter.[3] Lipset and Selznick report that 55 percent of their respondents, on the basis of their recollections some time later, claim they had no specific job plans while in school.[4]

The contention that the choice of a relatively specific occupation may not be salient for working-class youth receives some indirect support from Dubin's study of some 1200 industrial workers. He concludes,

> Considering the pattern of responses to all the questions, we found that only 24 percent of all the workers studied could be labelled job-oriented in their life interests. Thus, three out of four of this group of industrial workers did not see their jobs and work places as central life interests for themselves. They found their preferred human associations and preferred areas of behavior outside of employment.[5]

It may be that these attitudes developed as a result of job experiences. If, however, working-class youngsters learn early in life that work will not be a major source of satisfaction, they might not become as involved in a process of occupational choice. As a matter of fact, in a study of ninety-seven blue-collar and low-income white-collar families, Dyer (1957) found that children's attitudes were similar to those of their parents, that white-

[1] Eli Ginzberg and others, *Occupational Choice: An Approach to a General Theory.* New York: Columbia University Press, 1951; Donald E. Super, *The Psychology of Careers.* New York: Harper & Row, Publishers, 1957.

[2] The project is discussed in Super and others, *Vocational Development: A Framework for Research.* New York: Bureau of Publications, Teachers College, Columbia University, 1957.

[3] M. P. Carter, *Home, School and Work.* New York: The Macmillan Company, 1962.

[4] Seymour Martin Lipset and Reinhard Bendix, *Social Mobility in Industrial Society.* Berkeley, Calif.: University of California Press, 1959, p. 193.

[5] Robert Dubin, "Industrial Workers' Worlds: A Study of the 'Central Life Interests' of Industrial Workers," *Social Forces*: 3 (January 1956), 135.

collar fathers had a more favorable attitude toward their occupations, and that children of blue-collar fathers considered blue-collar jobs less prestigeful than white-collar jobs. This would suggest that working-class youth might aspire to white-collar occupations, but not necessarily that they would actively seek out alternatives or really believe them possible.

In his study of automobile workers, Chinoy collected some data on younger people. He concluded that working-class youth, in one particular community at least, were interested in work as a source of ready spending money, and do not become seriously concerned with occupational choice and careers until they get married.[6]

As a substitute for learning about the behavior of youth of different social origins with reference to the labor market, we must shift our attention to the issue of occupation plans and aspirations. In so doing, another anomaly must be noted. Ginzberg does not use the concept of "aspirations" as an element in his theory, nor do most psychologically oriented researchers interested in this area. The research concerning the origins and relevance of levels of occupational aspirations is done almost solely by sociologists concerned primarily with the relation of social class to human behavior. There remains the suspicion that both groups may be talking about the same thing.

In an early study of children's occupational preferences, Galler (1951) found that middle-class children chose occupations with higher status than did lower-class children. Empey (1956), reviewing this and similar research, argued that relative position should be taken into account in measuring aspiration and, further, that a distinction should be made between occupations children might prefer and ones they think they can actually enter. Using a state-wide sample of male seniors, he found that while middle- and upper-class students did tend to aspire to higher-status occupations, the lower-class students aspired to occupations at a higher level than those of their fathers.[7] Further, all students anticipated entering occupations less prestigious than those to which they aspired, though the downward revisions of lower-status students were somewhat larger. Youmans (1956), on the basis of data from a large sample of tenth- and twelfth-grade students, reported that while there was a relationship between social origins and aspirations, in each social stratum, boys tended to aspire to jobs they did not actually expect to achieve. He found, as did Empey, that the great downward revision was for sons of manual workers (and farmers). Caro and Pihlblad (1965) report similar findings.

[6] Eli Chinoy, *Automobile Workers and the American Dream*. New York: Doubleday & Company, Inc., 1955, 110 ff.

[7] A similar finding, based on a study of boys aged thirteen through fourteen in Australia, is reported by N. F. Dufty, "The Relationship Between Paternal Occupation and Occupational Choice," *International Journal of Comparative Sociology*: 2 (March 1961), 81–87.

While Empey was concerned with clarifying the importance of the relative measurement of aspiration, Stephenson (1957) focused on separating occupational plans ("What kind of work do you intend to do?") from occupational aspirations ("If you could do what you really wanted to do, what would you do?"). From a sample of 1000 ninth-grade students in four New Jersey communities, he produced evidence to show that students did distinguish plans from aspirations. While aspirations were high for all social statuses, they did decline with lower status, but not nearly as much as did occupational plans. Stephenson concluded that:

> . . . aspirations are relatively unaffected by class and, hence, reflect the general cultural emphasis upon high goal orientation, while plans or expectations are more definitely class based and, hence, may reflect class differences in opportunity and general life chances. [p. 212]

This formulation may help to explain the "unrealistically" high aspirations often attributed to Negro students. However, it appears to assume that all students do in fact have plans and does not touch on the problems raised earlier in this chapter. It cannot apply to those who have already "opted" out of the system.

A number of studies have been conducted exploring the influence of various factors in the relationship between social status and occupational plans and aspirations. Thus, for example, Caro and Pihlblad (1964) found that class differences in occupational aspirations remained when academic ability is held constant. For comparable levels of ability, those from higher social-class backgrounds continued to show a greater orientation towards high-prestige occupations. Sewell, Haller, and Strauss (1957) found that although intelligence was related to aspirations, there was an independent relationship between social status and aspirations. Examining the influence of peer relationships on aspirations, Haller and Butterworth (1960) found the evidence inconclusive, although somewhat supportive of a positive relationship. Krippner (1963) found father's occupational level of "striking" importance to both sons' and daughters' occupational preferences, while that of the working mother was significant only for the occupational preference of daughters. Goetz (1962) found that, among a group of male parochial-school students, there was a positive relationship between status and the value put on work. Low-status students desired money as much as the other students, but perceived less opportunity. Goetz also found, however, that low-status students did not show any greater acceptance of illegitimate means for obtaining money.

Simpson (1962), noting that both parental and peer influences were used to explain the middle class aspirations of some working-class boys, examined the interrelationship by means of a questionnaire to boys in the white high schools of two southern cities.[8] He found parental influence to be a factor in upward mobility aspirations for both working-class and middle-class boys. In addition, however,

> Mobile working-class boys were much higher than nonmobile working-class boys and somewhat higher than unambitious middle-class boys in the percentage who said that they had middle-class friends. In the number of extra-curricular clubs to which they belonged, mobile working-class boys were close to ambitious middle-class boys, substantially higher than unambitious middle-class boys, and more than twice as high as nonmobile working-class boys. . . . Our findings also extend the anticipatory socialization hypothesis to cover middle-class as well as working-class boys.

Simpson then concludes,

> A working-class boy was most likely to aspire to a high-ranking occupation if he had been influenced in this direction by both parents and peers, and least likely to be a high-aspirer if he had been subjected to neither of these influences. Among the middle-class boys, only those low in both influences differed significantly from the rest, though the direction of the relationships in all cases paralleled those found among working-class boys. Of the two types of influence, that of parents appeared to have the stronger effect. Working-class boys influenced toward upward mobility by either parents or peers tended to have higher aspirations than middle-class boys not influenced toward high aspirations by either parents or peers. [pp. 521–522]

In a study of fifth-grade boys, Stewart (1959) explored the interrelationships between socioeconomic status, awareness of social-class symbols, occupational interests, ideas of social class behavior, and reputation among peers. He found the boys to be aware of social-class symbols but this awareness did not seem to be shaped by the respondent's own status. Further, boys from various social classes were found to have similar ideas about children's social-class behavior. Occupational-level interest scores were independent of perceptions of class symbols and of ideas about social class behavior.

> Interest scores appeared to be a factor only in the occupation preference of high status boys. Reputation among peers, however, seemed to reflect, in part, the occupational level scores. [p. 129]

[8] It should be noted that Sewell, Haller, and Strauss inquired about occupational "plans" and Simpson refers to occupations boys "expected" to enter, as measures of aspiration. But Empey and Stephenson consider the response a measure of expectation, not aspiration.

Though most of the research in this area pertains to boys, there is at least one study that concentrates on girls. Davis (1964) has reported on the results of a questionnaire distributed in grades seven through twelve in seventy communities and returned by 2549 girls, of whom 925 were daughters of blue-collar workers. When asked the type of job they hoped for at the end of school, 42 percent gave "housewife" only. Over half the girls selected one of four occupations: secretary (240), teacher (122), nurse (101), and beautician (63). Only one quarter of the blue-collar girls expected to obtain the jobs they would most like to have. In explaining the sources of their occupational choice, these girls said most frequently that the choice was their own and that the most important influence in the selection was their parents. As noted earlier, Krippner (1963) found that the occupational level of girls' preferences was significantly related to the suggestions made by both mothers and fathers, but that the mothers' suggestions were not significantly related to her own job level.

Data comparing the occupational aspirations and expectations of blue-collar and white-collar youths in grades seven to twelve are available from Morland's restudy of "Kent" (1964). He found no significant difference in the occupational aspirations of mill boys (blue-collar) and town boys (white-collar). The occupational aspirations of the mill girls were significantly lower than that of the town girls, though both groups gave secretarial work and nursing as the two top occupational preferences. Queried concerning their occupational expectations, the proportion of mill children (63.3 percent) who thought they would enter their preferred occupation was significantly lower than that of town children (75 percent).

Most studies of the relationship between social class and occupational aspirations suffer from a common technical handicap. The measure of family status is static. Whether it relates to the family at the time of the respondent's birth, or at the time of the study, the measure does not allow for the effect of social mobility, either up or down, that the family may have experienced during the child's early years. That such mobility is significant has been suggested by Smelser (1963). Using longitudinal material, Smelser was able to classify ninety-three families into five categories based on their socioeconomic history between 1928 and 1946: high and low status stationary, high and low status upwardly mobile, and downwardly mobile. The sons of these families were then grouped according to these categories, which reflected their fate during their first eighteen years of life. Smelser concluded that mobility, or lack of it, was significantly related to both aspirations and subsequent careers. At age fifteen and one-half, for example, when aspirations were measured, the mean status ratings of high-status upwardly mobile and high-status stationary families were not significantly different, yet sons from the former type of family aspired to higher-status occupations than sons from the latter type. Similarly, the mean status of low-status upwardly mobile and low-status stationary families were comparable in 1928, yet at age fifteen and one-half, sons of the upwardly mobile families had higher occupational aspirations than sons of the low-status stationary families. Finally, with reference to present careers, Smelser noted that sons from low-status upwardly mobile families hold higher status positions than sons from downwardly mobile families. In general, downward mobility had about as strong a negative effect as constant low status.

From a study of the "wishes" of Negro high school seniors, Smith (1952) determined that there was the usual positive relationship between social class and occupational preferences. A higher proportion of upper-middle and lower-middle seniors aspired to professional jobs than was the case for seniors from lower statuses. Smith notes that "The lower classes were indefinite about their vocations," a finding usually hidden from view because it represents the proportion who fail to answer or who check "don't know." Likewise, Uzell (1961) found a significant relationship between levels of occupational aspiration and parents' education for another group of Negro male high school seniors, and a relationship between level of aspiration and success in school. Lack of money and inadequate school performance were mentioned most often as potential barriers to entry to preferred occupational choices.

Race and Class

A number of studies deal with race as well as class differences in occupational expectations and aspirations. Holloway and Berreman (1959) studied male students in grades six, seven, and eight in three elementary schools of one city. They found that the occupational aspirations of lower-class pupils were significantly lower than those of middle-class students, but that the aspirational level of Negroes and whites was substantially the same for each class level. Further, the occupational plans of lower-class pupils of both races remained as high as their aspirations, as was true for both groups of children with middle-class backgrounds. These findings, somewhat contradictory to others cited earlier, are supported by Gist and Bennett (1963), based on data from ninth- and twelfth-grade students. These authors report no great differences in the occupational aspirations of Negro and white students, for given social-class categories and measured intelligence. Furthermore, all students showed considerable uniformity between plans and aspirations, regardless of race or father's occupation.

The picture is not clarified when we examine results reported by Sprey (1962), based on ninth-grade pupils in two cities. The Negro children in the sample were, in the main, from blue-collar families, and so class comparisons within the Negro sample, or between Negroes and whites by class, are not warranted. Sprey found that while Negro and white girls showed comparable levels of aspirations, Negro boys had significantly lower aspirations than white boys and both groups of girls. The same pattern held for occupational plans, though there did not seem to be any significant differences, on the basis of race, in the relationship between aspirations and plans.

The Lotts (1963), in their study of Negro and white seniors in Kentucky, found occupational choice differences based on race, sex, and class. With respect to aspirations and expectations, Negro males were more likely to opt for jobs in the clerical, sales, or skilled-trades categories than the white males who were more likely to expect professional and business occupations. There was the expected decline in high-status choices between jobs aspired to and jobs expected. There were interesting differences in the findings for girls:

> A comparison of white and Negro girls indicates that proportionately more of the latter desire top status occupations . . . but that fewer desire glamour jobs or the role of housewife. It is noteworthy that not one of the 52 Negro girls stated a desire to be a housewife in 10 years. The findings are similar with respect to expectations: proportionately more Negro than white girls expect to have top status jobs, and proportionately fewer expect to be housewives or be in a glamour (in the arts or other out-of-the-ordinary fields) job. [p. 65]

There was no significant difference in the proportion of white and Negro males who expected to attain the occupations they desired. However, a greater proportion of Negro girls expected to do what they desired to do.

There would appear to be three hypotheses that have been put to the test in the above studies, but not all three in all studies. These are (1) low-income youth have lower occupational aspirations than higher-income youth; (2) Negro youth have lower aspirations than white youth, and (3) the gap between aspirations and expectations is greater (a) for low income youth and (b) for Negro youth. The findings on these hypotheses have been summarized in Table 5. Two of the studies find that Negro males have lower aspirations than white males, two find that they do not. Two studies find that Negro girls have lower aspirations than white girls, while the Lotts find they have higher aspirations. Two of the studies find that the gap between aspirations and expectations is not greater for low-income youth. Three of them find the gap is not greater for Negro youth, but the Lotts find it greater for Negro males and for white girls. The lack of consistency may be a function of the samples used and/or the techniques. But, on the evidence, one must consider the hypotheses "not proven."

It was noted in Chapter 2 (Education) that levels of educational aspirations and expectations are affected by the climate of the school. Given the relationship between educational and occupational aspirations, it is not necessary to repeat the evidence with reference to occupational aspirations and expectations at this point. An English study of some interest, however, is that of Liversidge (1962) who compared the occupational expectations and aspirations of boys and girls from grammar schools and modern (public) schools. He was able to show that, in general, the higher class and prestige schools had the effect of "raising" the occupational aspirations of lower-class youth, while the modern school had the effect of "lowering" levels of aspirations and expectations of upper-class youth. The evidence seems rather strong, then, that the occupational as well as educational aspiration and expectation levels of low-income youth are negatively affected to the extent that their educational experience is confined to schools in low-income areas that do not generate a very special climate.

TABLE 5.   OCCUPATIONAL ASPIRATIONS BY SEX, CLASS, AND RACE

	ASPIRATIONS ARE LOWER FOR		ASPIRATIONS EXCEED EXPECTATIONS MORE FOR	
	Low-Income Youth	Negro Youth	Low-Income Youth	Negro Youth
Holloway and Berreman				
Boys	Yes	No	No	No
Gist and Bennet				
Boys and Girls	No	No	No	No
Sprey				
Boys		Yes		No
Girls		No		No
Lott and Lott				
Boys		Yes		Yes
Girls		No		No

Considering the amount of research that has been done in the area of occupational aspirations and expectations, it seems relevant to note the remarks of Davis and Hess (1963) as a result of one of the few studies that even raised the question of the relationship between aspirations and future success:

Although the subjects' level of occupational aspiration (as reported in the high school phase of the study) was associated with academic success, such aspirations held no relation to actual occupational success later. Similarly, those whose parents held high occupational aspirations for them did well in high school but did not necessarily show occupational achievement as adults. Neither fathers' nor mothers' attitude toward college attendance of our subjects or actual level of parental education bore any relationship to the subject's success in high school or later. [pp. vii–8]

Such a finding strongly suggests the importance of additional follow-up studies to pursue the issue of the extent to which differences in aspirations of students and/or their parents do make significant differences in subsequent careers.

In the discussion of occupational aspirations and expectations, we have generally not paid attention to the question of just what occupations are favored by various groups of young people. Because of the wide range of possible choices, researchers have generally used some system of categories by which to collapse the many alternatives. Very little attention has been paid, however, to what has been called the "situs" dimension of occupations—that is, the fact that many occupations may be found in a range of settings. These settings themselves have status and prestige dimensions, the consequences of which may be masked when only the occupational dimension is used. One of the few instances, apparently, when the site dimension was utilized is reported by Opinion Research Corporation in a survey of 1723 high school seniors (June 1964 graduates) in 100 high schools.[9] Two questions that were asked with reference to nine "institutions" have been used to rank order the choices. The questions were (1) "When you start to work or start looking for work in a permanent job, in which of these do you feel you might be able to find the kind of job you want?" (used here as a measure of aspiration); and (2) "Which *one* of these will probably be your first choice as a place to work?" (used here as a measure of expectations). The results can be seen in Table 6. Large and small businesses rank high as desirable locations, with males, however, ranking the federal government high and expecting to work in a school or college although they do not particularly want to. Working in a service or welfare organization falls slightly over the middle in ranking on aspirations and expectations for girls, but is quite low for boys on both counts. Starting one's own business and working for a labor organization appear as neither desirable nor expected.

Early Work Experience

Though the generalization may not hold for the children of the lowest strata of American society, it would appear that high school students recognize the prestige hierarchy of occupations and, in varying degrees, their chances for reaching particular levels. In this section we will review some of the data on the work experience of youth while in school and during the period shortly after high school graduation. We have ignored data concerning post-college employment, since there is reason to believe that a small proportion of youth from working-class homes complete college. It should

[9] Opinion Research Corporation, *How Today's Youth View Careers and Corporations.* Princeton, N.J.: Opinion Research Corporation, 1965.

TABLE 6. RANK ORDER OF "ASPIRATIONS" AND "EXPECTATIONS" CONCERNING WORK SITES, OF HIGH SCHOOL SENIORS, BY SEX

WORK SITES	ALL		MALES		FEMALES	
	Aspira-tions	Expecta-tions	Aspira-tions	Expecta-tions	Aspira-tions	Expecta-tions
A leading corpora-tion	1	1	1	1	3	2
A small business	2	3	3	2	1	3
A school or college	3	2	6	2	2	1
Federal government	3	4	2	2	5	5
State or local gov-ernment	5	7	5	7	5	6
A service or welfare organization	6	5	9	8	4	4
Self-employed pro-fession	7	5	4	5	7	7
Start own business	8	8	7	6	8	8
A labor organization	9	9	8	7	9	9
Number	(1723)		(825)		(895)	

Source: By permission of the copyright owners, Opinion Research Corporation, Princeton, N.J. [Adapted from pp. A–5, A–6.]

be noted that, given the widespread practice of part-time work at the high school level, there is surprisingly little data available.

According to Hamel, on the basis of information from the October 1963 monthly survey of the labor force conducted by the Bureau of Census, about one quarter of the students age fourteen to twenty-four were working or looking for work.[10] The number of employed students rose by 300,000 over the previous year, to a high of 3,850,000. Most of the increase was contributed by sixteen- and seventeen-year-olds, reflecting population growth rather than an increased rate of participation in the labor force. Of the boys fourteen to seventeen years old, about half worked in the occupational category of farm or nonfarm labor. Just over three fifths (62 percent) of girls fourteen to seventeen years old were employed as private-household workers (including baby sitters) or in other service occupations. Davis (1964) found that 27 percent of her "blue-collar" girls worked after school or on Saturdays, over half of them as baby sitters. The proportion of girls who worked was about the same for those with higher-status fathers. Boys age fourteen to seventeen, according to Hamel, worked an average of ten hours per week, girls of the same age an average of nine hours. The unemployment rate for nonwhite students of this age group (19.3 percent) was better than

[10] Harvey R. Hamel, "Employment of School Age Youth, October 1963," *Monthly Labor Review*: 87 (July 1964), 767–773.

twice that of white students (8.6 percent), though the participation rates were comparable.

The evidence is strong, as seen in Chapter 2 (Education), that a high proportion of drop outs are from working-class or low-income families. We have not found any data comparing the early work experience of drop outs from varying social backgrounds. For example, while Bowman and Matthews (1960) show that some 90 percent of their drop outs were essentially working class in origin, when they compare the early work experience of drop outs and a control (non drop out) group, they do not explore the effect of social class. We will assume, for practical purposes, that data concerning the work experience of high school drop outs describe the fate of working-class youth. Similarly, while there is evidence that a higher proportion of middle- or upper-status youth go to college, there appear to be no studies comparing the early work experience of noncollege-going high school graduates of differing social origins. Here again, though with some reservations, we will assume that the early work experience of high school graduates is more typical of working-class than of middle- or upper-class youth.

Employment data for both drop outs and graduates presented by Perrella permit some assessment of their fate.[11] The unemployment rate, in October, for 1963 drop outs was 32 percent, almost double that of graduates (18 percent). Further, the proportion of drop outs working or looking for work (66 percent) was appreciably lower than that for graduates (79 percent), indicating an important number had apparently stopped looking for work. Perrella noted that 1961 drop outs had not significantly improved their relative occupational position during the subsequent two years. Incidentally, she notes that two thirds of the sixteen- to twenty-one-year-old women who had not graduated high school were married. The rates were sharply different for whites (68.6 percent) and nonwhites (48.6 percent).

Havighurst and his associates (1962) draw a similar picture for those in River City who drop out of high school or do not obtain education beyond high school graduation. "The best jobs are held almost without exception by high school graduates, while the drop outs hold the poorest jobs or are unemployed." [p. 134] But even the graduates were most likely to find semiskilled or low-level white-collar jobs. The ability to find and hold a job was related to such factors as social class, IQ, and measures of social adjustment in school.

The relative effect of dropping out or graduating from high school (for those not in college) during 1961 through 1963, by color, is shown in Table 7.[12] Better than half the white graduates were found in white-collar occu-

<hr>

[11] Vera C. Perrella, "Employment of High School Graduates and Dropouts in 1963," *Monthly Labor Review*: 87 (May 1964), 522–529.

[12] Adapted from Perrella. Table 5: "Major Occupation Group of High School Graduates Not Enrolled in College by Year of High School Graduation and of School Dropouts by Year Last Attended School, by Color, October 1963," p. 526.

TABLE 7.   OCCUPATIONAL LOCATION OF GRADUATES AND DROP OUTS,
            BY RACE

OCCUPATIONAL GROUPS	GRADUATES[a]		DROP OUTS	
	White	Nonwhite	White	Nonwhite
White collar, total [b]	53.4%	18.7%	13.3%	6.7%
Clerical and kindred	41.5	10.3	6.4	3.3
Blue collar				
Operatives and kindred	19.5	28.4	30.0	15.3
Laborers and farm foremen [c]	8.3	21.3	31.8	46.6

[a] Includes graduates of both January and June 1963, but only of June for other years.
[b] Includes professional, technical, and kindred; managers, officials, and proprietors, except farm; clerical and kindred; sales workers.
[c] Combines the categories of farm laborers and foremen; and other laborers, except farm and mine.

pations, which was true for only 13.3 percent of the nongraduates. Looking at the single largest white-collar category, clerical and kindred workers, we find about two fifths of the white graduates there, but less than one tenth of the nongraduates. Clearly, neither nonwhite graduates nor drop outs fared as well as the comparable white group. But if we look at the relative "pay off" for high school graduation to whites and nonwhites, certain interesting differences emerge. White graduates were about four times as likely to be in white-collar occupations as nongraduates, whereas the ratio for comparable nonwhites is about 3 to 1. The ratio of white graduates to nongraduates in the "operatives" category is about 2 to 3; for nonwhites, it is reversed and about 2 to 1. For the white student, graduation meant a white-collar job, for the nonwhite, it meant factory work, service work, or work in the "laborer" category. For the white student, nongraduation meant work in the "operative" category; for the nonwhite drop out, it meant work as a laborer. Roughly put, high school graduation means the difference between a blue-collar or a white-collar job for white students, but only the difference between unskilled and semiskilled work for the Negro student.

This analysis leaves out an important consideration alluded to earlier and discussed by Miller (1964). It does not take into consideration the differential access to the better jobs that might exist between working-class and white-collar youth who go to work from high school. But to the extent that white-collar jobs are dependent on the life styles much more likely to be found among middle-class youth, the latter may well be in a position to skim off the better jobs. As Miller puts it,

> . . . if we could partial out family status in viewing the relation of graduating to occupation, I believe that we would find that graduation does not make a great deal of difference for the working-class boy. It is the linkage of graduation with prior middle-class status that makes

the major difference in the over-all results of the relation of high school diplomas to occupations. [p. 128]

Some support for this contention is provided by Caro (1965). Two years after graduation, 61 percent of males and 40 percent of females not in college indicated that work was their major current activity. Whites with low social backgrounds, low aptitude ratings, and Negroes held white-collar jobs less often than others, though the association between social class and occupation was not statistically significant. Fifteen percent of the noncollege group had been unemployed for at least a month at one time or another. White males, Negroes, and those with low social background were significantly more likely to have experienced difficulty finding work.

Additional support is provided by Morland (1964) in the study referred to earlier. He points out that in his original study in 1948, just 3.5 percent of the schoolchildren said they wanted to become millworkers. Yet of the 132 children from fifty-eight of the ninety-six mill families included in the restudy, over half did become blue-collar textile workers. Only ten of the sixty-four boys entered white-collar work or were potential white-collar employees. Slightly less than half of the 132 children were graduated from high school, although this was a verbalized goal. While just over 15 percent of those who were graduated entered white-collar work, only one boy among the nongraduates did so. To some extent, this may reflect the level of opportunity in a Piedmont community of 5000. However, all fifteen mill children who continued their education beyond high school became or were potential white-collar workers. This suggests that it may take more than high school graduation to lift the working-class offspring into the strata of white-collar jobs.

The relationship of social class and education to subsequent employment is explored in a retrospective study of a Canadian community by Hall and McFarlane (1962). Recruits to nursing and teaching are shown to be high school graduates of predominantly manual-worker–father background. Five of seven accountancy students came from the families of manual workers. On the other hand, while slightly over one fifth of the respondents had parents or guardians in nonmanual occupations, three fifths of the university cohort were of this social origin. White-collar work is predominantly the province of girls and is a most convenient occupation for social mobility—a high proportion of the girls in such work come from the homes of manual workers. Seven eighths of the apprentices or apprentice-trained boys were sons of manual workers, and most of them had taken a vocational course in high school. At the level of semiskilled work, we begin to find high proportions of the children of manual workers who did not finish high school. The authors make the following interesting observation on the relative opportunities for upward mobility of boys and girls:

Over 60 percent of the boys from the families of non-manual workers are themselves employed in non-manual occupations, whereas 90 percent of the girls with a similar background are in the non-manual work. Of interest too is the fact that two thirds of the girls whose fathers or guardians are manual workers have found work in non-manual fields. This is in sharp contrast to the boys from the families of manual workers, where the proportions entering manual and non-manual occupations are the reverse, that is, two thirds of the manual workers' sons are engaged in manual occupations and one third in non-manual. [p. 59]

Morland makes an interesting point concerning the relationship of education to occupation. On the basis of conversations with mill officials and teachers, he concludes that a decision about occupation is made prior to a decision about education:

Teachers and officials reported that mill children would often ask if they should drop out of school to take a job in the mill. Those asked stated that they reminded the children that once they stopped school and entered the mill, they were in such work for life. The mill child's decision . . . to drop out or to go further in school rested, then, on a decision about what occupation he wished to enter. Stated in another way, it was not more schooling that led the mill child into white-collar work. Rather it was the decision to try for white-collar work that led to more schooling. [p. 139]

This formulation fits well with that offered by Stinchcombe (1964) to explain high school "rebellion." He contends that it is not social origin as such that determines attitude toward school, but rather the perception the student has of the relevance of school to his future occupational status. While the education is likely to appear irrelevant more often to those of low social origins who do not expect much in the way of future jobs, it will also appear irrelevant to middle-class children who, for whatever reason, have already decided not to participate in the race for a prestigeful job.

Though going to work is almost as certain as death or taxes, there appears to be little social-science concern with the problems of work adjustment of high school graduates or drop outs. While some data are available concerning the location of youthful workers in the labor force, we know little concerning their attitudes, values, and beliefs. In his study of the automobile worker, Chinoy did touch on this problem.[13] He found that young workers coming to the auto factory consider their jobs as temporary. "Working class youth may profess to be concerned with occupational success and advancement but they are likely to be more interested in a good time." [p. 114] This requires money, and the auto factory has the virtue of relatively high start-

[13] See footnote 6.

ing wages. The deviant pattern, according to Chinoy, is represented by those who decide quickly to shift to skilled work, through additional schooling or apprenticeship training. For the majority, however, concern with advancement and the future does not manifest itself until marriage or, sometimes, parenthood. But then the young workers are likely to find that they lack the training for advancement to skilled jobs, or that family responsibilities do not permit the luxury of additional schooling.

Himes (1964) has suggested that lower-class Negro youth are particularly disadvantaged with reference to socialization to the world of work. The relatives, neighbors, and peers with whom they associate are excluded from important segments of the labor force and therefore cannot serve as models for significant occupations, or pass on the occupational culture. They tend to do work that has no intrinsic goodness or importance and in which there is little evidence of a link between effort and advancement. Thus, according to Himes, lower-class Negro youth are excluded from the prevailing work ethos. They do not overhear shop talk and do not become familiar with tools, jargon, and custom. They are not likely to acquire the ideology and values of labor unions, nor are they likely to become familiar with the impact of such industrial arrangements as work shifts, pay periods, or vacation schedules. In a very real sense, they are culturally deprived. These elements of the industrial culture, normally taken for granted because they are learned painlessly by most people, may be equally alien to significant segments of white youth.

Labor-Management Relations

A major aspect of the adjustment to work has to do with the socialization of young people to the nature of organized labor-management relations. Yet we have been able to find only one study, that of Haire and Morrison (1957) that touches on the topic, and it deals with adolescents still in school. The authors gave five short tests to 755 subjects in grades seven through eleven in schools in the San Francisco area. They found that even at a young age, the perceptions concerning labor and management were related to socioeconomic origins. Children from lower socioeconomic families were more pro-labor, showing greater agreement and identification with workers. By comparing children from lower and higher socioeconomic families who attended schools dominated by the same or the other class, it was found that, for the younger children, the school was more important in shaping attitudes than the home.

The two groups differed in their perceptions of the union as an organization. Those of high origins tended to see the union as an aggregate of people with relatively unspecified functions and little organization structure. Those of low origins focused primarily on function, seeing the union's economic function as directly related to labor-management relations. One might interpret this finding as supporting the abstract-concrete dimension often cited as a crucial class difference, or as simply indicating that the students of low social origins knew what unions were about while the others did not.

There were also interesting differences in the way the two groups characterized "the boss" and "the worker." Younger children of higher origins noted that the boss was a leader, an important man who received a large salary. Older high-origin children shifted their emphasis to the education and intelligence of the boss, differentiated between brain and brawn in work, and stressed the fact of ownership. High-origin children stressed the subordinate position of the worker. Looking at the boss, low-origin children saw him as giving orders, telling other people what to do. These children saw workers as people who worked hard, earned a living, and did what they were told to do. These views may be interpreted as reflecting the differences related to class cultures, or as related to a projection of anticipated status. In either case, it is apparent that the sources, substance, and consequences of attitudes, values, and beliefs held by youngsters concerning the nature of labor, management, and their interrelationship are fruitful areas awaiting investigation.

In 1960, Opinion Research Corporation did a survey of 1130 students in grades seven, nine, and twelve in a four-county industrial and rural community in the Midwest.[14] Some of the items used in that survey give us clues to the attitudes of high school students toward labor and management. As can be seen from Table 8, the students may be considered somewhat pro-union. It is also evident that these attitudes are related to social-class background, as measured roughly by the educational level of the chief wage earner of the respondent's family.

Conclusions

What do we know about the occupational aspirations and expectations of working-class youth and their subsequent occupational fate, as compared with other youth? It seems apparent that, broadly speaking, most American children, regardless of class, aspire to work careers that represent upward mobility as compared to the careers of their parents. Working-class youth seem less likely to aspire to the professions, and as a means to these occupations, to a college education. But when their aspirations are viewed in relative terms, there is no doubt that most of them are aware that "getting ahead" is expected of them. It may be that working-class youth are not as optimistic as higher-placed youth—the gap between aspirations and expectations may be greater—but the evidence is not conclusive.

There is some evidence that the level of occupational aspirations is

[14] Opinion Research Corporation, *How Children Form Their Views of the Business World*. Princeton, N.J.: Opinion Research Corporation, 1961.

TABLE 8.   PROPORTION OF STUDENTS EXPRESSING AGREEMENT, BY
FAMILY EDUCATION LEVEL

ITEMS	TOTAL	LESS THAN HIGH SCHOOL	HIGH SCHOOL	SOME COLLEGE OR COMPLETED
Labor unions are very necessary to protect the workingman	74%	80%	74%	63%
Labor unions have become too big and powerful for the good of the country	51	47	49	63
One of the faults of the business system . . . is that the owners get too much of the money companies make, compared to what employees get	55	57	58	47
There's too much power concentrated in the hands of a few large companies for the good of the nation	48	53	49	40
Money invested in new machinery and equipment has increased output. The workers have got some of the increase, but the larger share has gone to the owners	71	75	72	63
Total	(1130)[a]	(455)	(387)	(259)

Source: By permission of the copyright owners, Opinion Research Corporation,
Princeton, N.J. [From pp. A–16, A–19, A–21, to A–23.]
  [a] This figure does not agree with the total number of responses reported (455 +
387 + 259 = 1101); the explanation is probably that some respondents did not answer
all items.

an important factor in setting the level of educational aspirations. But it
is not clear how predictive, if at all, occupational aspirations are of future
occupational fate. As Caro has indicated, it would seem that a sizable proportion of each youth cohort may have to settle for less than what they
expected, let alone what they aspired to. Davis and Hess argue that the
importance of posthigh school experiences is more significant in careers
than much of school experience, except for the level of school achievement.
And several authors have pointed to the role of school climates as equal
to or possibly greater than the influence of family background in shaping
future orientation.

It would seem that the "structural" or objective side of the analysis has been neglected. That is, there is considerable research on individual values and goals, and attempts to relate these to such factors as family background, peer relations, and so on. But aside from using father's occupation as a measure of status, there has been relatively little concern with that occupation in terms of its meaning to the family, and how the particular configuration affects the children's definition of particular occupations and the broader world of work. Nor do we have much knowledge about how the school systematically (or otherwise) passes on values, attitudes, and beliefs about work—what is a good job, and why; what kinds of people get good jobs, and how. To what extent and in what ways do schools seek to guide working-class youth into "socially" appropriate careers? This is a subject about which much has been written on the basis of minimal evidence.

In recent years, there has been some discussion of the inadequacy of the mechanisms designed to rationalize the transition from school to work. The U.S. Employment Service, since the passage of the Economic Opportunity Act, has moved toward specialized facilities for assisting youth to find employment—with unevaluated results as yet. Hall and McFarlane (1962) report that neither school guidance counselors nor employment-service personnel were significant in the job-hunting efforts of their respondents. But to understand the occupational fate of young people we must look beyond the transition to the first job and see the relationship between such entry points and long-range careers.

One such effort is a study by the National Committee on Employment of Youth which examined industrial practices with reference to the employment and training of high school drop outs and graduates.[15] Here we get a picture of the barriers raised by employers, some rational, others based on prejudice, and thus some understanding of the opportunity structure facing such youth. As the study points out, such variables as the nature of the labor force, the occupational mix of the particular firm, and management policies on training and promotion significantly shape the opportunities of young people. Furthermore, it is apparent that comparable firms may vary greatly in whether they perceive possibilities for upward movement from jobs of lesser skill, and whether they are willing to provide the training programs that are a necessary link between aspirations and realistic opportunities. Unfortunately, we have no way of knowing to what extent there is accurate or distorted knowledge about these contingencies among high school youth and how such knowledge, or the lack of it, acts to shape aspirations and expectations long before the youth even reach the labor market.

[15] National Committee on Employment of Youth, "Getting Hired, Getting Trained." New York: The Committee, 1964. Processed.

Chapter Four

FAMILY OF PROCREATION

At some points and in some ways most American adolescents are either pushed, pulled, or wander out of their families of orientation into some interim "debottling" version of a "youth culture," and into some form of protective organization such as schools, colleges, the Army, or cliques or gangs. From this interim phase, they are presumably again pushed, pulled, or wander (or rush or are dragged) into their own families of procreation, which then have some kind of relationship (from alienation to close involvement) to their own and their spouses' families of orientation and to the "youth culture."

To describe these processes as they occur in the lower, or any other, class, would be to describe the "points" and the "ways" at which each of the transitions is made, the nature of the felt costs and rewards of making and not making them, the content of the particular youth culture, the processes of pairing off, and the nature of the new unit and its relationships to the old ones.

Curiously enough—in view especially of the general American infatuation with sex and with the alleged spontaneity, potency, and troublesomeness of lower-class persons—there is, in fact, very little detailed information on any of those issues for the current or recent period. We have, to begin with, no real knowledge of the relative numbers or proportions of lower-class youth of different ages who have varying degrees of attachment to their families of orientation, who feel varying degrees of responsibility to them and varying degrees of control by them. A single exception to this is a 1946 questionnaire study by Nye (1951) of 1472 adolescents from grades eight and eleven of fifteen Michigan public schools. Nye found that lower-class students were significantly more poorly adjusted to their parents than high-status students, and that this difference remained after controlling for rural-urban residence and for broken homes.

But qualitatively, we know little of a reliable nature about their time schedules—how much time is spent in family enterprises or surroundings, how much in peer activities, how much in heterosexual or homosexual relations (and how much of those are "sexual" in which kinds of ways); and we know even less about the significance of such time allocations in the psychic economies of these youth.

Smith (1962) contrasts the adolescent clique and the gang as the respective middle-class and lower-class interim socializing and controlling structures, pointing to the gang's greater monopoly of control over its members, greater alienation from families of orientation and the general adult world, and greater tendencies to violence, exploitation, and other forms of deviance. These are largely impressionistic sketches, however; and we do not know anything about incidence and proportions.

With respect to strictly sexual experiences, Kinsey's[1] data from the 1940s are still the most extensive. They indicate that lower-class males as contrasted with others have greater frequencies of orgasm of all types, masturbate less, have fewer nocturnal emissions, are erotically aroused by a narrower range of stimuli, are much less likely to pet to climax, and are much more likely to have premarital sexual intercourse, to have it at earlier ages, and to have it more frequently. They are also more likely to use prostitutes, but a smaller proportion of their premarital intercourse is had with prostitutes. They are more likely to have homosexual relations leading to orgasm (but Kinsey himself was suspicious of the reliability of the low rates indicated by his data for middle- and upper-class men).

As far as heterosexual relations in general are concerned, there has been some interest in the differences in class practices with respect to "dating." What is meant by "dating," however, is not always clear. If we define it as the practice in which a boy asks a girl some time in advance to go with him at his expense to some recreational activity, and then escorts her there and home, several axes of possible differences become apparent: how far in advance the asking conventionally takes place, the types of recreational activity typically engaged in, the mode and manner of escorting, the expensiveness of the occasion, its typical frequency, the number of girls a boy typically dates over a period of a month or more, the kind of *quid pro quo* expected of the girl, the dyadic or "group" nature of the enterprise.

Hollingshead (1961) found that the frequency of dating was lower among lower-class youth, but it is not clear whether this means that lower-class youth had less social interaction with members of the opposite sex or that their interaction less often took the form of dating. Hill (1955) found in a study of 229 high school students in Florida that the higher a student's social class, the greater his number of dating partners, but again it is not

---

[1] Alfred C. Kinsey, Wardell B. Pomeroy, and Clyde E. Martin, *Sexual Behavior in the Human Male*. Philadelphia: W. B. Saunders Company, 1948.

clear just what this means. With respect to the other axes of differentiation, we know even less.

Whyte's[2] well-known study of Cornerville painted the by-now familiar picture of lower-class boys' classifying girls into "virgins," whom one might ultimately marry, and "lays," whom one would rather not. Walter Miller[3] has provided the most vivid picture since Whyte in his, as yet unpublished, report on the Roxbury Youth Project of the Boston University School of Social Work. The lower-class adolescents (all gang members) described by Miller have a complex image of women as being "pigs and bitches"; highly desirable; agents of control ("ball and chain"); agents of nurturance; and loyal supporters and allies. It is not, moreover, that different females are in each category; all females are in all of them.

In this group, boys and girls start going steady at age sixteen or seventeen, the relationship being much like marriage, with an "of course" expectation of sexual intercourse. A high proportion turn into actual marriage, *via* the route of premarital pregnancies. [Hollingshead (1961) relates in this connection that in 83 percent of marriages of lower-class youth in Elmtown, premarital pregnancy was suspected. Kinsey, however, found that lower-class girls—as measured by education and by father's occupation—were *less* likely than others to have premarital coitus, although when age of marriage was controlled, the class differences disappeared.]

When marriages occur, according to Miller, they sweep the gang in a wave—"as if in response to a signal which said, 'Now is the time for group members to take a wife.' "

Miller offers an interesting explanation of the abrupt shift from the gang to marriage; namely, that with the end of adolescence the gang cannot provide the nurturance and control these men need, or at least not without the growing cost of continuing an image of self as somehow not fully grown up. Miller puts it in a striking way: "the simple explanation, 'Those wedding bells are breaking up that old gang of mine,' could just as well be phrased, 'The break-up of that old gang of mine is bringing on those wedding bells.' "

No study reports, however, on the process by which final sorting out of mates occurs; and we have almost no picture of how this situation looks from the girls' point of view.

Rainwater (1960) suggests a pattern of simply drifting into marriage —"I don't know why or how but we just did." [p. 62] Pavenstedt (1965) similarly notes with respect to her sample of thirty relatively stable working-class families, "In the history obtained of the courtship . . . there was little evidence of a love relationship of any great depth." [p. 2] Havighurst and

---

[2] William Foote Whyte, *Street Corner Society*. Chicago: University of Chicago Press, 1943.

[3] See footnote 11, Chap. 1.

his "River City" associates (1962) have a slightly different, but by no means inconsistent, hypothesis concerning early marriages among lower-class youth, especially girls. Their cohort study of almost 500 children from the time they were eleven until they were twenty found that three fourths of the Class D girls were married by the age of twenty, as compared to only one fourth of the Class A girls. Their suggestion is that early marriage may be the only path to maturity for girls whose class and/or intellectual background prevents them from using school as such an avenue. Boys, they suggest, among whom they found no relationship between class and early marriage, may have other alternatives. Caro's (1965) findings point in the same direction.

We are somewhat better off when it comes to knowledge about the structure and operation of the lower-class family of procreation itself, once formed. This is due in largest part to the impressive study by Cohen and Hodges (1963) of some 2600 male heads of families in four different classes (lower-lower, upper-lower, lower-middle, and upper-middle) in California. They report, to begin with, a marked tendency for lower-lower family members to maintain closer ties to former kinship solidarities than do higher classes. They visit neighbors, relatives, or other friends twice as frequently as do upper-middle-class families; are more than three times as likely to say that "relatives," rather than neighbors or friends, are the people they invite to their homes most frequently; and are over twice as likely to respond that three or all of their four closest friends are relatives.

Cohen and Hodges report further that, unlike the middle-class pattern, *each* of the spouses in the lower-lower family tends to cling to his or her *own* former kinship ties, instead of relating to them as a unit. "For men," they write,

> prospects in the world of work are not sufficiently optimistic to permit turning one's back on any relationships that might provide some cushion against insecurity. For women, there is not the same assurance as in the middle class, derived from marriage to a stably employed male, of an economically stable future, and they are reluctant to weaken their ties to any trusted and dependable kinsmen. [p. 309]

On the other hand, as Cohen and Hodges report, other studies comparing patterns of giving and receiving help in lower-class and middle-class families (an issue not directly investigated by Cohen and Hodges) do *not* show any class differences. Cohen and Hodges feel that within the very lowest class, older kin ties may, however, be more important than is revealed by other studies which fail to distinguish between lower lower and upper lower, and that this importance is especially great in the case of such difficult-to-measure "objects of exchange" as "recognition and response, relief from boredom and loneliness, and the toleration and indulgence of idiosyncrasies and failings." [p. 313]

Some differences in this connection among different sections of the lower class are reported by Stone and Schlamp (1965), who interviewed almost 400 husbands of families that had never been on welfare and over 200 husbands of families that had been on welfare for a long time. They found that the major difference between the "never-on-aid" group and the "long-term-welfare" group was that the never-on-aid families had much more contact and mutual aid relations with extended kin than the other group. This difference, moreover, was independent of both ethnicity and rural-urban residence.

The comparative underemphasis on the conjugal family as a source of emotional support and a focus of psychic energy is suggested by Miller (see footnote 11, Chap. 1), who describes a pattern in which the male, after relinquishing his gang, "spends some period of time as a member of a husband-wife household, gradually shifts his associations back to the all-male group, returns to the husband-wife arrangement, and so on." Gans'[4] observation that the marriage partners of his Boston low-income area "are much less 'close' than those in the middle-class" is supportive of this. "They take their troubles," says Gans, "less to each other than to brothers, sisters, other relatives, or friends." [p. 51]

Pavenstedt (1965) describes a similar pattern, although in so doing she suggests the existence of a conspicuously more family-centered pattern in certain cases. Speaking of the relatively stable working-class families in her sample, she notes, in the first place, that

> The young couple rarely attempted to discover common interests or ideas. . . . Bowling and roller skating had been the chief interests of the mothers prior to marriage; the movies and visiting with family members and occupational friends now took their place. We were surprised how many of the young women tolerated the continuation of their husbands' adolescent group relationships and activities—the poolroom, ball games, etc. [p. 2]

Komarovsky (1964) reinforces this picture for the sixty working-class couples (white, Protestant, semiskilled, less than high school education, 80 dollars per week income) she studied. The ready acceptance by wives of their husbands' independent social lives is explained by one of Komarovsky's female respondents in an interesting way:

> Regular guys don't mess around with women except when they want what a woman's got to give them. Men and women are different; men

[4] Herbert Gans, *The Urban Villagers*. New York: The Free Press of Glencoe, 1962.

don't feel the same as us. The fellows got their interests and the girls got theirs, they each go their separate ways. [p. 150]

Moreover, Pavenstedt's description of the women's reluctance to leave their jobs strikes a consistent note. "When we first saw them [in a prenatal clinic], the women were still in factory, clerical, or sales jobs engaged in upon leaving school. . . . They were reluctant to cease working in the seventh month of pregnancy, fearing the loss of companionship and routine activity and their relative financial independence." [pp. 2–3]

A different note is struck, however, when Pavenstedt continues with the observation that "Many of the men were taking courses under the GI Bill to improve their employment. Most abandoned these as they were confronted by the cost of the delivery and the responsibilities of becoming fathers. Instead, they took on extra jobs." (There were, however, only thirty of these "stable" working-class families to begin with, so it is uncertain what the significance of "many" or "most" might be.)

Once the family of procreation has "settled down" to a more or less stable routine, what is it like? The Rainwater, Coleman, and Handel study (1959) of workingmen's wives gives a picture, from the woman's point of view, of dullness and hopelessness, mixed with a "determination to keep going." [p. 61] These wives feel a lack of variety or relief from monotony, they fear loneliness, they are pervaded by a sense of immobility. Reality is seen as flat and unvarnished, but at the same time filled with uncertainties. They wish for more brightness in their lives, but they do not always do much to put it there. They are emotionally volatile, and rather concerned about being so. They feel "vulnerable to sexual temptation"; but probably yield to it very infrequently, if at all. [p. 70] They are afraid of their husbands, and feel unable to control their marital ups and downs.

Komarovsky again supports and illumines this condition: she notes that the idea of contemporary families as specializing in the "tension-management" of spouses, or as being "companionate," may not apply to working-class families. Even though the spouses in working-class families may idealize such a relationship (as wives are more likely to do than husbands), they lack the social-emotional and communicative skills for actually practicing it. In any case, she writes, "these men and women do not turn to one another for emotional support, and it is uncertain whether the net effect of the marital relationship is to relieve or to increase personal tension." [p. 327]

Some evidence on the latter point is suggested by an NORC study of 393 men in four communities in Illinois (Bradburn, 1963). Lower-status men were found to be almost twice as likely as higher-status men to report that their marriages were only "average" or "not too happy"; but they were *less* likely to report "high marital tension." They were, however, more likely than upper-status men to say that their marriages were unhappy, regardless of the level of tension reported—in fact, among all men with low marital tension, lower-status men were about twice as likely to say that their marriages were "unhappy."

Although, as Rainwater, Coleman, and Handel report, the working-man's wife often feels dependent on and afraid of her husband, she has a great deal of autonomy in the management of the household. This seems to have given rise to some uncertainty among observers as to just what the power structure of lower-class families is. On the one hand, as Cohen and Hodges report, lower-class males are more likely than others to express, in response to questionnaire items, sentiments of an authoritarian patriarchal nature such as, "Men should make the really important decisions in the family." On the other hand, they report that in fact lower-lower-class women "take the major share of responsibility for budgeting, bill-paying, and child-care—to a greater degree, in fact, than is true in the other class levels." [p. 326] Blood and Wolfe[5] also found that lower-class wives were more "dominant" in decision making than wives in other classes; and that their working tended to increase this dominance. [p. 31] (We shall return below to the issue of wives' participation in the labor force by class.)

Cohen and Hodges offer what seems to be the best tentative resolution available of the apparent contradiction. They suggest that the lower-lower-class male probably has a greater "compulsive" need to affirm his power.

> This does not mean that he will attempt to run the household; he will leave that to his wife. But he will need from time to time to make a demonstration of his power, to be ascendant in a contest of will in order to reassure himself of his status. In most matters concerning the internal affairs of the household, however, effective power will be actually wielded by the wife, not because she would be more successful in a showdown, but because, by the husband's default, she is left in effective command most of the time. [p. 327]

Blum (1964) cites evidence to show that the upshot of these marital relationships is to leave lower- and working-class spouses more discontented with their marriages than other categories of the population. Blood and Wolfe provide support for this from their study of Michigan wives, indicating that the higher the social class the greater the proportion of wives who express satisfaction with their marriages. [pp. 253–254]

Blum links both the fact of discontent and the alleged fact that given levels of discontent lead less often to divorce, to the pattern of conjugal role segregation. On the one hand, he suggests, "As the close-knit [non-familial] network increasingly comes to serve as a source of gratification

<hr/>

[5] Robert O. Blood, Jr., and Donald M. Wolfe, *The Dynamics of Married Living.* New York: The Free Press of Glencoe, 1960.

for working-class spouses, their own inter-personal relationships deteriorate and suffer." [p. 201] On the other hand, following Bott (1957), he notes two characteristics of the spouses' extrafamilial networks that other writers have tended to pass by, and that soften, or at least alter, the impression of sharp isolation of the spouses. The first of these is that the networks of each spouse are themselves interconnected. As Bott puts it, "Male relatives of the wife are likely to be friends or colleagues of the husband, and, after a marriage has continued for some time, the husbands of a set of sisters are likely to become friends." [p. 254] In consequence,

> In spite of the conjugal segregation in external relationships the overlapping of the networks of husband and wife tends to ensure that each partner learns about the other's activities. Although a wife may not know directly what a husband does when with his friends, one of the other men is likely to tell his wife or some female relative and the information is passed on. Similarly, any important activity of the wife is likely to be made known to her husband. [p. 255]

A second characteristic of these networks that refine the picture of husband-wife isolation, Blum suggests, is that their very interconnectedness, when combined with their near monopoly of informal normative control over members, holds the spouses locked, as it were, in their marital relationship, in spite of their discontent and role segregation. Nonetheless, as Goode shows, divorce rates are inversely related to socioeconomic status, service workers' "index of proneness to divorce" being over three and one-half times that of professional and semiprofessional workers, or proprietors, managers, and officials; and low-income recipients' (less than 1000 dollars) being over two and one-half times that of persons with incomes of 4000 dollars and over.[6] Education, also, is inversely related to divorce proneness (except, interestingly, for Negroes, among whom there is a positive relationship, perhaps, reflecting, as Goode suggests, a continuation of the pattern in which desertion is the poor Negro's divorce).

Glick and Carter (1958) similarly observe that over a fourth of persons with elementary school education have been married twice or more, while only a tenth of college graduates have been.

In commenting on these relationships, Goode, by the way, offers an interpretation directly contrary to Blum's generalization. "The network of both kin and friends is larger and more tightly knit among the upper strata than among the lower strata, so that the consequences of divorce are likely to be greater. It is easier for the lower class husband simply to abandon his marital duties." [p. 419]

[6] William J. Goode, "Family Disorganization," in Robert K. Merton and Robert A. Nesbit, eds., *Contemporary Social Problems*. New York: Harcourt, Brace & World, Inc., 1961, pp. 390–458.

The contradiction, of course, is probably more apparent than real, since Goode is referring to "lower class" and Blum to "working class," but the juxtaposition of their observations highlights the need in this area for more research with more careful distinctions among strata.

Two recent studies focus attention on the impact of increased prosperity on working-class family patterns; and in so doing may foreshadow the problems that will occupy social scientists and the caretaking professions when the current ones of poverty are solved. Hurvitz (1964) interviewed twenty-four working-class couples "born in the lower class . . . and moving into the middle class," who have had a materially middle-class level of living "thrust" upon them by a booming California airplane industry fed by defense contracts. Their sudden affluence, Hurvitz observes in an unusually sensitive and suggestive analysis, has, to begin with, made them uneasy. "They feel that somehow they are lying about themselves because their [middle-class] appearance does not reflect their [lower-class] self-evaluations." [p. 95]

The wives tend to develop middle-class definitions faster than their husbands through their exposure to "the ubiquitous Dr. Spock," as well as to "pediatricians, schoolteachers, PTA speakers . . . daytime TV programs, the family or women's section of the daily newspapers, and so forth." [p. 95] The husband, however, continues to regard himself

> . . . as the victim of circumstances—not their creator—even though those circumstances are presently benign and are enabling him to prosper. He . . . describes himself as less adequate than his material possessions . . . [and] his negative self-evaluation permeates his relationships with other people, his wife included. [p. 96]

On the wife's side, her acculturation to middle-class orientations, while she is married to a man who, by those standards, is not a success, creates special problems for her—and for her husband. She handles her problem, Hurvitz suggests, by transferring "her loyalty from her husband to her children almost as soon as they appear and she attempts to prove her worth as a person by her effectiveness as a mother." [p. 97] The result is an incongruity in the respective conceptions of wives and husbands of their own and their spouses' "most important" roles.

Both agree that the husband's most important family function is "earning the living and supporting the family" and that the wife's is "caring for the children's everyday needs"; but after that their rankings of their own and one another's roles diverge in ways that are at the root of their marital strains. To the husband, his relations with his wife come next in importance, and he thinks this should be true for her also. To her, however, her relations with her children come next, and only after that her companionship role with her husband. Her sexual role not only comes far down on her list, but she tends to use it as a bargaining counter with her husband in order to have her way in other areas to which she attaches more importance—being a "friend, teacher and guide" to her children, homemaking, managing finances, practicing the family religion or philosophy, serving as a model of woman for her children.

The net impression is of a man who feels so vulnerable in the economic role both he and his wife agree is his most important one that he is unable to satisfy a wife whose aspirations and values require, but whose own feelings of inadequacy have prevented her from capturing, a much more middle-class-like husband.

In addition, Hurvitz notes a phenomenon that is made the focus of the Rainwater and Handel (1964) analysis of the impact of prosperity; namely, an attenuation of the traditional pattern of a close-knit network of relatives and long-time friends and a correspondingly greater focus of attention on the nuclear family. Moreover, they report that a related effect "is a shift away from a pattern of highly segregated conjugal roles . . . toward more mutual involvement" between husband and wife. The husband "is less likely to have his own friends, and his wife, her separate set of friends." [p. 72]

The Rainwater and Handel paper is based on what is apparently a reanalysis of interviews with working-class couples conducted for three other studies in which the authors were engaged. (These interviews were with "1000 upper lower class men and women" in Chicago, 300 working-class couples and 100 middle-class couples in five cities across the country, and 150 middle- and lower-class couples in Chicago.) The authors use the difference between conjugal-role segregation and mutual involvement as an index of "traditional" versus "modern" working-class family structures; but it is not clear how those types are related to the more usual distinction between "lower lower" and "upper lower" class families, as in the Cohen and Hodges study. Nor is it clear to what extent the "modern" families are working-class families who have become "modernized" after experiencing something like the affluence of Hurvitz's couples, or to what extent they simply represent a more middle-classlike segment of the working class that has always been that way.

They *are* different, however, in several ways. Concerning the power dimension, for example, Rainwater and Handel write that, although the "modern" husband

> . . . may not define himself as being as powerful as his traditional counterpart, he actually has more influence on what goes on at home because he is there more and because he expects to cooperate with his wife both in making decisions and in carrying them out. [p. 72]

The substitution by "modern" working-class couples of a close mutual involvement for the traditional conjugal-role segregation, however, does not make these couples middle class. Rainwater and Handel note that very few working-class couples talk of themselves, as lower-middle-class people do, as being socially active or as cultivating individual intellectual or artistic interests. "For the lower middle class, such interests are seen as enriching the conjugal relationship; in the working class, they are more likely to seem dangerous distractions, harbingers of conjugal segregation in a new guise." [p. 73] Additional differences appear in the area of marital sexual relations, and will be discussed below.

Before turning to the sexual and reproductive patterns, however, we should note here the omissions from the literature of information about many aspects of the nonsexual quality and content of lower-class marital relations. The daily round, the levels and styles of communication, the depth of understanding, the nature of affection and the means and manner of displaying it—on none of these issues do we know much. In fact, there is little basis on which even to assess the contemporary accuracy of the Lynds' comment on the difference between Middletown's working-class and business-class couples of over a generation ago: "There is less frankness in the relationship and more confusion and disagreement on subjects that are of mutual concern, such as birth control."[7]

We do know some quantitative things about physical sexual relations, as of almost a quarter of a century ago, from Kinsey—to wit, that the lower the level of education, the less does marital intercourse account for all "outlets" in the early years of marriage, and the *more* does it do so in later years. (More educated males, as they move into the later years of marriage, masturbate more, have nocturnal emissions more, and have more extramarital intercourse.) As of the Kinsey period, further, lower-class couples frowned on nudity, on extensive foreplay, and on "fancy" positions, as compared with middle- and upper-class couples. Frequency of marital intercourse was similar at all class levels.

Rainwater (1960) provides more qualitative information on the sexual relations of the ninety-six lower-lower and upper-lower men and women in his sample, as well as on other dimensions of marital relations. His attention was focused on contraceptive attitudes and behavior, but in the context of the couples' over-all sexual practices and general interaction.

The picture that emerges of sexual relations is aptly summed up by J. Mayone Stycos in his preface to Rainwater's (1960) book: "It would seem, in short, that fewer of the good things of life are free than has commonly been supposed. The lower classes seem underprivileged not only in

[7] Robert S. and Helen M. Lynd, *Middletown*. New York: Harcourt, Brace & World, Inc., 1929.

terms of sexual knowledge but, at least by several measures, in terms of sexual gratification as well." [p. x]

Stycos' comment comes immediately after his efficient summary of the Kinsey findings on the American female [p. x]:

1. American women in lower educational groups do not have sex relations more frequently than higher educated women.
2. The lower the educational level, the less likely it is that pre-marital relations occurred.
3. Attitudes toward nudity are more conservative among lower class women.
4. Erotic arousal "from any source" is lowest among the women of least education.
5. Fewer women in the lower educational groups have ever reached orgasm in marriage.
6. The frequency of achievement of orgasm is considerably less among the poorly-educated women.

Lower-class women seem, from Rainwater's observations, to enter marriage with a depth of ignorance about sex and procreation that is wildly inconsistent with popular images about the free and easy sex lives of the lower classes. Yet, on the other hand, Rainwater reports that

> Three-fifths of the lower lower class women in our sample ranked being a good lover first or second in importance for a good husband, yet less than five percent of the lower lower class husbands ranked this role as high, and three-fifths of them put it in the "least important category." [p. 67]

This incompatibility seems to work in reverse also: men think that what is important in wives is being good mothers and housekeepers, but wives think it is being good lovers and friends to their husbands. (Note the contrast between this observation and those of Hurvitz, quoted above.)

"One result," remarks Rainwater, "is that in most working class families sharing experience tends to be limited," with the wife's affectional needs often not being met [p. 69] and with wives in general more or less resignedly adjusting to their powerlessness, dependence, and insecurity. The Lynds' impression of "less frankness" and "more confusion and disagreement" would appear to be as apt today as then.

Men's tendency to rate "being a good mother" as very important in their wives may reflect, Rainwater notes, a desire to be mothered themselves; and some of the interviews quoted support this suggestion vividly. "She is good to me and the kids" is a refrain among many of the men who are satisfied with their wives; and uneasiness about their wives' independent sexuality or their expressions of affectional needs is a theme of dissatisfaction.

In their 1964 paper, Rainwater and Handel note several differences between "modern" and "traditional" working-class couples in the area of sex. Among the modern couples, as contrasted with the traditional ones

1. Both spouses are much more likely to say that sexual relations are highly gratifying to them.
2. Husbands are less likely to have greater interest in sex than wives.
3. Husbands are more likely to express a "strong interest" in sex.
4. Husbands are more likely to consider it important for sexual relations to be mutually gratifying.
5. Both spouses are more likely to emphasize the social-emotional aspects of sex over their purely physical aspects.

Reproduction

Pregnancy, Rainwater suggests in the 1960 study, is something that establishes for lower-class women "their legitimacy as mature females"; [p. 83] and, although less urgently, impregnating women serves a similar function for men. Moreover, for the man, having his wife frequently pregnant allays his anxiety about her turning "bad." When children come, the wives tend to be pleased; but one receives the impression that their pleasure is partly that of a validation of their own capacities, and partly that of being pleased with a new plaything, at least for the initial and early births. They do not see the children as individuals in their own right, and often come, at length, to feel ineffective and powerless in their mother roles also.

It is clear, however, that these generalizations do not apply to all lower-class couples. They apply mostly to the lower-lower class. In addition, one of Rainwater's divisions is between "effective" and "ineffective" users of contraception, the effective users being the exception to the foregoing portraits. The frequency and the sources of the differences, however, have not been studied.

All evidence available points to a single picture of lower-class efforts to control the births of children; namely, one in which the lower-class parents are much like all other parents in their conceptions of an ideal family size (two–four children); much like them also in that they make some effort to limit conception; but very different in their effectiveness. They are different also in the point in their child-bearing careers at which they begin the use of contraceptive techniques, and in the techniques they use.

The Freedman, Whelpton, and Campbell (1959) study in 1955 of a national sample of over 2,700 white married women found that young women of all classes want about the same number of children, but that lower-class women (as measured by education) both have more and *expect* more. They reported also that whereas 68 percent of college women used contraceptives before their first pregnancy, only 24 percent of grammar school women had done so. Ninety percent of the former, compared to 29 percent of the latter used some form of contraception before the second pregnancy. As far as methods are concerned, the condom is used in all classes, but only 17 percent of grammar school women had used diaphragms, compared to 57 percent of college women.

The 1960 Growth of American Families Study, as reported by Jaffe (1964), discovered essentially similar patterns: lower-class husbands (incomes under 3000 dollars) wanted only an average of 3.1 children, whereas husbands with family incomes of 10,000 dollars or more wanted 3.3; and nonwhite wives wanted fewer children than white wives. But in this study, too, *expectations* of the number of children they would have were higher among lower-income women.

By 1960, moreover, virtually everyone was using some kind of contraceptive—although still only 72 percent of grade school wives, as compared to 93 percent of college wives. One institutional factor that may contribute to the lower efficiency of lower-class women's practice of contraception is suggested by Jaffe. The more effective contraceptive techniques, he notes, are those dispensed by, or requiring the advice of, private physicians or other professional workers, who are in the first place largely inaccessible, and in the second place often unhelpful to lower-class women.

> Among [the] obstacles are those who manage to transform what has become an everyday practice for most American families into a traumatic experience, such as the case worker who told a Planned Parenthood field worker not long ago, quite seriously, that she "wouldn't dream of suggesting birth control to a client unless the client had been in deep therapy for at least two years." And, of course, there are the very physical arrangements of many public institutions, not to speak of the attitudinal problems of the serving professionals. How many middle class couples would be practicing birth control if it required first that the wife spend half a day in a dingy clinic waiting room, only to find that she has to defend her integrity against the indifference and hostility of a doctor who tells her that she ought to stop her sex life if she doesn't want children? [p. 470]

Rainwater's (1960) study points to some of the reasons for ineffectiveness in the lower-class couple themselves. The central reasons would appear to be a mixture of husbands' refusal to cooperate responsibly, wives' ignorance, embarrassment, and fear of examination by doctors, and the pervasive inability on the part of both spouses really to feel that such control, over anything, is within their power.

One aspect of this inability appears to be an uneasy feeling both that doing something about the number of children is somehow "unnatural" and "strained," and that deliberately intruding some planning element into the impulsiveness of sexuality is also "unnatural" and "artificial." In addition, Rainwater suggests, the inability of spouses to communicate sympathetically with one another about sexual matters narrows the possibility of joint rational planning.

Whatever the causes, the result is higher fertility for lower-class women. In 1960, the average woman forty-five years old or over with less than a grammar school education had had 3.6 children; her college-educated sister had had 1.6. The wife of a "professional, technical, or kindred worker" had had 1.9 children; the wife of an urban laborer had had 3.1 (and the wife of an unemployed man had had 2.7). The wife of a man who earned under 2000 dollars had had 3.1 children; that of a 7000 dollars or over man had had 1.9 (*Statistical Abstract of the United States,* 1964, Table 56, p. 53).

What happens to these children in lower-class families we have reviewed in Chapter 1.

Labor-Force Participation

Both the nature of the conjugal relationship and the experiences of children in their families of orientation are likely to be affected by the wife-mother's participation or nonparticipation in the labor force. In this section, therefore, we shall summarize the apparent facts about such participation.[8]

It seems reasonable to suppose that married women's labor-force participation rates reflect the interaction of several variables. Because pressures toward participation include incentives to augment the family income, those pressures might be supposed to be greater the lower the husband's income. Incentives to pursue something like a career as a fulfillment of some nonfamilial part of the self might be supposed to be greater the *higher* the husband's income (on the assumption that more-educated women are more likely to have such incentives and are more likely to marry men with high earning capacities). As probable *deterrents* to participation are the factors of the tradition of women's place being in the home (which might be supposed to be more pervasive among less-educated women); lack of marketable skills (presumably related to class in the same way); and the presence of dependent children (which is presumably related to class only as much as fertility is class related).

We shall look at each of these factors, and where possible their interplay, insofar as they help to illuminate class differences.

[8] This section is not a "survey of the literature"; it is based chiefly on *Special Labor Force Report No. 40,* Bureau of Labor Statistics, U.S. Dept. of Labor, 1964; and on figures supplied by the Commissioner of Labor Statistics, Dr. Ewan Clague, in a personal communication, for which we are much indebted.

The expected tendency for "higher" class women to participate more by virtue of their "career" seeking may be reflected in the fact that among married women with no children under eighteen years, the *higher* the husband's income, the *greater* the rate of participation.[9] A clearer indication of the tendency is the fact that the higher the educational level of married women, the greater their tendency to be in the labor force.[10]

The deterrent effect of children is shown in the fact that among all married women (with husband present) 22 percent of those with children under six years are in the labor force, as compared to 38 percent of those with no children under eighteen years. The further fact that 42 percent of those with children aged six through seventeen are labor-force participants may suggest that the deterrent of *young* children has been reduced, at the same time that the pressure to augment family income for the sake of still-dependent children is enough to push the rate above that for women with no dependent children.

Indeed, at every level of husband's income below 7000 dollars, the lowest participation rates are for women with children under six, and the highest are for women with children six through seventeen, with women having no children under eighteen displaying in-between rates.

The effectiveness of the children-under-six deterrent, however, is a function of husbands' incomes. Not surprisingly, the lower the husband's income, the less, apparently, can the pressure on wives to concentrate on child care overcome the pressure to augment the family income. (Thirty percent of women with children under six whose husbands earn less than 3000 dollars are in the labor force, as compared to 15 percent of those whose husbands earn 7000 dollars or more.) The same class pattern is found for women with children aged six through seventeen; 53 percent of those whose husbands earn less than 3000 dollars seek to augment the family income, but only 33 percent of those with husbands making 7000 dollars or more a year.

This fairly obvious relationship of class to women's working or seeking work is, moreover, in nearly all cases the same for both white and nonwhite women—a difference being that among nonwhites, participation is higher in each category. Among whites, the difference between the participation rate of "poor" women with young children (under six years of age) and

[9] *Special Labor Force Report No. 40.,* Table L, p. A–14. A qualification of this is that there is a downturn of the participation rates at the income class "7000 and over," which may suggest a curvilinear relationship over the entire range of husbands' incomes.

[10] *1962 Handbook on Women Workers,* Bulletin 285 of Women's Bureau, U.S. Dept. of Labor, Washington, D.C., 1963, Table 5, p. 109. Data are for 1959. An exception to the above generalization is that married women with "some" college have slightly lower participation rates (32 percent) than those with "high school" education (34 percent).

TABLE 9.   THE EFFECT OF CHILDREN UNDER SIX ON LABOR-FORCE PARTICIPATION OF NONFARM MARRIED WOMEN, BY INCOME OF WOMEN'S HUSBANDS AND BY COLOR OF WOMEN, MARCH 1963 (IN THOUSANDS)

	WHITE HUSBAND'S INCOME (DOLLARS)								NONWHITE HUSBAND'S INCOME (DOLLARS)							
	Under 3000		3000–4999		5000–6999		7000 and over		Under 3000		3000–4999		5000–6999		7000 and over	
	Wives in Labor Force	Wives Not in Labor Force	Wives in Labor Force	Wives Not in Labor Force	Wives in Labor Force	Wives Not in Labor Force	Wives in Labor Force	Wives Not in Labor Force	Wives in Labor Force	Wives Not in Labor Force	Wives in Labor Force	Wives Not in Labor Force	Wives in Labor Force	Wives Not in Labor Force	Wives in Labor Force	Wives Not in Labor Force
Children under 6 years	393 (29)[a]	985	649 (25)	1979	840 (22)	2973	513 (15)	3009	176 (35)	322	182 (37)	307	73 (37)	121	15 (29)	37
Children 6–17 years only	530 (50)	517	865 (46)	994	1415 (47)	1673	1233 (38)	2564	173 (65)	94	113 (49)	118	83 (47)	94	19 (63)	11
No children under 18 years	1417 (29)	3423	1342 (40)	1948	1379 (43)	1175	1208 (33)	1957	334 (49)	347	165 (56)	129	90 (55)	72	33 (57)	25

Source: Calculated from Table N, p. A–15 of *Special Labor Force Report No. 40*, Bureau of Labor Statistics, U.S. Department of Labor, Washington, D.C., 1964; and from figures supplied by Commissioner Ewan Clague.

[a] Figures in parentheses are the percentages of all women in the indicated income, color, and children's ages categories who are in the labor force.

that of "richer" women is the difference between 29 percent and 15 percent; among nonwhites, it is the difference between 35 percent and 29 percent.

An exception to this parallel between whites and nonwhites appears in the case of women with children aged six through seventeen. Among whites, the higher the husbands' income the less the wives' labor-force participation, without exception. Among nonwhites, however, there is an exception: although participation rates decline from 65 percent among women whose husbands earn less than 3000 dollars, to 47 percent among those with 5000–6999 dollars husbands, the rate leaps up to 63 percent for women whose husbands earn 7000 dollars or more.

These data are shown in Table 9.

Chapter Five

RELIGION

In his *American Society,* Robin Williams notes that although American social scientists have apparently neglected religion as an area of investigation, this is no reflection of its importance in American society, for in no other modern state does religion play a more significant role.[1] We are concerned with religion here in two senses: (1) what is the nature and extent of affiliation, participation, and belief among low-income urban youth, and (2) what consequences do these have for their behavior and values in other aspects of their lives?

Williams speaks of religion as providing men with a way of facing the problems of ultimate and unavoidable frustration, of "evil," and the generalized problem of meaning in some nonempirical way. Some of these problems are death, imperfect or limited control of physical nature and society, and evil. More specifically, he defines religious matters as those entities and events that are interpreted as being beyond the range of ordinary human understanding and control. Religion is essentially concerned with the sacred as opposed to the profane.

Adult Religious Life

There is a serious paucity of material dealing with the religious life of American youth. Therefore it will be necessary, more so than in most areas, to lean heavily on those studies of adults that provide some data on differences by social class. Having reviewed this material, we will then discuss the literature dealing with youth that we have been able to find.

Religious Affiliation

In a comprehensive study of the religious factor in American life, Lenski (1961) analyzed the class structure of Detroit in terms of religious affiliation. Categorizing the population into four groups—white Protestant,

[1] Robin Williams, *American Society*. New York: Alfred A. Knopf, Inc., 1957.

Negro Protestant, Catholics, and Jews—he found that Catholics and Negro Protestants were disproportionately represented in the working class, while Jews were disproportionately represented in the upper-middle and middle classes. White Protestants were almost evenly divided between the working and middle classes, with a slightly higher representation in the middle class. Thus, the major difference between the working and middle class would seem to be in terms of its Jewish and Negro Protestant members. While these results could not be expected to hold in the South because of the prevalence of Protestants there, it would seem typical of northern industrial cities with a Negro and Jewish population.

A similar finding is possible from Moberg's data (1962) concerning the status hierarchy of American churches. He ranks the denominational families in America from higher to lower in the following order: Episcopal, Unitarian, Congregational, Presbyterian, Christian Scientist, Jewish, Friends, Methodists, Disciples of Christ, Lutheran, Catholic, Baptist, Mormon, Eastern Orthodox, Assembly of God, Pentecostal, Holiness, Jehovah's Witness. The higher-status groups are largely white Protestants and Jewish, while the lower status are Catholic, Negro Protestant. In short, affiliation with the Catholic church or certain sects of the Protestant church is most likely for the urban poor.

Religious Participation

As indicated by Stark (1964), there is widespread evidence to support the contention that the lower classes are least likely to be church members or attend Sunday worship. One explanation of this phenomenon is offered by Dotson (1961), who notes the lack of participation of the working class in all types of associational activity. This position is also held by Lenski, but Stark (1964) contends, on the basis of poll data, that "Whether they belong to several organizations or to none, blue-collar workers are less likely than white-collar workers to attend church." [p. 700] In the case of British workers, at least, Stark argues that involvement in "radical" politics is a substitute for involvement in religion. An apparently contradictory finding would be that of Lynd (1929), who described the working class as believing more ardently, with religion operating more prominently as an active agent of support and encouragement. This may only be an apparent difference since strength and influence of beliefs may not be equated with extent of participation.

There appear to be subgroup variations from the dominant patterns. According to Lenski, working-class Jews participate more extensively than do middle-class Jews. Frazier (1940) and Lewis (1960) have pointed to the importance of the church in Negro life, with particular reference to low-income families. While Wright and Hyman (1958) report a lower rate of membership in voluntary associations for Negroes than for whites, they did not include church membership. On the other hand, Babchuk and Thompson (1962) show a high rate of participation for their sample of Negroes and conclude that "The hypothesis that Negroes belonged to fewer associations than whites was not supported by the data." [p. 650] The authors note also "a direct but slight relationship between occupational rank and multiple membership," with this relationship holding for educational achievement and family income. They conclude that, on the whole, Negroes tended to be affiliated with formal religious organizations to a significantly greater degree than "is probably characteristic of the adult population as a whole." With reference to the husbands of her respondents, Peil (1963) reported that "The Negroes were slightly better represented in church groups and the white husbands, in fraternal groups." [p. 56]

Responding to the speculation about a religious revival in the United States, particularly in the suburbs, Berger (1960) found no indication of any in his working-class suburb. About a quarter of his respondents said that subsequent to moving to the suburbs their church going had increased, but just about the same proportion claimed it had declined. Just over one half the respondents said they attended church "never or rarely." Further, 81 percent said they never participated in other church activities. Nor was there any appreciable increase in church going for those who most clearly approximated white-collar status. "What is true is that the most obvious pattern is for the lowest status groups to manifest most religious interest and activity." [p. 49] Berger notes that the lowest-status groups were heavily "Bible-belt Baptists," who accounted for a major share of all church activity.

Religious Beliefs

In his study, Lenski distinguishes between devotionalism and ortho-doxy, and reports a positive relationship between devotionalism and social status, but no such relationship between orthodoxy and social status. Doctrinal orthodoxy refers to a set of beliefs which stresses a "belief in God who watches over them like a heavenly father, who answers prayers, who expects weekly worship, a belief in Jesus as God's only son and a belief in punishments and rewards in a life after death." (Lenski's definition applied only to Christians.) Devotionalism refers to an orientation which "values direct, personal communication with God through prayer and meditation, and which seeks divine direction in daily affairs."

Moberg (1962) found that working-class individuals hold views similar to those of upper-class persons about death. Both adhered to spiritual, transtemporal, and fate-or-luck orientations. Middle-class individuals were more likely to have secular, temporal, and means orientations. These findings are in keeping with those of Lynd, who observed some thirty years earlier that "in general the working class believe more ardently than the business class and accumulate more emotionally charged values around beliefs." He notes a shift in status of certain religious beliefs in the business class, the concept of heaven and hell having declined in importance and the belief in God having become more vague.

The Impact of Religious Beliefs

Lenski explored in some detail the relationship of religious impact and secular behavior, with particular reference to economic, political, and family systems. In discussing the effect of religious commitment on economic behavior, he noted that "Protestantism and Judaism develop in their adherents attitudes, values, beliefs and behavior patterns which are in keeping with the spirit of capitalism to a greater degree than those developed by Catholicism." Attitudes of socioreligious groups were related to such indices as vertical mobility, aspirations and ambition, attitudes toward work, attitudes toward the labor movement, self-employment, belief in the possibility of success, spending, and saving. On the great majority of variables either the Jews or white Protestants ranked first with the other second, the Catholics usually ranked third, and the Negro Protestants fourth. To the extent, as indicated earlier, that Catholics and Negro Protestants are overrepresented in the low-income segment of society, there is a consistency between religious affiliation, class position, and economic attitudes. Among white Catholics and Protestants, Lenski found that those who were not so orthodox were twice as likely to express a positive attitude toward work as the more orthodox.

Lenski found that involvement in the Protestant and Catholic churches seemed to have differential consequences for mobility. Those persons more active in the Protestant churches seemed to be upwardly mobile (middle-class sons of working-class fathers). Among working-class fathers, those who were more devout tended to have upwardly mobile sons. The findings were somewhat different for those who were active in the Catholic church in that there was no relationship between activity and mobility.

Working-class members who were more active in the Protestant churches more closely approximated middle-class persons than those who were not active, with reference to political behavior. In addition, those who were more orthodox were more likely to favor the Republican party.

According to Lenski, strong church associations tended to weaken family ties for Protestants, while for Catholics a high degree of involvement seemed to strengthen family ties. The effects of the Negro Protestant churches is intermediary between white Protestants and Catholics.

A study by Cox (1957) sheds some light on the effects of religious participation on other aspects of religious experience, though her sample was limited to forty-one high-status families. She found that there was generally a "high degree of religious identification and formal religious activity in the home, satisfaction in religious denomination and high religious values in the family." More specifically, there is a positive relationship between the frequency of church attendance and other formal religious activity in the home, higher religious values, and degree of satisfaction with religious denominations.

Adolescent Religious Life

On the basis of the material presented at the beginning of this chapter, one would predict lower rates of religious participation among low-income youth, with the possibility that low-income Negro adolescents would show higher participation rates than comparable white youth. Some evidence on this point is provided by Remmers and Radler (1957). As can be seen from Table 10, according to reports, the parents of low-income youth attend

TABLE 10. PROPORTION OF YOUTH REPORTING CHURCH ATTENDANCE BY THEIR PARENTS AND THEMSELVES, AND PRAYING, SELVES, BY INCOME LEVEL

RELIGIOUS PRACTICES	INCOME	
	Low	High
My father attends church at least twice a month		
Yes	37%	48%
Don't know, no response	16	8
My mother attends church at least twice a month		
Yes	54	66
Don't know, no response	11	4
On the average I go to religious services		
More than once a week	26	32
About once a week	40	44
Less than once a week	34	25
On the average, I say prayers including grace at meals		
Less than once or twice a day	43	38
About once or twice a day	36	40
More than once or twice a day	19	19
No response	2	3

Source: Adapted from Remmers and Radler (1957), pp. 167, 174.

church less often than do the parents of high-income youth, and low-income youth themselves go less frequently than do other youth. Further, they appear to make less frequent resort to prayer. While the differences are small, they are all in the same direction. Using the ratings of clergymen, Havighurst and others (1962) found "a marked relationship between church participation and social class, with higher status youth much more active in church." [p. 91]

In a study of Jewish youth, Rosen (1965) found that 17 percent of the respondents claimed to attend services at least once a week, 26 percent said they went at least once a month, and 55 percent admitted to going only on the High Holidays. The rate of claimed attendance was considerably lower than the rate that the respondents themselves considered appropriate. Though the sample was essentially middle class in social origin, the attendance rate is considerably lower than that reported in the Remmers and Radler poll, but may be in line with Lenski's finding, noted earlier, that working-class Jews participate more extensively than do middle-class Jews.

A few studies deal directly with the question of religious beliefs among adolescents. Hollingshead describes most of the students of Elmtown as holding "an amorphous body of beliefs symbolized by awesome words." Summing up available studies, Ausubel found that the majority of adolescents

> . . . belong to a church, have a favorable attitude toward the church, rely upon prayer, and believe in a personal, omnipotent, omniscient God, who, although bodyless, participated in the writing of the Bible and guided the affairs of men and nations.[2]

One source of this description are some of the items reported by Remmers and Radler. As can be seen from Table 11, the differences by income level are slight, with low-income youth just somewhat more likely to have a vision of God as all powerful and all knowing. Rosen (1965) reports similar findings for his Jewish sample. Over two thirds of the adolescents expressed belief in a personal God; 23 percent believed God to be impersonal; and just 5 percent did not believe in God. About half the respondents accepted the idea of heaven and hell, while a third rejected it.

As noted earlier, Lenski found a positive relationship between devotionalism and social status, but no such relationship between orthodoxy and status, as he defined those terms. Some of the items reported by Remmers and Radler have been taken as indices of orthodoxy in Table 12. Less than one third of the respondents believe religious faith should be accepted without question, suggesting a "liberal" bent, yet little more than one third are willing to accept the notion that man has evolved from lower forms of animal life. Likewise, just about one third believe the good society can be built without divine assistance and over two thirds believe that behavior here and now has consequences for the hereafter. Clearly, a majority of the

[2] David P. Ausubel, *Theory and Problems of Adolescent Behavior*. New York: Grune & Stratton, Inc., 1954, p. 268.

TABLE 11.　ADOLESCENT PERCEPTIONS OF GOD, BY INCOME LEVEL

PERCEPTIONS	INCOME	
	Low	High
God controls everything that happens everywhere		
Yes	61%	57%
Don't know, no response	22	21
God knows our every thought and movement		
Yes	84	82
Don't know, no response	13	13
God is		
A human-looking being	21	18
A bodiless spirit which exists everywhere	66	68
Only a symbol of man's ideals	8	10
No response	5	4
The first writing of the Bible was done under the guidance of God		
Yes	57	57
Don't know, no response	30	27

Source: Adapted from Remmers and Radler (1957), pp. 172, 173.

respondents tend toward "orthodoxy," with this orientation somewhat more frequent among low-income youth. It is interesting to note that here, as well as in most other instances, low-income youth show a consistently higher rate of "no answer" or "don't know" designations than high-income youth.

But what relationship is there between religious participation, however measured, religious beliefs, religious origins, and the behavior and attitudes of youth? As might be expected, given the paucity of knowledge concerning participation and beliefs, little can be known about their relationships to other aspects of adolescent life.

In a modest study, Kvaraceus (1944) found no difference in the participation rates of juvenile delinquents in Passaic and church membership for adults in New Jersey. Numerous investigators have commented on the low rate of juvenile delinquency among Jews (and Chinese). Several of the studies of alcohol use among teenagers, cited in Chapter 7, note that those who attend church regularly are less likely to be users of alcohol.

Havighurst and others (1962) found that adolescents who were more intelligent, who received more education, and who were better adjusted tended to have a closer relationship to the church, as reported by clergymen. Likewise, those with higher personal and social-adjustment scores also were more likely to be interested in church than those with lower scores. One finding of interest was that two thirds of those selected by clergymen as showing a high level of leadership in church activities were not leaders in school activities, indicating that the church provides an alternate outlet for some youngsters. Rosen (1959) found Catholics to have a lower achieve-

TABLE 12. INDICATIONS OF "ORTHODOXY" AMONG YOUTH, BY IN-
COME LEVEL

ITEMS	INCOME	
	Low	*High*
One should accept religious faith without question		
Yes	29%	24%
No	54	63
Don't know, no response	17	13
Man has evolved from lower forms of animals		
Yes	34	38
No	39	42
Don't know, no response	27	20
Our fate in the hereafter depends on how we behave on earth		
Yes	70	69
No	8	11
Don't know, no response	22	20
Men working and thinking together can build a good society without any divine or supernatural help		
Yes	33	31
No	44	51
Don't know, no response	23	18

Source: Adapted from Remmers and Radler (1957), pp. 171, 172.

ment-motivation score than Protestants, Greek Orthodox, and Jews, but suggested that a significant part of the difference was due to class differences.

Conclusion

It seems eminently clear that the research reported above tells us little about the behavior and values of working-class youth, even if we try to extrapolate from materials on adults and other social classes. The dearth of data is pointed up by examining the findings reported by Berelson and Steiner:[3]

1. With reference to the relationship between age and religion, they summarize as follows:

> (3–10) Children are considerably religious, at first holding fairy tale beliefs, later accepting the standard ideas of their group. (10–18) Intellectual doubts start at a mental age of 12, followed by emotional stress; these conflicts are often resolved at about the age of 16 either by conversion to religion or by a decision to abandon the religion of childhood. . . . There is no general increase in religious activity during these years. (18–30) There is a sharp decline in all aspects of religious activity, the years 30–35 being the lowest point in the life-cycle. [p. 392]

[3] Bernard Berelson and Gary A. Steiner, *Human Behavior: An Inventory of Scientific Findings.* New York: Harcourt, Brace & World, Inc., 1964.

2. With reference to the relationship between class and religion, they note that (1) participation in organized religious activity is higher in the middle class; (2) church affiliation is tied to social class; and (3) the most deprived groups in the society are the most likely to engage in salvationist religions.
3. Finally, with reference to the relationship between race and religion, they claim that "some minority groups develop strongly aggressive religions to help them get more of the world's rewards." [p. 394]

Berelson and Steiner also conclude that religion has an influence on political attitudes, marital relations, and other facets of life. But there are basic issues that remain untouched. There has been considerable discussion about the revival of religious interest in the growing suburbs. Aside from the issue of the meaning of any revival to those involved, there is the question of what is happening, in terms of long-time trends, to religious activity among the urban poor. If there is no revival going on in the urban core, what implications does this have for the influence of religion on the coming generations of youth in low-income areas?

Church membership and participation has come to mean involvement in a wide range of activities, not necessarily related to religious practice. To what extent are such opportunities available in low-income areas; to what extent are they utilized; and what are their consequences, if any, on the values and behavior of the youth who are involved? The available scattered evidence suggests that working-class youth are likely to be somewhat more conservative or orthodox in their beliefs than other youth and to be somewhat less attached to the church. There is the suggestion that participation in church activities is part of a larger syndrome of participation in school organizations and organizations in general, and it may well be that working-class youth who do follow this path are more oriented to "playing the game" than others.

Chapter Six

GOVERNMENT AND LAW

Youth, of any social background, may come into contact with a variety of political and legal agencies, ranging from the local political machine to the FBI. Our primary concern is the experience of working-class youth with the instruments of law creation and enforcement, and with their perceptions of this experience. In addition, we are interested in the nature of the beliefs and attitudes toward law, authority, and justice as abstract principles and as they are embodied in operating agencies.

Despite the tremendous concern in recent years with problems such as juvenile delinquency, drug addiction, and sexual promiscuity, there is remarkably little empirical data for our purposes. Studies, such as those by Chapman (1956) and Reckless, Dinitz, and Murray (1956), which utilize empirical data, tend to confine their analyses to intragroup patterns. Further, much of the work in this area—by Smith (1962) and Bloch and Niederhoffer (1958), for example—does not usually distinguish among strata within the working class and lower class. If the latter distinction is as significant as Miller and Riessman (1961) claim, then ignoring these differences can seriously distort conclusions drawn from the evidence.

Experience with Law Enforcement Agencies

The general consensus has been that there is a higher rate of delinquency among low-income youth than among youth of higher social status, as well as a higher rate in low-income areas than in more affluent ones. One would therefore conclude that low-income youth have significantly more contact with law enforcement agencies. Nye, Short, and Olsen (1958) question this contention with evidence showing some relationship between institutionalization and status, but no significant relationship between subjective reports of actual delinquent behavior and status.[1]

[1] The literature on juvenile delinquency is far too extensive to be dealt with adequately in this general review. It should be noted, however, that there is consider-

In a social-area analysis, Polk (1957–1958) found that areas of low economic status, low family status, and high ethnic status showed high rates of delinquency, though none of the independent variables alone was associated with delinquency. This suggests that the interaction of these factors is significant for high delinquency rates. Gottlieb and Ramsay (1964) suggest that the stereotyping of the lower-class slum youth as a delinquent leads to increased police expectation of crime on their part, hence to increased arrests and convictions—which, in turn, helps to support the stereotype. Higher rates for Negro delinquency, they suggest, might be explained by the same process, with the additional factor of high Negro visibility.

It may be, then, that low-income youth do not engage in delinquent acts at greater rate than other youth, but that they are more likely to be apprehended and so do have a greater incidence of experience with probation, incarceration, and parole and with the agents assigned to assist in these functions—social workers, probation and parole officers, juvenile court judges, employees of reformatories, and so on. However, there seems to be no data showing how social class origins affect the career of the delinquent as he passes through these treatment agencies nor how such experiences differentially affect the attitudes and values of youth of varying social origins.

Attitudes toward Justice and Law Enforcement

One study relevant in the above context is by Chapman (1956). It deals with the attitudes of delinquent and nondelinquent youth toward various law enforcement agencies. In a sample of adolescents who might all be considered working class, Chapman found that delinquents were more hostile toward all of the legal agencies and toward the police. The differences were smaller with reference to the juvenile court, probation bureau, and reformatories, from which he concluded that the methods of treatment of

---

able disagreement, particularly on the basis of self-report studies, on the relationship between reported delinquency and social status. Thus, for example, Robert A. Dentler and Lawrence J. Monroe ("Social Correlates of Early Adolescent Theft," *American Sociological Review*: 26 (October 1961), 733–743) support Nye, Short, and Olsen. On the other hand, Albert J. Reiss, Jr., and Albert L. Rhodes ("The Distribution of Juvenile Delinquency in the Social Class Structure," *American Sociological Review*: 26 (October 1961), 720–732) find more serious delinquent deviation in the lower stratum and career-oriented delinquency only in that stratum, while John P. Clark and Eugene P. Wenninger ("Socio-Economic Class and Area as Correlates of Illegal Behavior among Juveniles," *American Sociological Review*: 27 (December 1962), 826–834) find significant differences in the incidence of illegal behavior among communities differing in predominant social-class composition in the same metropolitan area. What seems likely is that while self-reported delinquency may show no or little relationship to social class, delinquency as reflected in official statistics does, indicating that low-income youth are more likely to come into contact and have dealings with such agencies as the police, the courts, probation, and parole.

the latter were more acceptable to delinquent boys than were the methods of the police.

Approaching the problem from a broader perspective, a basic theme running through descriptions of working-class culture is the worker's feeling of alienation from the basic institutions of our society. The worker, it is said, is ready to believe in the corruptness of leaders and has a generally negative feeling toward "big shots." Nevertheless, he favors discipline, structure, order, and strong leadership. He expects obedience from his children and operates on the belief that wrongdoing requires punishments as a deterrent. Thus, while he believes in the efficacy of punishment and the necessity of strong leadership, at the same time he is alienated from the institutions that fulfill these functions in the complex society.

This theme of alienation is found in the literature concerning working-class youth as well. According to Smith (1962), "lower class youth is largely isolated from the mainstream of the dominant American cultural heritage and institutions." The gang, which is the more typical transitional institution of lower-class adolescents, has developed norms that diametrically oppose adult middle-class values and conflict with the formal institutions that enforce conformity. This results in withdrawal and sabotage of youth programs and concentration on commercial recreation, which may contribute to delinquency.

This is not to suggest that the lower-class youth is therefore to be viewed as a potential anarchist. It may be, as has been suggested, that he maintains a loyalty to authority that leads him to behave in ways that may conflict with the larger culture. Although Bloch and Niederhoffer (1958) suggest that the gang is not peculiar to the lower class, they do conclude that lower-class gangs are characterized by a "more formal almost military structure." All gangs, however, have a similar and well-defined pattern of leadership and control. The gang has both formal and informal patterns of leadership and will coerce members to obtain conformity to its norms.

On the other hand, Goodman (1956) and Finestone (1957) do see the adolescent as increasingly anarchic in his relation to authority. His reference point is himself and he is completely skeptical of the ability of others to provide suitable models for behavior. Goodman attributes the problem to the failure of society to provide a coherent and viable culture into which the adolescent can grow: "Tradition has been broken without a new standard to affirm, resulting in a culture that is eclectic, sensational and phony." Although Goodman sees these problems as typical of adolescents in general, the problem may be intensified for the lower-class adolescent who cannot afford the luxury of conspicuous conformity.

While the theme of alienation is frequently found in the literature concerning the lower classes, that of rebellion is frequently found in writings concerning adolescents. Alienation is usually conceived of as leading to withdrawal, resignation, apathy; rebellion leads to an active effort to establish a new set of norms. Yet writers do not always treat the two categories as mutually exclusive. There is some feeling that the expression of rebellion is increasingly assuming a more ominous and antisocial tone in the lower class. Smith (1962) depicts the contrast between working-class and middle-class adolescents in terms of the differential consequence of their developmental patterns. Whereas the middle-class adolescent may be temporarily and superficially isolated from adult society by his cliques, clubs, special language, these are transitory stages through which he proceeds to resolve his own sense of independent identity with the demands of organized society. In contrast, the lower-class youth tends to engage in behavior which moves him further away from the attainment of adult status and consequently away from a more satisfactory relationship with the authorities of the adult world. Behaviors such as gang formation, drug addiction, and school withdrawal tend to perpetuate the youngster's subservience to authority in the form of limited independence of choice and increasing supervision by legal institutions. Thus, while it might appear that the lower-class youngster is more rebellious, his behavior leads to greater control.

Differences are noted not only in contrast to the middle-class but also in comparison with the working-class youth of the prewar era. The characterological type emerging is alienated from the culture at large and even from the subculture of his community. By contrast, Whyte's "street corner society" (1943) shows a strong sense of group, the dominant value of loyalty to one's friends, and the firm identification with the culture of Cornerville. The Cornerville youth is ambivalent in his attitudes toward middle-class values, but not so disaffected that he cannot be moved to participate in settlement houses, politics, and other neighborhood enterprises. The values that form the basis for his behavior are manifestly drawn from the American value system. In contrast, Finestone's "cat" (1957) or the youngster described by Goodman (1956) is almost totally alienated from the surrounding culture. His behavior is escapist in nature, the cultural goals are no longer accepted, and the behavior is merely a means of expression at a more primitive level.

In discussing a particular minority group, Puerto Ricans in New York City, Padilla (1958) notes the formal manner in which they relate to officials of the larger society. She attributes this to the fact that few of them are in official positions themselves. They see themselves as being somewhat inadequate to deal with the problems they face and try to use intermediaries to facilitate their dealings with the larger society. This is reminiscent of Gans' (1962) description of the Italian-Americans in their "urban village." Thus it may be generic to groups who see themselves disadvantaged in relation to the larger society.

Knowledge, Values, and Attitudes Concerning the Political System

On the basis of available evidence, Easton and Hess (1961) suggested that political socialization begins earlier in life than expected, and seems to be relatively complete by age twenty-one. They went on to suggest that "for those who go on to higher school there is little evidence of substantial development during the whole of the high-school period, at least in the area of governmental orientation." [p. 240]

In addition, the authors provide a useful framework for viewing the process of political socialization. They suggest there are three major objects about which consensus is crucial for the maintenance of a political system: (1) the government, or day-to-day authorities; (2) the regime, or the basic form and norms of the system; and (3) the community in which the government and regime operate. The political orientation to these elements of the system is composed of three elements: knowledge, values, and attitudes. Political socialization, then, is

> . . . a process of acquisition, not only of information and attitudes toward political persons and institutions, but modes of relating to the society, particularly to those elements invested with authority, in ways that may at a later, adult period determine specific political behavior and commitment. [p. 235]

Hess and Torney (1965), on the basis of a study of children in grades two through eight in eight cities have provided a valuable fund of information on political socialization and on the role of such factors as family, school, religion, peers, intelligence, and social class on the process. Their report deals with attitudinal development in five areas: (1) attachment to the nation; (2) attachment to political figures and institutions; (3) compliance and response to the law; (4) influencing government policy; and (5) participation in the process of elections. For our purposes, we must restrict ourselves primarily to their discussion of the consequences of differences in social origins.

The authors find the acquisition of political attitudes to be affected by both social class and intelligence, but in different ways. High intelligence appears to accelerate the acquisition of attitudes, while social-class differences are more likely to be reflected in the content of the attitudes.

Attachment to the nation is not influenced by intelligence level or social class, suggesting it represents a fundamental consensus. In the second area, attachment to figures and institutions of government, intelligence and class are both related to conceptions of the system. Intelligence is strongly related to knowledge concerning the function of Congress; social class is positively, though not as strongly, related to a tendency to personalize government

Working-class children tend to have a more positive attachment to the president; a projection, the authors feel, of the ideals they do not find in their own fathers.

Young children tend to conceive of law as just and unchanging, to believe that punishment invariably follows wrongdoing.[2] However, high social status and high intelligence both lead to a more flexible view, with intelligence showing a stronger relationship than status. In the realm of influencing government policy, participation in political discussions and concern with political issues were more frequent among children with high intelligence and social status. Highly intelligent children were more likely to question the competence of government, but differences based on social class were not consistent. The authors conclude that:

> . . . lower status children more frequently accept authority figures as right and rely on their trustworthiness and benign intent. There is, therefore, more acquiescence to the formal structure and less tendency to question the motivations behind the behavior of government and governmental officials. [p. 276]

With regard to attitudes concerning participation in the election system, voting is more salient as a symbol of government to highly intelligent children, but the influence of social class is not consistent. Likewise, while a larger proportion of highly intelligent children believe that the good citizen is the one who votes, the influence of social class is negligible. Political activity, on the other hand, is higher in children of high intelligence and social class. The authors find that social status is not related to choice of party until after grade five. The authors summarize their findings in this area as follows:

> The basic attachment to the nation and the government, and the acceptance of compliance to the law and authority are relatively unaffected by social class and by the mediation of intelligence in the learning process. These are also areas in which the family and community play strong supporting and socializing roles. . . .

> The acquisition of more active and initiatory aspects of political involvement . . . is strongly affected by I.Q. and, to a lesser degree, by social status. [p. 304]

[2] This is in agreement with the findings by Kohlberg that "Law and government are perceived quite differently by the child if he feels a sense of potential participation in the social order than if he does not." Lawrence Kohlberg, "Development of Moral Character and Moral Ideology," in Martin L. Hoffman and L. W. Hoffman, eds., *Review of Child Development Research*, Vol. 1. New York: Russell Sage Foundation, 1964, pp. 383–431.

The authors consider the family as the crucial source of class differences. They find that children from high-status families see their fathers as more powerful within the family and as more instrumental teachers of political attitudes than do lower-status children. In addition, children from lower-status families tend to see their fathers as less effective in influencing others and less interested in government and current events than do higher-status children. Consequently, the lower-class child is more oriented to the school and teacher for political socialization.

> Not only does the lower class child perceive his father as lower in status (of low power and less interested in politics), but these children do not regard their fathers as potential sources of information about politics and citizenship. The relationship of these items to social class suggest the possible *source* of some social class differences. [p. 196]

The findings of Greenstein (1965), from a somewhat similar study in New Haven, are not in complete agreement with those of Hess and Torney. Using respondents from grades four through eight, Greenstein found that lower and upper socioeconomic groups did not differ significantly in expressed willingness to vote "when you grow up," in the belief that elections "are important," or in level of political information. He did find significant differences in political preferences, with lower socioeconomic groups being more Democratic and upper socioeconomic groups being more Republican in persuasion.

According to Hess and Easton (1962), the family is also the crucial source of attachment to a political party. On the other hand, the findings of Levin (1960) and Cohen and Hodges (1963) suggest significant withdrawal from the political process by low-income groups, and an attitude of cynicism. All the evidence from voting studies show a positive correlation between socioeconomic status and registration, as well as voting. It would follow, then, that discussion of the political system within low-income families would have a low order of priority and, when it does occur, would not likely to be supportive of the system.

It is often noted that there are no political movements involving American youth. But to Easton and Hess (1961) the problem is not the lack of involvement of youth. They argue that the problem is the circumstances under which, in this one area, youth seem to be a faithful mirror of adults. Just as their parents do, young people seem to accept the regime and community components of the political system with little question, and to participate only peripherally in the governmental component. This position is supported by the findings of Maccoby, Matthews, and Merton (1954), and those of Middleton and Putney (1963) and Lane (1959). There is little sign of adolescent rebellion against parental standards. What needs to be explained, they contend, is the lack of differentiation in this area, given the evidences of rebellion and age conflict in so many other areas of contemporary life.[3]

Hess and Torney consider the schools important sources of political socialization, particularly for lower-class youth. However, according to Smith (1962) and Horton (1963) the schools do not provide the kind of information and experience necessary for the development of citizenship qualities or the ability to perform in a democratic political role. Horton found there was no relationship between completion of high school courses in this area and his measures of basic orientation. In this respect there may be no difference between working-class youth and those of other classes, except that working-class youth have less exposure resulting from their tendency to leave school at an earlier age. Comparing ninth graders with twelfth graders, Horton finds only a slight increase in acceptance of the Bill of Rights, a difference that could be attributable to maturation rather than to the intervening school experience.

> And, since a considerable proportion of those entering high school will "drop out" before graduation, the difference between ninth graders and twelfth graders may be one of *selection* rather than *education*. For the majority of the "drop outs" come from families of lower income level and lower level parental education, and, as we have seen, it is precisely those pupils of such background who are least likely to believe in the Bill of Rights. [p. 58]

Litt (1963) has explored the role of the school in political socialization in relation to the surrounding community by examining the content of civics education in three communities of varying social status. In all three, he found instruction in the equalitarian creed of democracy and a rejection of political chauvinism. But, he maintains, the students in the three communities "are being trained to play different political roles, and to respond to political phenomena in different ways." In the working-class community, there is little emphasis on political participation. In the lower-middle-class community, knowledge about the formal process of democracy is buttressed by an emphasis on the responsibilities of citizenship.

> Only in the affluent and politically vibrant community are insights into political processes and functions of politics passed on to those who, judging from their socio-economic and political environment, will likely man those positions that involve them in influencing or making political decisions. [p. 74]

[3] One may wish to argue that the activities of the Student Non-Violent Coordinating Committee, the Students for a Democratic Society, as well as the Free Speech Movement at Berkeley and the anti-Vietnam activity on many campuses, refute this statement. It may be too early to decide whether we are faced with a fad or with a change. It is interesting to note however, that these evidences of youthful revolt appear to be dominated by middle-class students.

Another source of learning about the political system is to observe it in operation at a familiar level. On the basis of Whyte's work (1943), it is possible to suggest that the working-class child, as described in *Street Corner Society,* may gain a more intimate knowledge of politics by being involved in the operations of the political machine at the local level. Certainly there was widespread evidence during the 1964 election campaign of the involvement of teenagers in a variety of activities. But there does not seem to have been any research into the class origins of those involved, the nature of the learning experience if any, and other implications of this activity for the process of growing up in the city.

Remmers and Franklin (1963) offer data about the attitudes of high school students toward relevant applications of the Bill of Rights, and how these have changed from 1951 to 1960. These responses might be viewed as clues to the values and attitudes toward the regime component of the political system—the basic rules of the game.

High school students are not particularly in favor of freedom of the press. In 1951, 45 percent agreed and 41 percent disagreed with the statement "Newspapers and magazines should be allowed to print anything they want except military secrets." In 1960, only 29 percent agreed, but just 51 percent disagreed with the statement. This finding is supported by another. In 1951 and 1960, 60 percent of respondents agreed that police and other groups should have the power to ban or censor certain books and movies, while those opposed declined from 27 to 24 percent. Finally, just under two thirds of respondents in both 1951 and 1960 would support laws against "printing or selling any communist literature."

There is somewhat greater support for freedom of speech, but it is not overwhelming. Those who disagreed with the statement "The government should prohibit some people from making public speeches" declined from 53 percent in 1951 to 51 percent in 1960, while those who favored it declined from 34 percent to 25 percent, a significant change. The shift was into the "uncertain" category, which grew from 13 percent in 1951 to 22 percent in 1960. The result was better with regard to public meetings, where almost two thirds of respondents disagreed, in both time periods, with the statement "Certain groups should not be allowed to hold public meetings even though they gather peaceably and only make speeches." Roughly one third each agreed, disagreed, and were uncertain in response to the statement "Some of the petitions which have been circulated should not be allowed by the government." Finally, barely a fifth of respondents think that the Communist party in the United States should be allowed on the radio during peacetime.

There is fairly strong and consistent support for the right to trial by jury, protection against arrest without formal charge, and protection against search without a warrant. Better than three fourths of respondents disagree in both 1951 and 1960 with the statement "In some criminal cases a trial by jury is an unnecessary expense and shouldn't be given." Disagreement in both periods is even higher in response to the statement "Some criminals are so bad they shouldn't be allowed to have a lawyer." About three fourths of respondents reject the suggestion that "Local police may sometimes be right in holding persons in jail without telling them of any formal charge against them." The results are a little different, however, in response to the proposition "In some cases, the police should be allowed to search a person or his home even though they do not have a warrant." In 1951, 26 percent agreed, and by 1960, this number had risen to 33 percent. Similarly, 58 percent agreed, in 1951 that, "The police or F.B.I. may sometimes be right in giving a man the 'third degree' to make him talk." And while this proportion had dropped to 42 percent in 1960, those in disagreement had only grown from 27 percent to 32 percent. On the other hand, there was sharply increased support for protection of the right against self-incrimination.

While these data give us a time perspective, they are not analyzed with reference to a social-class variable. However, to the limited extent that this has been done by Horton (1963) with similar data, there is reason to believe that more liberal responses will be found in the higher economic groups.

Conclusion

If, as some authors contend, political socialization begins relatively early and basic political orientations are firmly established by the early teens, then the dearth of basic data of the kind needed here is particularly distressing. Much has been written concerning alienation in general, the alienation of youth, and, in particular, their abstinence from political involvement. But these findings seem to grow out of the projection of a concept, alienation, rather than from detailed and sophisticated observation of young people. We know nothing about the involvement of young people with political machines and political campaigns, as though any involvement other than that in the tradition of the 1930s was of no social significance.

It is likely that working-class youth will have more experience with certain aspects of the political and legal structure—the police, the courts, the welfare system—than other youth. But there is little evidence of a systematic nature concerning the broad pattern of such contacts by youth and how these vary by social class. Nor is there much evidence that such differential contact, if it occurs, is reflected in systematic differences in attitudes and values.

The work of Hess and Greenstein (1965) on the political socialization of adolescents should lead to some rethinking of our ideas about working-class youth. There appear to be subtle but important differences in the orientations and attitudes of some of these youth as compared to those of middle-class origin. A larger proportion of working-class youth are likely to be less well-informed, somewhat less interested in the political process, but more positively and less critically oriented to the authority structure. The work of Horton shows working-class youth to be less accepting of many provisions of the Bill of Rights. Taken together, these findings suggest the elements of a working-class authoritarianism as propounded by Lipset (but criticized by Miller and Riessman [1961]).

With or without a label, the more positive but less critical orientation of working-class youth is not compatible with the image, from other sources, of youth who are indifferent to or defiant of authority. One explanation of the incompatibility may be that the latter image is appropriate for a relatively minor segement of those usually included in the working class, a problem to which we have alluded several times. Another approach is a developmental one: somewhere beyond the eighth grade, experiences, either common to all youth or unique to working-class youth, cause some working-class youth, because of their pre-existing "dogmatic" orientation, to swing to an equally uncritical nonacceptance of authority. If such youth are more prone to leave school before graduation, the process may go undetected in studies of youth in school. Whatever the explanation, if the above-mentioned findings are accepted, the educational process as it now exists for many such youth would seem more likely to lead to withdrawal or blind rejection of authority rather than to creative rebellion on the part of disenchanted working-class youth.

Chapter Seven

LEISURE-TIME ACTIVITIES

Distinguishing between "free time," "leisure time," and recreation has led to innumerable difficulties, as evidenced, for example, by the comments of Anderson and Smigel.[1] What we are concerned with here is how the adolescent makes use of time not committed to his roles as family member, student, or employee. In these roles, he is obligated to utilize varying amounts of time assisting in household chores, studying, or working. Beyond this, he is reasonably free to engage in leisure-time or recreational activities. In fact, there are cultural expectations that the adolescent will seek to use as much of his time as possible in this way.

Our primary focus is on the ways in which working-class adolescents use their free time and how this pattern compares with the usage by youths of other socioeconomic groups. We are interested in content of the activity, the extent to which it involves formal organization, and the various sites at which the activity occurs.

Leisure in General

Guide lines for the analysis of leisure-time activities of youth are available in the growing body of literature on leisure as a general problem or activity. While relatively little attention has been paid to youth in the growing concern with leisure, there has been interest in class differences. Thus, for example, Clarke (1956) found significant differences in the use of leisure related to occupational prestige. The lowest prestige group (based on the prestige of their occupations) participated most in the following activities: watching television, playing with children, fishing, playing card games other than bridge, driving or riding in cars for pleasure, attending

[1] Nels Anderson, *Dimensions of Work*. New York: David McKay Company, Inc., 1964, pp. 91–103; Erwin O. Smigel, ed., *Work and Leisure*. New Haven, Conn.: College and University Press, 1963.

drive-in theater, spending time in taverns, spending time at zoo, attending baseball games. Those in the highest prestige group were most involved in attending theatrical plays and/or concerts, attending special lectures, visiting a museum or art gallery, attending fraternal organizations, playing bridge, attending conventions, community-service work, reading for pleasure, studying, entertaining at home, attending motion pictures. Clearly, much of the difference relates to styles of life rather than directly to income.

Dividing his population into four classes—upper middle, lower middle, upper lower, and lower lower—White (1955) found a relationship between leisure activity and social class:

> The rate of use of parks and playgrounds by class rises sharply from the upper-middle class rate through other classes for both males and females. The same regular progression is shown in attendance at church services and, with slight variations, for a single class in rate for community-chest services, museums, and ethnic-racial organizations. For libraries, home activities, and lecture-study courses the trend is reversed and decreased from upper middle downward. The rates for commercial amusements differ: low for upper-middle-class females and a lower and almost even rate for the others. [p. 146]

By dividing his respondents into two groups, one age six to seventeen, the other age eighteen and over, White was able to show that differences were more consistent for the older groups, inferring that the differences in life styles become sharper and more consistent as the individual takes on adult roles.

There is extensive evidence for the minimal participation of lower income groups in voluntary associations. In a study conducted in Bennington, Vermont, in 1947, Scott (1957) found that more than one third of persons in the sample had no membership in a voluntary association other than in a church. He concluded that "The persons in the lower social class, in manual occupations, with Catholic religious affiliations and with only elementary education have even higher percentages of non-affiliation." [p. 318] Using national samples as well as NORC studies of localities, Wright and Hyman (1958) showed that nearly half of the families and almost two thirds of the respondents in the samples belong to no voluntary associations. Further,

> Whichever index to status is used, an appreciably higher percentage of persons in higher status positions belong to voluntary associations than do persons of lower status. . . . Furthermore, there is an increase in the percentage of persons who belong to *several* organizations as social status increases. [p. 288]

Finally, Wright and Hyman (1958) note that membership in voluntary associations is somewhat more characteristic of whites than Negroes.

In his study of a working-class suburb, Berger (1960) found that 70 percent of his 100 respondents belonged to no clubs, organizations, or associations and only 8 percent belonged to more than one. Participation was meager for those who did belong. The above figures exclude membership and activity in union and church. Most of the respondents were union members but 27 percent said they never attended meetings, and 48 percent attended them rarely. Examining informal social relations, Berger concluded that his data supported Dotson (1951) in the latter's emphasis upon the importance of informal social participation *within* the working-class family but did not support his data about such relations with friends.

Among other forms of leisure, Berger found watching television to be dominant. More than half the respondents go to the movies "never" or "rarely," while more than half the sample spend more than sixteen hours a week watching television. They do not watch the most prestigious shows: westerns were mentioned sixty-eight times, sports events sixty-four times, and the next important category, adventure, was mentioned twenty-nine times. There was some evidence of reading in that there were thirty-one reported subscriptions to *Reader's Digest,* sixteen to *Life,* nine to *The Saturday Evening Post,* and eight each to *Look, Good Housekeeping,* and *The Ladies' Home Journal.* There were no reported subscriptions to journals of serious commentary or discussion.

Much of the data on social characteristics related to membership and participation in voluntary associations has been summarized by Hausknecht (1962) in his analysis of data from national-sample studies by NORC and AIPO. He concludes that between one third and one half of all American adults belong to voluntary associations, although no more than one quarter of the population belongs to more than one. As in other studies, Hausknecht finds that membership is positively related to educational level, income, and occupation, but negatively related to community size. The youngest (age twenty-one through twenty-five) and the oldest (age sixty-five and over) groups have the lowest membership rates. Generally speaking, membership rates for younger and older groups increase with higher income, education, and occupation. Whites appear to be more active in associations than Negroes, except for church-related organizations and political and pressure groups.

Hausknecht makes the point that not only do those with less income and education belong to fewer organizations, they also belong to different types of organizations.

> The fact that such organizations [local chamber of commerce or Parent-Teacher Association] are comprised predominantly of middle class in-

dividuals means that on the local community level, at least, the dominant voice is that of the middle class. Or, to put it more simply, the low rate of working class voluntary association membership, and in this kind of association in particular, means that this class does not avail itself of one of the means of political leverage, and as a result is left in a relatively weak position within the power structure.

The membership rate of the working class is obviously related to educational level, but it is important to see that this is only one part of a complex process. A low level of education means a low level of interest in and knowledge of the uses of voluntary associations, and therefore the low rate of membership. But this rate, especially as it applies to membership in civic and service organizations, has the further consequence of maintaining the low level of interest and knowledge of institutionalized means of achieving individual and group ends, i.e., voluntary associations. As a consequence, in conflict situations working class interests cannot be achieved, and this may result in a sense of alienation among members of this class. This sense of alienation, in turn, would result in reinforcement of initial lack of interest and knowledge of the use of voluntary associations. [pp. 81–82]

Viewing reading of books, newspapers, and magazines as links to the larger world, and in this sense functionally equivalent to associations, Hausknecht finds that nonmembers do not read as much as members. Thus, for example, in the NORC study, 51 percent of nonmembers read no magazines, as contrasted with 23 percent of those who belonged to two or more associations. Fifty-eight percent of nonmembers spent no time in reading books as compared with 21 percent of those who belonged to two or more associations. Even when education is held constant, the relationship holds. Thus nonreading is part of the syndrome of low income, low education, nonmembership, and consequent marginal involvement in the larger world.

The evidence presented above, as well as the reports of other studies, would lead one to expect some differences in the patterning of leisure-time activities by adolescents from different socioeconomic backgrounds. Except for Hausknecht, however, there has been little concern with the meaning of the above-mentioned differences, or with their possible consequences for other aspects of the lives of people differentially situated within the social system.

Out-of-School Activities

The boys and girls in the public high schools that formed the basis of Coleman's study (1961) were asked, "What is your favorite way of spending your leisure time?" and the results are shown in Table 13.

TABLE 13. FAVORITE WAY OF SPENDING LEISURE TIME, BY SEX

	BOYS	GIRLS
1. Organized outdoor sports—including football, basketball, tennis, etc.	22.0%	6.9%
2. Unorganized outdoor activities——including hunting, fishing, swimming, boating, horseback riding	14.7	11.3
3. "Being with the group," riding around, going uptown, etc.	17.2	32.5
4. Attending movies and spectator sports—athletic games, etc.	8.5	10.14
5. Dating or being out with the opposite sex	13.6	11.6
6. Going dancing (girls only)		12.0
7. Hobby—working on cars, bicycles, radio, musical instruments, etc.	22.5	20.1
8. Indoor group activities—bowling, playing cards, roller skating, etc.	8.0	8.1
9. Watching television	19.4	23.6
10. Listening to records or radio	11.2	31.7
11. Reading	13.7	35 5
12. Other, e.g., talking on telephone	7.1	9.3
13. No answer	8.1	3.7
Number of cases	(4020)	(4134)

Source: Reprinted with permission of The Free Press from *The Adolescent Society* by James S. Coleman. Copyright © 1961 by The Free Press, a Corporation. [p. 13]

The results indicate that boys like to spend considerable time in outdoor pursuits, being with their friends, or engaged in hobbies. Girls spend considerably more time than boys "being with the group," listening to records or the radio, and reading.

A sense of the wide range of activities involved is provided in a study conducted for the Boy Scouts of America (1960). The study reports at least thirty-eight different activities in six categories: (1) team sports, (2) individual sports, (3) outdoor activities, (4) formal social activities, (5) informal social activities, and (6) hobbies. Using a possession index as a measure of status, it was found that boys with more possessions (higher social status) have had more opportunities to participate in most of the activities than boys with fewer possessions. The only item for which this was reversed was in reading comics. Certain activities appeared to be fairly equally available to all classes: teaching sports; individual sports such as swimming, roller skating, horseback riding; outdoor activities such as fishing, hunting, camping, hiking; formal social activities, that is, parties; informal social activities like going to movies, listening to radio or records, indoor games, bicycling; and some hobbies.

There were, however, certain activities in which boys of higher social status showed a higher degree of participation. These included skiing,

skating, skin diving, water skiing, outboard motoring, sailing, outdoor cook-
ing, dancing, bowling, making things like model airplanes or radios, working with a chemistry set, playing a musical instrument ,and collecting stamps
or coins. The basis for these differences seems largely economic since the
higher-status activities require income or access to facilities and equipment
that would tend to exclude working-class adolescents.

A comparable study was conducted for girls (1956) and the findings
relating to class are even more striking. In twenty of twenty-nine activities,
a greater proportion of high-status girls say they have had some experience
than do girls of low status. Most of the activities where the differences are
most apparent involve special equipment. Roller skating is one activity involving special equipment in which low-status girls have a preponderance
of participants. However, even here the high-status girl is likely to have
participated. In three of four creative activities (music, arts and crafts,
writing) high-status girls show a distinct advantage, while in the fourth,
dramatics, there is essentially no difference.

Data are presented by de Grazia from an Opinion Research Corporation study, based on a national probability sample, concerning leisure-time
activities engaged in on the previous day.[2] A portion of these data is presented in Table 14. Looking at the variations by income, watching television
is the only activity that shows a marked difference for low-income respondents. Activities such as reading magazines, pleasure driving, hobbies, and
participation in sports show a slight positive relationship with income.
Visiting with friends or relatives and going to meetings do not show the relationships found in most other studies.

Comparing the youngest group (age fifteen through nineteen) with the
over-all sample, it is apparent that listening to records and spending time
at "hang-outs" is markedly a youth activity, as are, to a lesser extent, visiting, going pleasure riding, and going to the movies. Working around the
yard and garden, by the same token, is an activity more characteristic of
older people. It is difficult to compare these findings with those of Coleman
noted earlier. But there appears to be a significant discrepancy between
the proportion (about one fifth) who reported watching television as a
favorite activity in the Coleman study, and the proportion (better than
half) who reported watching television on a specific day in this study.

A number of studies based on smaller samples touch on some of the
same themes. A "pre-television" study by MacDonald (1949) of public
school children aged ten to twelve turned up systematic class differences in
participation in organized recreational groups and in certain individual
activities, such as taking music lessons. The middle-class child took part

[2] Sebastian de Grazia, *Of Time, Work and Leisure*. New York: The Twentieth
Century Fund, 1962, pp. 460–462. Source: "The Public Appraises Movies," *A Survey
for Motion Picture Associates of America, Inc.* Princeton, N.J.: Opinion Research
Corporation, 1957.

TABLE 14. PERCENT OF POPULATION ENGAGING IN VARIOUS LEISURE ACTIVITIES "YESTERDAY,"[a] BY PERSONAL CHARACTERISTICS

ACTIVITY	PERCENT OF ALL RESPONDENTS	ANNUAL FAMILY INCOME				AGE 15–19
		Under $3000	$3000–4999	$5000–6999	$7000 and over	
Watching television	57	47	60	59	59	56
Visiting with friends or relatives	38	39	38	38	39	46
Working around yard and in garden	33	35	30	33	34	20
Reading magazines	27	23	25	27	33	31
Reading books	18	20	16	18	20	21
Going pleasure driving	17	13	17	18	17	25
Listening to records	14	13	12	14	15	35
Going to meetings or other organization activities	11	11	10	11	11	11
Special hobbies (woodworking, knitting, etc.)	10	8	12	11	11	11
Going out to dinner	8	6	7	7	12	7
Participating in sports	8	3	8	10	11	8
Playing cards, checkers, etc.	7	5	6	8	8	12
None of those listed	7	10	8	5	6	3
Spending time at drugstore, etc.	6	5	6	7	7	20
Singing or playing musical instrument	5	5	4	5	4	10
Going to see sports events	4	3	4	5	5	7
Going to movies in regular theater and drive-in	7	4	6	5	6	15
Going to dances	2	2	2	1	1	8
Going to play, concert, opera, lecture, etc.	2	1	2	2	2	2

Source: By permission of the copyright owners, Opinion Research Corporation, Princeton, N.J. [pp. 460–462]

[a] Day prior to that on which respondents were visited.

mainly in Scouts and YMCA while the lower-class child was involved primarily in two centers or clubs for "underprivileged children."

The importance of "cultural" activities for children of upper social levels is demonstrated by Cramer (1950) on the basis of a sample of children from an upper-class private day school. Almost 35 percent of the respondents spent at least five hours per week in music lessons and practice. With reference to six "cultural" activities, it was found that 85.4 percent of the group were engaged in dancing lessons (70 percent said they did not like their dancing lessons). Almost half the group belonged to and participated in organized activities.

The differential importance of organizational membership was also found by Crichton and others in a study of a sample of fifteen- to eighteen-year-old boys and girls in Cardiff.[3] Nearly 60 percent of the grammar school group (higher status) as against 47 percent of the secondary modern school group (lower status) paid subscriptions to some formal organization. Watching television was the main leisure-time activity in the home, though this became less so with age. An interesting finding was that while the grammar school group read little more than the other group, there were sharp differences in the type of reading:

> Roughly similar proportions of each educational group read newspapers, magazines and paper backs, but the grammar section had a considerably lower proportion of readers of comics and a considerably higher proportion who had read any other printed matter. . . . Almost two-thirds of the grammar section were using a library of some sort, compared with less than a quarter of other teenagers. [pp. 203–209]

Logan and Goldberg (1953), studying a slightly older group, found comparable differences in reading, but not in leisure-time activities.

The effort, in recent years, to "expand the horizons" of low-income youth arises in part out of the realization that such youth appear to grow up in a relatively confined ghetto. This is the picture that emerges from the research of Whyte and Gans, where the focal point of recreational life is the neighborhood, and the outside community is viewed as alien territory.[4] Bernard (1939) found that the higher the social status, the earlier neighborhood patterns of associational relationships are displaced, occurring at age fifteen in the highest status group and age seventeen in the middle status group. The neighborhood pattern is most pronounced in the lowest status group and tends to endure into adulthood.

The other side of this coin is reported by Cramer (1950) for his privileged children. About four fifths of them had taken outside trips during the school year and a significant proportion had missed a week or more school for that purpose. Similarly, Crichton and others found that a much larger proportion of their higher status students had been away on vacation during the previous summer, and, while over half of that group had gone abroad, only 8 percent of the lower status group had traveled to that extent.

One recreational pattern not discussed in the larger studies referred to above is the use of alcoholic beverages. While there have been a number of studies of the use of alcohol by high school youth, they generally suffer

---

[3] A. Crichton, E. James, and J. Wakeford, "Youth and Leisure in Cardiff, 1960," *The Sociological Review*: 10 (July 1962), 203–220.

[4] William F. Whyte, *Street Corner Society*. Chicago: University of Chicago Press, 1943; Herbert J. Gans, *The Urban Villagers*. New York: The Free Press of Glencoe, 1962.

from relatively unsophisticated analysis, and, important for our purposes, unconcern with class differences. Nevertheless, because the findings tend to be consistent, we have assembled those most relevant for us in Table 15. Three of the studies, those by Hofstra College in Nassau County (1953): the University of Kansas, comparing a metropolitan with a nonmetropolitan area (1956);[5] the University of Wisconsin in Racine County (1956); used essentially the same design, method, and questionnaire. The fourth study, by Globetti and McReynolds (1964) is a comparison of white and Negro high school students in two communities in Mississippi, one a hill community, the other a delta community.

The results indicate that the use of alcoholic beverages is negatively related to attendance at church, and that Catholics are more likely to have permission to drink at home, and are more likely to drink than Protestants. Use of alcohol is also positively related to measures of social status. It is negatively related to grades in school; somewhat related, negatively, to number of offices held in school organizations; but not related to participation in school organizations, with two exceptions. The Kansas study found that girls who participate in interscholastic athletics are more likely to use alcohol than those who do not, although this relationship does not hold for boys. The Mississippi study found no significant differences in the pattern of use between Negro and white youth.

Though none of the authors discuss the issue, the finding that lower-class youth report drinking less than middle- and upper-class youth would seem to contradict popular expectations. One possible explanation is that lower-class youth who remain in high school do not indulge, partly because they adhere to different norms than do their peers who leave school, and partly because, in relation to higher-status peers, they simply have less money. Maddox and McCall (1964), in their study of teen-agers in the eleventh and twelfth grades of three public high schools, throw some light on this issue because they used a variety of measures of social class and aspirations. When the census classification of the father's occupation is used as a measure of status, the users are concentrated in the lower occupational classifications. Using Warner's Index of Status Characteristics as a measure, they find users more often at the upper and lower ends of the class structure with nonusers in the middle range. They sum up as follows:

> When the occupation of the fathers alone serves as an indicator of status, users are more likely than others to come from a family in which the father has a blue-collar occupation. However, when additional

[5] This study is also reported in E. Jackson Baur and Marston M. McCluggage, "Drinking Patterns of Kansas High School Students," *Social Problems*: 5 (Spring 1958), 317–326.

TABLE 15. RELATIONSHIP FOUND BETWEEN USE OF ALCOHOLIC BEVERAGES AND CERTAIN SOCIAL FACTORS, IN FOUR STUDIES OF HIGH SCHOOL YOUTH

SOCIAL FACTORS	NASSAU 1953	KANSAS 1956	RACINE 1958	MISSISSIPPI 1964
Religion				
Attendance at church	—ᵃ	negative	—	negative
Catholic rather than Protestant	—	positive for use and parental permission to use	—	
Status				
Father's occupation	—	—	—	positive
Number of rooms in house	—	positive	—	
Education				
Grades	negative	negative	negative	
Participation in school organizations	none	none	slight negative	
Number of offices held	—	negative	none	
Participation in interscholastic athletics	—	positive for girls	—	

ᵃ Indicates factor not discussed.

criteria are used to place students in a hierarchy of social classes, users are more likely to be found in upper and lower classes, the nonusers in the middle class. Among boys, use of alcohol appears to be related to the preference and expectations of upward social mobility. Among girls, the relationship between potential upward social mobility and use of alcohol is less clear. Girl nonusers, however, are more likely than others to expect such mobility. [p. 55]

Clearly, these findings contradict those of the earlier studies reported.

School-Related Activities

An early work often cited in this connection is *Elmtown's Youth* (1961). Hollingshead reports that lower-class students are in a disadvantaged position in extracurricular activities as well as in larger community experiences. Youngsters tend to associate with members of their own class, to date within these groupings, and to extend these relationships to other social activities. Lower-class youth were found to engage more frequently in the less socially acceptable activities such as drinking, gambling, and extreme sex play. This style of life serves to stigmatize these youth and to lead to their exclusion from the more prestigeful school-based activities.

An earlier study by Smith (1945) showed similar findings. Using a questionnaire to determine the extent of student participation, he found that extracurricular activities generally tend to be related to socioeconomic status, with higher-status adolescents more often being participants. More recently, Havighurst (1962) reached similar conclusions.

These three studies involved particular schools that may have been dominated by middle-class populations. This leaves open the question, what is the nature of extracurricular participation for lower-class youth in schools that are not dominated by a middle-class population? Coleman (1961) found that while the lower class is excluded from participation and leadership positions in schools where the middle-class predominates, the former takes the lead where they are in a majority. The pattern of the school follows the pattern of the community. However, where the class lines are sharply drawn and family background is a major determinant of association, adolescents from the dominant class tend to dominate the schools, and other adolescents find it hard to break in.

Coming from a good family is important in terms of prestige and for the economic advantage it usually provides the youngster. For the boy, it means that a car is more likely to be available, an important determinant of social success, particularly in the suburbs. For the girl, more money assures a more extensive wardrobe, which has an important bearing on popularity and prestige. Finally, despite the fact that public education is nominally free, the many expenses related to participating in the social life of the school result in family income being an important determinant of the extent of participation.

Conclusion

Given the vast amount of time that young people spend in leisure activities, relatively little is known about the dimensions of that activity, except possibly by marketing research agencies, which are loathe to make their findings public. There is some indication of what constitutes favorite activities and, for a few specific activities, how much time is spent by select samples of the population. But little seems to be known about the pattern of the allocation of time for groups characterized by social status, race or ethnicity, or value systems. There is no indication of the meaning of an activity such as pleasure riding, for example, for groups differentially located in the social structure. If there is an inverse relationship between family income and time spent at wage work by young people (there is little evidence on this point), then the greater scarcity of free time among youth from low-income families must have consequences for the structuring of allocations. But we do not know. Nor is there any information on the kinds of adult recreation possibly created by the pattern of youthful leisure.

From the available literature we do have the beginnings of a picture of some of the differences between working-class adolescents and their more affluent peers in terms of recreational experience. The working-class adolescent appears to be less involved in what might be called cultural or artistic activities. He tends to be less involved in extracurricular activities except possibly for team sports, and less involved in the activities of formal associations of a "character-building" nature. His recreational life is more centered in his own neighborhood and in activities of an out-of-door, physical nature. Finally, there is some evidence that the lower- or working-class youth who remains in high school drinks no more, and possibly less, than his higher-status peers in school.

Part Two

APPENDIX

Introduction

This appendix is a series of annotated references designed to serve several interest groups. For the teacher, it can be a source of material, a reference to the major research in our area of concern. It provides, in outline or condensed form, the essentials of social-science inquiries into the problems of low-income youth in the urban United States. For the student, it is a guide to the literature in that it provides enough information to point to what needs to be read. The appendix is not a substitute for the original material. For the researcher, it provides a summary of what has been done, how it was done, as well as the weight of evidence in support of alternative findings. Finally, for the policy maker, new to the area of concern, here is the empirical evidence that can serve as an additional ingredient in the process of decision making.

As was noted earlier, the annotated references are based primarily on material produced between 1950 and mid-1966. The core consists of research reports that we were able to locate with findings relevant to our concern. Also included are some more general theoretical and speculative works of special interest. Research studies with obvious deficiencies of method or suspect findings have been included to save the time of those coming after us. The literature dealing with similar problems in other countries is usually footnoted in the relevant review chapter and is annotated only when it is of special interest.

We know that certain areas or disciplines are inadequately represented here. No effort was made to review the psychoanalytic literature except that of more general interest in the *Journal of Orthopsychiatry*. Nor was the psychological literature covered fully—we restricted ourselves primarily to the area of educational psychology, with occasional forays into social psychology. Finally, the problem of juvenile delinquency has an immense literature of its own, with many attempts at review and integration, and is not included except for a few items dealing with the relationship between delinquency and social class. Other significant omissions must be attributed to human frailties.

As to the format of the annotations, for empirical studies, we have tried to outline the purpose of the research, the sample and method used, and the conclusions. This pattern is varied for nonresearch materials.

The sections of the appendix follow in the same order as the chapters in Part One. When the same item is used in several chapters, it is usually annotated with reference to the earlier mention and cross-referenced in later sections.

In our review of the literature, we tried to bring some order to the materials collected and to indicate areas of agreement or disagreement, overlap and underdevelopment. In the annotations, we have tried to indicate the limitations of some of the research, as well as intellectual and methodological ties that may have been overlooked by the authors. Our purpose was not the development of a rapid system of classification, but the erection of guide posts to assist the hurried or inexperienced traveler.

Annotated References for Chapter One

Bell, Robert R.
"Lower Class Negro Mothers and Their Children"
Integrated Education: 2 (December–January 1964–1965), 23–27

Purpose: To ascertain lower-class Negro mothers' aspirations for their children.

Sample: 202 Negro mothers, living in a lower-class neighborhood of Philadelphia, with a minimum of two children, one of whom was in either kindergarten or nursery school. Sample subdivided into four categories:

1. Thirty-seven "low status" mothers (zero to eight years of education; seven or more children)
2. Forty-three "middle status" mothers (zero to eight years of education; six or fewer children)
3. Twenty-nine "middle status" mothers (nine or more years of education; seven or more children)
4. Ninety-three "high status" mothers (nine or more years of education; six or fewer children)

Method: Interviews by two Negro female graduate students, using a schedule containing 102 items.

Conclusions: High-status mothers were significantly more likely than low-status mothers to want a college education for their sons and daughters, to want children to marry at later ages, to want them to have *more* children, and to believe that "hard work and ambition" (rather than "playing up to" or "socializing with") the boss was important for getting ahead. They did not differ in respect to their occupational aspirations for their children, or in their idea of "any young man with ability and hard work" being able to earn 10,000 dollars a year. (About three quarters of both groups were optimistic in this respect.)

Blood, Robert O.
"Social Class and Family Control of Television Viewing"
Merrill-Palmer Quarterly: 7 (July 1961), 205–222

Purpose: An examination of class difference in parental control of television viewing.

Sample: 102 lower- and middle-class families in Ann Arbor, Michigan, in 1957.

Method: Pretested interviews consisting of twenty-four open-end questions administered by student interviewers to mothers of children between two and eighteen years of age.

Conclusions: Most families control the use of TV by their children. The lower class, however, has a deviant minority with a laissez-faire approach toward

TV interference with bedtime, toward quarrels over what program to watch, and especially toward the number and kinds of programs their children watch. The lower class views TV most enthusiastically as a boon to their family life. When there is conflict over control of the TV, it is apt to be resolved by direct manipulation of the set itself or by simple personal manipulation. By contrast, middle-class families are more concerned about keeping TV under control but are more flexible and less frustrating in their methods. Substantially briefer viewing time is achieved in the middle class by moving the TV set out of the living loom, limiting the viewing time allowed, and encouraging alternative activities. For the sample as a whole, the data revealed relatively little difficulty in the use of the TV in the family. Most families have definite preferences about what their children should and should not see on TV and find that their children are gradually being socialized into acceptance and self-maintenance of these values.

Boek, Walter E., Marvin Sussman, and Alfred Yankauer
"Social Class and Child Care Practices"
Marriage and Family Living: 20 (November 1958), 326–333

Purpose: To explore the relationship between social class and child practices.
Sample: 1433 mothers from upstate New York, with children ranging in age from three to six months.
Method: Mothers were interviewed concerning (1) family planning, (2) prior employment, (3) child-care literature, (4) feeding practices, and (5) aspirations for her child. Social class was measured by Warner's ISC.
Conclusions:

1. There were variations in planning by social class, but these were not large.
2. The proportion of mothers working before they became pregnant was about the same for all classes.
3. About one fifth of the sample did not report any child-care literature as especially helpful, and the lower the class, the more likely the respondents were not to list any literature as helpful.
4. A slightly higher proportion of the two highest-class mothers were breast-feeding at the time of the study. There was an inverse relationship between length of breast-feeding and social class. There was no significant difference among social classes in the type of feeding mixture used. For the mothers who were feeding solids at the time of the interview (97 percent of the sample), there was no significant difference by social class in the age of the baby at which time solids were introduced.
5. There was a positive correlation between social class and college aspirations, although over half of the mothers in the lowest class wanted their child to go to college. There was a positive relationship between social class and a tendency to answer that the selection of an occupation was up to the child to make when he grew older.

Brooks, Deton J.
"Parents of School Dropouts: Some Aspects of Culture,
  Environment and Attitudes. Preliminary Report"
Chicago: Cook County Department of Public Aid,
  September 24, 1964 (mimeo)

"This is a preliminary report of a full scale research undertaking which basically examined some aspects of the culture, environment, and attitudes of a group of women who had two factors in common—they were mothers of children who had not completed high school and they were recipients of public assistance." [p. 1] The group of 296 mothers (92 percent Negro) ranged in age from thirty-one to sixty-five. They were interviewed and given three tests: the Revised Beta Examination (a nonverbal IQ test), the New Stanford Reading Test, and the New Stanford Arithmetic Test. These were administered by thirty-two second-year graduate students from Loyola University School of Social Work. The reported data deal with social characteristics, family background, migration history, living conditions, parent-child interaction, cultural interests, reading, religious and social activity, and knowledge and use of community resources.

Brooks, Edna Earl, J. Buri, E. A. Byrne, and M. C. Hudson
"Economic Factors, Parental Attitudes and School Attendance"
Social Work: 7 (October 1962), 103–108

Purpose: To learn the characteristics of children with attendance problems and the situations or stresses that serve as barriers to school attendance.

Sample: 476 parents of children selected from 135 public elementary schools in all areas of St. Louis, Missouri.

Method: Precoded stimulus-response questionnaire designed to get at parental attitudes toward education, the school, and school attendance. Twenty-five socioeconomic factors considered to influence these attitudes and attendance were studied.

Conclusions: Over-all parental attitude was strongly related to school attendance, with positive attitudes being associated with best attendance. However, there was little evidence of a relationship between socioeconomic factors and attitudes.

> Twelve socioeconomic factors, namely, age of child, school grade of child, age of respondent, age of spouse, respondents' level of completed education, number of times family moved in a two-year period, gross family income, number of years family lived in neighborhood, number of persons living in the home, status of home ownership, type of work of respondents' spouse, and source of family income, were positively and significantly related (at the 10 percent level or lower) to attendance. Six factors showed non-significant relationships . . . and included sex, race, parental structure of the

home, rural-urban background, and respondents' presence in the home when children left for school or when they returned home. [p. 108]

There was no effort to explain the relationship found.

Burchinal, Lee, Bruce Gardner, and Glenn R. Hawkes
"Children's Personality Adjustment and the Socio-Economic
   Status of Their Families"
Journal of Genetic Psychology: 92 (June 1958), 149–159

Purpose: To test the hypothesis that rural and small-town children coming from higher socioeconomic status families show fewer indications of personality maladjustments than do children of families with lower socioeconomic status.
   Sample: Stratified probability sample of 256 fifth-grade children.
   Method: The Rogers Test of Personality Adjustment was administered. This test yields subscores of (1) feelings of personal inferiority, (2) social maladjustment, (3) family relationships, and (4) daydreaming.
   Conclusions: There is a significant inverse relation between children's total scores and their personal inferiority scores on the one hand, and the prestige of their father's occupation on the other. When father's occupation was used as the stratification criterion, only differences in total mean scores were significant. On every scale, however, the children whose father had had post-college graduate educations had higher ("worse") scores than children of less-educated fathers.

Carroll, Rebecca Evans
"Relation of Social Environment to the Moral Ideology and
   the Personal Aspirations of Negro Boys and Girls"
School Review: 53 (January 1945), 30–38

Purpose: To determine the relation of adolescents' SES (socioeconomic status) to conception of right and wrong, and ideas of persons they would like to resemble.
   Sample: 300 Negro adolescents attending a segregated school in East Baltimore, Maryland.
   Method: Students were asked to write answers to such questions as (1) What is stealing?, (2) Why is it, or is it not, right to steal?, and similar questions regarding cheating and lying. Students were asked to write essays on the subject "The Person I Would Like to Be."
   Conclusions: Lower-class adolescents tended to express aversions to lying, cheating, and stealing in "materialistic" terms; middle-class adolescents, in "altruistic" or "social" terms.
   Middle-class adolescents were judged to have reached a high degree of moral development. Lower-class adolescents were more likely to choose glam-

orous adults as their ideal selves, and to stress physical beauty, personal liking, and fame; while middle-class adolescents stressed moral, intellectual, and altruistic qualities.

Davis, Allison
"Language and Social-Class Perspectives"
(Processed, no date)

This is a comparison of the "language-culture" differences that exist in all social classes. The author notes that

> . . . lower-class children, on the average, exhibit less skill in the solution of abstract verbal problems, and in understanding or using abstract oral English. . . . This is not to say that lower-class groups do not exhibit facility and sophistication in spoken language. Their dialects are highly intricate and effective in the expression of action, thought, and emotion. But in the schools and in the libraries, only that particular dialect which is called "standard" English counts.
>
> The choice of a symbol-system in which to express thought, feeling, and fantasy, . . . depends not only upon the individual, but also upon the cultural values and perspectives in which he has been trained by his group. The basic problem is not so much a matter of the degree to which the expression is abstract or specific, as of a perspective upon life which emphasized ratiocination, on the one hand, or action and emotion, on the other. [pp. 4–12]

Deutsch, Martin
"The Disadvantaged Child and the Learning Process," in
    A. Harry Passow, ed.
    Education in Depressed Areas
New York: Bureau of Publications, Teachers College,
    Columbia University, 1963, pp. 163–179

Purpose: To discuss the interaction of social and developmental factors and their impact on the intellectual growth and school performance of the child, with special reference to urban children from marginal social circumstances.

Sample: Findings and hypotheses based on on-going work at the Institute for Developmental Studies.

Conclusions: The author argues that children from low-income homes, particularly Negroes from ghetto slums, suffer from "stimulus deprivation." "By this is not necessarily meant any restriction to a segment of the spectrum of stimulation potentially available." This deprivation has effects on both the formal aspects of cognition (the behavior by which stimuli are perceived, encouraged, and responded to) and the contentual (the actual content of the child's knowledge). Therefore, experiential poverty probably results in a child falling considerably short of his maturational ceiling.

Following are some of the specifics in the child's environment, and their effects on the development of the formal, contentual, and attitudinal systems, as discussed by Deutsch:

1. "The sparsity of objects [in the household] and lack of diversity of home artifacts which are available and meaningful . . . gives the child few opportunities to manipulate and organize the visual properties of his environment and thus perceptually to organize and discriminate nuances of that environment." [p. 170]
2. The lower-class home is not verbally oriented, although it may be noisy; a situation not conducive to the development of auditory discrimination skills and attentiveness.
3. "The combination of the constriction in the use of language and in shared activity [with adults] results, for the lower-class child, in much less stimulation of the early memory function."
4. The lower-class child lacks orientation to the expectation of reward for performances and for especially successful task completion, which reduces motivation. [p. 171]
5. He lacks opportunity "to use the adult as a source of information, correction and reality testing involved in problem solving and the absorption of new knowledge." [p. 173]
6. He lacks practice in word use, which, it is hypothesized, is strongly related to reading skills and other conceptual verbal activity.
7. He demonstrates a lack of syntactical organization and subject continuity in speech.

Douvan, Elizabeth
"Social Status and Success Striving"
Journal of Abnormal and Social Psychology: 52 (March 1956), 219–223

Purpose: This study was designed to contrast the members of two social groups, middle and working class, with respect to the degree of achievement motivation.

Sample: 313 high school seniors in a medium-sized midwestern community. Class membership was determined by (1) occupational index based on data derived from school records, (2) a questionnaire in which the subject was asked to describe father's work and conditions of employment.

Method: Subjects were given a series of tasks under two reward conditions: (1) reward limited to personal satisfaction derived from attaining a norm, (2) material reward added. Following failure experiences, to induce deprivation, subjects in each condition were given McClelland's projective test for achievement motivation.

Conclusions:

From the results it is concluded that the pattern of achievement motivation a child develops depends on the class subculture in which he is trained, and is functional to the values and behavior requirements with which he will be confronted as he assumes adulthood within that setting. [p. 223]

Downing, Gertrude L., R. W. Edgar, A. J. Harris, L. Kernberg,
and H. F. Steren
*The Preparation of Teachers for Schools in Culturally
Deprived Neighborhoods*
Washington, D.C.: U.S. Office of Education, Cooperative Research
Project No. 935, 1965

Purpose: To provide a testing ground for current assumptions about the learning process and about reaching the educationally disadvantaged, and to provide a realistic base for proposals for modification of future teacher-education programs.

Sample: All children were from a "special service" junior high school in a depressed area of South Jamaica, Queens, New York. Eighty-five students were selected at random from an incoming seventh grade, forty boys and forty-five girls. The control group consisted of fifty boys and sixty-one girls. All were Negro except for twelve Puerto Ricans and three others.

Method: Four studies were pursued: (1) A curriculum study in which three teachers taught the four main academic subjects to the same eighty-five pupils for three years, (2) a psychological study using both individual and group intelligence tests as well as personality and achievement tests, (3) A teacher-education project, (4) A field-experience project in which prospective teachers participated in informal after-school programs in "difficult" schools.

Conclusions: Based on the Rosenzweig Picture-Frustration Test, the study and control groups were found to be considerably less mature than the norm for twelve to thirteen-year-olds. From administration of the Rorschach, the authors conclude that, compared to a middle-class group which also scored higher on measured intelligence,

> . . . the Project group emerges as being less productive, less controlled, less constricted, less mature, more impulsive, emotionally more responsive to social stimulation and also more sensitive to nuances of interpersonal relationships. Their ability to see the world as do most others does not seem notably different on the average from the normative group. Nor do they appear, as a group, inclined toward markedly greater stereotype of perception. [p. 143]

The authors also concluded that

> . . . It is very doubtful that every new teacher can, through training and experience, develop the understandings and skills that are necessary to work with these children, even with the best of supervision and the most adequate provision of materials and equipment. [p. 215]

They suggest that the good teacher of the culturally disadvantaged (1) should be emotionally mature, (2) should have unusual physical stamina, (3) should have the ability to feel interest and enthusiasm for his subject, (4) should be capable of considerable objectivity, (5) should be able to individualize his classroom procedures, and (6) should be able to use the arts as stimulants to the learning of academic subjects.

Haller, Archibald O., and Shailer Thomas
"Personality Correlates of the Socio-Economic Status
   of Adolescent Males"
Sociometry: 25 (December 1962), 398–404

Purpose: To investigate the degree of correlation between personality factors and socioeconomic status.

Sample: 440 seventeen-year-old boys from one culturally homogeneous Michigan county. Data collected in 1957.

Method: A version of the Sixteen Personality Factor Test was used to measure all personality dimensions except intelligence; Test of G: Culture Free used for intelligence; California Test of Personality used as an empirical link to previous research; SES based on a form of the Sewell socioeconomic-status scale.

Conclusions: Correlation between SES and personality is limited to certain personality factors and even here the correlation is low. The exception is measured intelligence that correlates 0.41 with SES. The personality variables that have a statistical significance in relation to SES, in order of magnitude, are as follows: relating to high SES—cyclothemia, superego strength, adventurous autonomic resilience, sophistication, will control and character stability, lack of nervous tension; and relating to low SES—dissatisfied emotionally, lack of internal standards, inherent withdrawn schizothymia, rough simplicity, lack of will control and character stability, nervous tension.

Havighurst, Robert, and Myra Robinson
"The Development of the Ideal Self in
   Childhood and Adolescence"
Journal of Educational Research: 40 (December 1946), 241–257

Purpose: To describe the development of the ideal self or ego ideal as it is revealed by self-reports during childhood and adolescence.

Sample: There is no specific sample indicated, although data are said to be drawn from boys and girls of different social and ethnic backgrounds ranging in age from eight to seventeen.

Method: The definition of ideal self used was "the integrated set of roles and aspirations which direct the individual's life." The subjects were asked to write a brief essay on the topic "the person I would like to be like." The responses were classified on the basis of six categories.

Conclusions: The results indicate that there is a developmental trend in the ideal self commencing with the parental figure in childhood, moving to the glamorous ideal in middle childhood, and culminating in late adolescence as a composite of desirable characteristics that may be symbolized by an attractive young adult. Children from the lower socioeconomic classes as a group lag behind the middle-class child in progressing through the stage of glamorous adult as an ideal model, indicating possible immaturity.

Hess, Robert D., Virginia Shipman, and David Jackson
"Early Experience and the Socialization of Cognitive Modes in Children"
Child Development: 36 (December 1965), 869–886

Purpose: To discover how teaching styles of mothers induce and shape learning styles and information-processing strategies in their children.

Sample: 163 Negro mothers and their four-year-old children: forty from college-educated, professional, executive, and managerial levels ("upper middle"); forty-two from skilled blue-collar occupational levels with not more than high school education ("upper lower"); forty from unskilled or semiskilled occupational levels, with predominantly elementary school education ("lower lower"); and forty-one from unskilled or semiskilled occupational levels, with fathers absent and family supported by public assistance ("ADC").

Method: (1) Mothers were taught several simple tasks, such as sorting and classifying objects in various ways, and then were asked to teach their children. Analyses were made of the mothers' verbal and nonverbal styles of teaching and of the children's success in learning; (2) mothers were asked how they would handle their child in various circumstances, and analyses were made of several dimensions of verbal styles of answers.

Conclusions: Lower-class mothers are significantly more likely than middle-class mothers to provide "a cognitive environment in which behavior is controlled by status rules rather than by attention to the individual characteristics of a specific situation and one in which behavior is . . . [impulsive rather than] mediated by verbal cues or by teaching that relates events to one another and the present to the future." In short, "the meaning of deprivation is a deprivation of meaning." In consequence, middle-class children learned the tasks more successfully. There were no class differences in affective aspects of mother-child interactions.

Himmelweit, Hilde L.
"Socio-Economic Background and Personality"
International Social Science Bulletin: 7 (Fall 1955), 29–35

Purpose: To ascertain the degree to which the Davis hypothesis, concerning the greater socialized anxiety developed in middle-class children, could be confirmed in England using a broader and more representative sample than Davis'.

Sample: Over 600 thirteen-to-fourteen-year-old boys in the third grade (equivalent to U.S. seventh grade) of "state schools" in London ranging in class status from middle middle to lower working, categorized on the basis of the prestige of their father's occupation.

Method: A variety of techniques was used, including structured questions, problem-solving situations, sentence-completion items, and projective techniques, in a total of seven hours over several sessions.

Conclusions: Davis' and Warner's findings of more rigorous supervision of middle-class children (in the areas of early training practice, performance in school, and leisure activities) were confirmed. Consequently, the middle-class children showed a more rigid value system, considered themselves as having to do more things, and believed more strongly that the infringement of rules required punishment. However, there was no evidence to indicate that the middle-class child experienced greater over-all anxiety, this being attributed to the greater child-centeredness of middle-class homes. On all questions dealing with family relationships, the middle-class child felt more accepted, felt he could discuss things with his parents, and felt that they shared his interests. It was concluded that pressure exerted in a cushioned environment can be tolerated without undue anxiety and that the lower-class child, while less pushed, is emotionally less protected and thus his needs for dependence may be less well-satisfied than those of the middle-class child.

Kahl, Joseph
"Educational and Occupational Aspirations of Common Man's Boys"
Harvard Educational Review: 23 (Summer 1953), 186–203

Purpose: To explore the social influences on ambitions of high school boys of working-class background.

Sample: 24 boys drawn from a sample of 3971 on whom questionnaire data were available.

Method: The preliminary questionnaire, used on the larger sample drawn from eight towns that are part of the Boston metropolitan area, elicited information on current educational plans, occupations of fathers, and IQ scores. The interviews, which are not described in detail, explored the influence on choice of aspiration level of boys of similar class and intelligence.

Conclusions: The interviews disclosed that dissatisfaction with working-class life as communicated by parents was the major factor in determining the aspiration level of the boy. These parents trained their sons to take school seriously and use education as a means of social ascent. It was also shown that if a boy does not take advantage of schools to climb, his later chances for occupational achievement will be slim. Even in homes where the pressures from parents were not obvious, the sons sensed the parents' dissatisfaction with their status or felt that the parents supported their aspirations even though they did not initiate them. Few of the boys derived intellectual satisfaction from their school experiences but viewed them in a completely utilitarian manner.

Kantor, Mildred B., J. C. Glidwell, I. Mensh, H. R. Demke, and
  M. L. Gildes
"Socio-Economic Level and Maternal Attitudes toward Parent-Child Relationships"
Human Organization: 16 (Winter 1958), 44–48

Purpose: To examine the relationship between socioeconomic level and maternal attitudes.

Sample: A group of 815 mothers of third-grade public school children was divided into three groups—upper, middle, and lower socioeconomic level—on the basis of occupation of head of family, education of head of family, and gross family income.

Method: A seventeen-item attitude questionnaire was administered, designed to identify maternal attitudes believed to be significantly related to the adjustment of children.

Conclusions: Low SES mothers were more likely than high SES mothers to agree that "jealousy is just a sign of selfishness in children"; that parents cannot influence some children; that standards of discipline and conformity are hard to establish; that the most important thing children should learn is obedience to parents; that the sexual problems of children were difficult to deal with; and that children have more fun than grown-ups.

Kohn, Melvin L. (a)
"Social Class and Parental Values"
American Journal of Sociology: 64 (January 1959), 337–357

Purpose: To investigate the difference that might exist between the values and attitudes of middle- and working-class parents.

Sample: The sample was drawn from parents of fifth-grade students in lower- and middle-class neighborhoods in Washington, D.C., excluding those census tracts with 20 percent or more Negro population, as well as those in the highest quartile with respect to median income. Two hundred families were randomly selected from among those in which the father had a white-collar occupation and 200 from those with a father in a manual occupation. Working-class families are stable working class rather than lower class.

Method: Interviews were scheduled with all mothers and with every fourth father. The main instrument for obtaining a measure of values for their children was derived from Kluckhohn's definition of values.

Conclusions: Although middle-class and working-class parents share many values in common, there are differences:

1. Middle-class parents value honesty as an indication of self-control, while working-class parents see honesty as a personal characteristic and group it with obedience and good manners.
2. While middle-class parents had a similar set of values for boys and girls, working-class parents valued dependability, being a good student, and

ambition as desirable for boys and happiness, good manners, neatness, and cleanliness as desirable for girls.
3. Obedience to parents was more important to working-class than to middle-class parents.

Kohn, Melvin L. (b)
"Social Class and the Exercise of Parental Authority"
American Sociological Review: 24 (June 1959), 352–366

Purpose: To compare the modes and conditions under which working-class and middle-class parents punish their preadolescent children.

Sample: 400 representative white middle- and working-class families in Washington, D.C., each family having a fifth-grade child.

Method: All mothers were interviewed. In every fourth family an interview was also arranged with the father and the fifth-grade child. The interviews pertained to the kinds of punishment used and the conditions which evoked punishment.

Conclusions: No class differences were found in the extent to which each parent participates in decision making, in family members' evaluation of which parent is stricter, or in use of physical punishment. Differences were found in the conditions under which middle- and working-class parents use physical punishment. Working-class mothers find "wild play" of an aggressive or destructive sort and physical fighting with brothers and sisters more tolerable than do middle-class mothers. Middle-class mothers punish or not on the basis of their interpretation of the child's intent. They find loss of temper, when it takes violent form, intolerable.

Kohn, Melvin, and Eleanor E. Carroll
"Social Class and the Allocation of Parental Responsibilities"
Sociometry: 23 (December 1960), 372–392

Purpose: To trace the effects of middle- and working-class parents' ideologies of child rearing upon the division of responsibilities between mother and father for support and constraint of children.

Sample: 400 representative white working- and middle-class families in Washington, D.C., each family having a fifth-grade child.

Method: All mothers were interviewed. In every fourth family the father and fifth-grade child were interviewed as well.

Conclusions: Results indicate that middle-class mothers emphasize the father's obligation to be as supportive as the mother, his role in imposing restraints is secondary. Working-class mothers want husbands to be more directive, the importance of constraints being more important. In relation to daughters, middle-class fathers feel this is more the mother's domain. Working-class fathers play neither the directive nor supportive role, and they view child rearing as the wife's responsibility.

Leshan, Lawrence L.
"Time Orientation and Social Class"
Journal of Abnormal and Social Psychology: 47 (July 1952), 589–592

Purpose: To compare time orientations among lower-, middle- and upper-class children.
Sample: 117 children, ages eight to eleven.
Method: Examination of children's stories.
Conclusions: The results indicate that the time orientation of the various classes differ in the directions predicted. Lower-class children are oriented to temporal goal orientations that involve quick sequences of tension and relief; in the upper-lower, middle, and lower-upper classes longer tension-relief sequences are more typical. This involves planning action into the future, and regularity of activity. In the upper-upper classes the individual sees himself as part of several or more generations and his orientation is backward to the past.

Lipset, Seymour M.
"Working Class Authoritarianism," Chapter 4, in *Political Man*
New York: Anchor Books, Inc., 1963, pp. 87–126

This paper presents a view of the prevalence and basis for authoritarian attitudes in the working class. The analysis is based on secondary sources, many of which have been gathered outside this country.

In summing up, Lipset states that the lower-class individual is likely to have been exposed to punishment, lack of love, a general atmosphere of tension and aggression since early childhood—all experiences that tend to produce deep-rooted hostilities expressed by ethnic prejudice, political authoritarianism, and chiliastic transvaluational religion. His education is less, his associations are limited, and he is surrounded on the job by others with a similarly restricted cultural, educational, and family background. From early childhood he has sought immediate gratifications, rather than engaged in activities that might have long-term rewards. All of these characteristics produce a tendency to view politics and personal relationships in black and white terms, a desire for immediate action, an impatience with talk and discussion, a lack of interest in organizations with a long-range perspective, and a readiness to follow leaders who offer a demonological interpretation of the evil forces which are conspiring against him.

Maas, Henry S.
"Some Social Class Differences in the Family Systems and
   Group Relations of Pre- and Early Adolescents"
Child Development: 22 (June 1951), 145–152

Purpose: A descriptive study, primarily concerned with the psychological and social distances that characterize the subjects' relations with their parents, siblings, and peers.

Sample: 21 subjects representing two subcultural groups, the lower-lower strata and the core culture, represented by a combination of upper-lower class and lower-middle class.

Method: Flexibly structured interviews.

Conclusions: Lower-class family systems appear to be hierarchical and rigid. Parents are seen as closed or inaccessible to the child's communication. Fear of parental authority and its explosive anger mutes the child until he explodes in a similar manner or redirects his hostile aggression and tender feelings toward siblings and peers.

McKinley, Donald S.
Social Class and Family Life
New York: The Free Press of Glencoe, 1964

Purpose: To explore "How and *why* . . . the methods of socialization vary from class to class."

Sample: 73 "upper class" boys, 94 "middle class" boys, and 96 "lower class" boys, all from the eleventh and twelfth grades in three schools in and near Boston. In addition, sixteen fathers (fifteen of them middle class or upper-lower class); and reanalysis of interviews conducted by others with 360 other fathers of kindergarten-aged children in suburban Boston.

Method: Questionnaires administered to high school boys; interviews conducted with sixteen fathers.

Conclusions: As a result of experiencing greater frustration in their occupational roles, lower-class fathers are more aggressively severe and hostile toward their adolescent sons than are higher-status fathers, although "frustrated" fathers at all class levels are more likely than satisfied/successful fathers to be severe.

Mitchell, James V., Jr.
"Identification of Items in the California Test of
   Personality That Differentiate Between Subjects
   of High and Low Socio-Economic Status at the Fifth and
   Seventh-Grade Levels"
Journal of Educational Research: 51 (December 1957), 241–250

Purpose: To discover some specific problems of adjustment that are characteristically reported with greater frequency by children from one or the other status groups and which consequently must be related to the different social climates operative for each group.

Sample: From eleven fifth and seventh grades in a midwestern community, a group of high and low socioeconomic status were selected using Warner's ISC. There were 108 subjects, an equal number of boys and girls.

Method: An elementary form of the California Test of Personality was administered to all.

Conclusions: At both grade levels a significantly higher proportion of low-status children showed evidence of having problems such as: (1) economic worries; (2) feelings of rejection or persecution, and consequent aggressive tendencies; (3) feelings of insecurity; (4) psychosomatic complaints or nervous symptoms; (5) unfulfilled desires for increased independence; (6) unfulfilled desires for new experiences; (7) troublesome anxiety reactions. There was some evidence that the cumulative burden of problems such as these tends to increase the low-status child's sense of frustration and discouragement as he grows older.

Moles, Oliver C., Jr. (a)
"Training Children in Low-Income Families for School"
Welfare in Review: 3 (June 1965), 1–11

The author succinctly reviews some of the literature in such areas as the development of intellectual skills, achievement motivation, and the opportunity for study at home, as these relate to children from low-income families, and relates the findings to on-going federal programs of service and research.

Moles, Oliver C., Jr. (b)
"Child Training Practices among Low-Income Families"
Welfare in Review: 3 (December 1965), 1–19

Purpose: To compare the child-rearing practices among three categories of low-income mothers.

Sample: 800 families with children in twelve inner-city schools in the fifth and sixth grades, divided into 208 families who had received from one to twenty-nine months of welfare assistance ("Low Recipients"); 214 "High Recipients" (thirty to thirty-six months of assistance); and 378 nonrecipients.

Method: Interviews with mothers; questionnaires to children.

Conclusions: There were virtually no differences among the three types of families. Among all types, 93 percent of the children said their mothers thought they should finish college; 43 percent of the mothers said they wanted their children to finish college; 67 percent would be dissatisfied with low-prestige manual occupations for their children; 51 percent of the children said their mothers helped most of the time with homework; 70 percent of the mothers said they read stories to their children at least once a week during the child's preschool period; 80 percent of the children perceived their mothers as expecting better school work than the children felt it possible to do; 41 percent of the mothers said their first choice of action if the child had a poor report card would be to speak to the teacher; and 76 percent agreed that obedience and respect for authority are the most important virtues children should learn.

Pavenstedt, Eleanor
"A Comparison of the Child-Rearing Environment of
   Upper Lower and Very Low Lower Class Families"
American Journal of Orthopsychiatry: 35 (January 1965), 89–98

Purpose: To observe and describe the atmosphere in the homes of families at the two extremes of the lower socioeconomic class.

Sample: 30 stable families contacted in a prenatal clinic in connection with their first pregnancies, and an unspecified number of "disorganized" families contacted after they had one to three children. All cases are from an urban East Coast area.

Method: Observation, interviews, and psychological testing focused on personality functions, courtship histories, marital relationships, and child-rearing practices of the "stable" group; apparently only observation of child-rearing practices was used for the "low lower" or "disorganized" groups. Theoretical framework was psychoanalytic. Number of visits per family is unspecified but amounted to many.

Conclusions: Regarding stable families: conscious marital goals seldom went beyond simple security; husbands often were studying under GI Bill but quit to take extra jobs when first baby arrived; mothers' personalities were restricted; "we would not have dared to propose psychological testing" to the husbands; little intellectual stimulation for children, but little overt neglect and much talk to children; emphasis was on obedience training; and "as children came of school age, parents showed more concern that they conform to the teacher's expectations than about learning per se." [p. 92]

Regarding disorganized families: adults were in constant crises; they were intensely reluctant to let children attend a special nursery school, were filled with suspicion and distrust, possessed extremely poor self-images; housekeeping was desultory and disorganized; children were focused on short-run gains and losses, were pseudo-independent, and also possessed very poor self-images.

Peil, Margaret
"The Use of Child-Rearing Literature by Low-Income Families"
Ph.D. Dissertation, Department of Sociology, University of
   Chicago, 1963

Purpose: To investigate the reading habits, interests, and sources of information on child rearing of white and Negro parents of low education and income to determine the amount and type of reading done, the influence of specific types of reading material, the child-rearing problems considered most important, and the racial differences in reading patterns.

Sample: 98 Negro mothers and 82 white mothers, all of them parents of first graders in three Catholic schools in Chicago.

Method: Interviews, half-hour to an hour. At the end of the interview, the respondent was given a pamphlet on reading. A week later she received a pamphlet on attitudes toward children. Another pamphlet on schooling was delivered the third week. About a week after the third pamphlet was delivered, the respondents were interviewed again as to their knowledge and understanding of the contents of the pamphlets.

Conclusions: Two results considered significant were: (1) racial differences in reading habits are greater than differences in education, age, or size of family. Negro women were greater readers than the white women studied. At least one half of the Negro women studied, read magazines regularly, and books occasionally. While few read books, especially among the white women, or used the library, almost all the women read the advice of "experts" if the material were readily available.

> Pamphlets which were delivered or made available were not spurned. . . . It is the increased availability of well-written, up-to-date information on child-rearing in the types of literature these women already read that is likely to have the greatest effect on their child-rearing practices. [p. 48]

Rainwater, Lee
"A Study of Personality Differences between Middle-Class
   and Lower-Class Adolescents: Szondi Test in Culture-
   Personality Research"
Genetic Psychology Monograph: 54 (1956), 3–86

Purpose: To study personality differences between middle- and lower-class adolescents, assuming that different styles of child rearing and different social environments will produce personalities that differ significantly in ways of handling basic psychological needs, drives, and tensions.

Sample: 25 adolescents from eighth-grade classes in lower- and middle-class schools.

Method: The Szondi test, a projective technique designed to investigate personality in terms of eight postulated psychological drives or need systems, was administered to all subjects. Validity was checked by a prediction experiment using sociologists and Szondi experts as judges. On the basis of blind analysis of the data, Szondi experts were able to predict lower and middle class at less than the 1 percent level, while sociologists were able to match social class groups with responses on the Szondi at the 0.1 percent level.

Conclusions: The results indicate that middle-class girls and lower-class boys are at opposite poles of personality organization, with differences between the sexes being smaller for both groups. The middle-class adolescent is found to be more dependent on people and more likely to work through people to derive gratification. The lower-class adolescent has little acceptance of a dependency drive, and is more oriented toward manipulation of objects for purely egocentric satisfactions without regard to the human nature of the object. Id impulses are more transformed in the middle-class group and, over-all, the middle-class adolescent has a better-oriented psychic pattern that involves stable bound energy, lesser emphasis on sexual area, and tighter control of libido. Finally, the findings indicate that the middle-class adolescent develops a personality more strongly committed to verbal and symbolic processes.

Rainwater, Lee, Richard P. Coleman, and Gerald Handel
Workingman's Wife
New York: Oceana Publications, Inc., 1959

A description of the psychosocial world of the workingman's wife and the way in which this affects her as a consumer. For this group, poverty is more a psychological than an economic problem because there is usually enough income to provide the essentials of life, if little else. In addition, differences in aspirations, purchasing habits, and increasing leisure have increased the demands for greater income. Although prosperity has increased in this group, other social problems have increased also, such as juvenile delinquency and psychosomatic disease.

Four hundred-twenty housewives in four cities, Chicago, Louisville, Tacoma, and Trenton were interviewed using three main interview guides. The interviews covered, generally, personality, social and consumption aspects of the woman, specific questions relating to these areas, and specific questions relating to consumption habits and family relations. The interviews were open end in design and had a conversational character. They usually lasted about one and one-half hours. In addition, a psychological personality analysis was made utilizing the Thematic Apperception Test and several special projective questions to get at particular aspects of the personality, and the Draw-a-Person Test was used. One hundred and twenty middle-class women were studied with the same procedures, as a contrast group.

Riessman, Frank
The Culturally Deprived Child
New York: Harper & Row, Publishers, 1962

The cleavage between the deprived child and the school is the concern of this book. The author attempts "to show how an understanding of the psychology of the deprived can perhaps produce much greater academic success than is presently envisioned." Included is a critical evaluation of the Higher Horizons Program, which Riessman feels does not go far enough, but which he calls "undoubtedly the best contemporary [early 1960s] project aimed at educating deprived children." The sources for the book are the author's experience with lower socioeconomic groups as a researcher, participant-observer, and teacher of underprivileged youngsters, and a survey of the literature on lower socioeconomic groups.

Rosen, Bernard C.
"The Achievement Syndrome: A Psychocultural Dimension
    of Social Stratification"
American Sociological Review: 21 (April 1956), 203–211

Purpose: To test the hypothesis that "social classes in American society are characterized by a dissimilar concern with achievement, particularly as it is expressed in the striving for status through social mobility." Two components of this achievement orientation were thought to be (1) a psychological factor called "achievement motivation" that provides an internal drive to excel, and (2) "a cultural factor consisting of certain *value orientations* which define and implement achievement motivated behavior."

Sample: 120 white boys, ages fourteen through sixteen, sophomores in two large public high schools in the New Haven area. The group was stratified by the social position of the family wage earner, through data supplied by a questionnaire according to the Hollingshead Index of Social Position.

Method: The Thematic Apperception Test developed by McClelland and his associates was administered to groups of twenty to thirty in a schoolroom. Following the test, the subjects filled out a structured questionnaire, part of which contained items designed to index their value orientations.

Conclusions: The findings of the study support the hypothesis, indicating that middle-class individuals tend to have considerably higher need-achievement scores than those in the lower social strata.

Rosenberg, Morris
Society and the Adolescent Self-image
Princeton, N. J.: Princeton University Press, 1965

Purpose: A survey of adolescents "attempting to understand how they saw themselves, how they felt about themselves, and what criteria for self-evaluation they employed."

Sample: 5024 students from ten high schools selected by random procedures from the roster of public high schools in New York State. High schools were stratified by size of community, and the ultimate selection was made by means of a table of random numbers. Since the sampling unit was the high school rather than the individual, the adequacy with which the sample represents the population of students cannot be determined.

Method: Anonymous questionnaires were distributed by teachers in class. The measure of self-esteem was a ten-item Guttman scale that has satisfactory reproducibility and scalability. High self-esteem in these scale items expresses the feeling that one is "good enough." Low self-esteem, on the other hand, implies self-rejection, self-dissatisfaction, self-contempt.

Conclusions: Among boys, results indicate that the higher the social class, the more likely is the boy to be concerned with intellectual values. The lower the class, the more likely is the boy to consider important, or care about, whether or not he is good at working with his hands, good at fighting or wrestling, or tough, not afraid of a fight. Two general points made are (1) "the higher classes are less likely to accept the lower-class values than the lower classes are to accept the higher-class values," and (2) "The values of the educational system are those distinctive of the higher classes and are antagonistic to many of the values distinctive of the lower classes." In contrast to the boys, the self-values of girls in the various social classes are strikingly similar.

Sewell, William H., and A. O. Haller
"Factors in the Relationship between Social Status and
   the Personality Adjustment of the Child"
American Sociological Review: 24 (August 1959), 511–521

Purpose: To explore the nature of the relationship between social status and personality adjustment in terms of scores on personality-test items.

Sample: 1462 children, grades four through eight, living in an urban community. The social status of the child was indexed by the father's occupational level, parental educational attainment, and the prestige of the child's family in the local community.

Method: Thirty test items found to be closely associated with social status in previous studies were selected for the questionnaire. The items were factor analyzed and four factors were found to account for 90 percent of the variance. These were concern over status, concern over achievement, rejection of family, and nervous symptoms.

Conclusions: The results indicate that lower-class children tend to exhibit more concerns and symptoms than do higher-status children. The authors attribute this to the lower-class child's internalization of familial values and images that conflict with the values and behavior characteristics he encounters in the larger community.

Stendler, Celia B.
"Social Class Differences in Parental Attitude
   toward School at Grade 1 Level"
Child Development: 22 (March 1951), 37–46

Purpose: To test the hypothesis: there are social-class differences in parental belief in and support of the school at grade one level.

Sample: 212 first-grade children.

Method: Two interviews were conducted with mothers, one prior to entrance and the second after the child had been in school for two months. Questions were specifically related to five areas under study: (1) preschool attendance, (2) parental educational aspirations for the child, (3) preparation for school, (4) parental criticism of school, (5) parental reception of report card.

Conclusions: Results showed that a child's chances of attending preschool decrease as one goes down the social ladder, even where economic factor is not relevant. Although parents become less ambitious as one goes down the social ladder, one half of the lower-class mothers expected their children to finish high school. There is more preparation for first grade in terms of teaching of the alphabet, writing or reading by middle-class parents. Counting was taught by all groups. No social-class differences were found in parental criticisms of the school. Parents were found to differ somewhat in reaction to report cards, with lower-class parents attaching less significance.

In general, differences do exist which may have some implications for the socializing role of the school.

Stone, Robert C., and F. T. Schlamp
"Characteristics Associated with Receipt or Nonreceipt of
   Financial Aid from Welfare Agencies"
Welfare in Review: 3 (July 1965), 1–11

Purpose: To determine whether families dependent on financial aid from welfare agencies are different from or similar to other low-income families in life style.

Sample: Equal numbers of white, Negro, and Spanish-speaking families in each of two categories: 600 families currently (1964) receiving aid to families with dependent children; and 600 families not currently receiving assistance whose incomes were matched with the 600 AFDC cases. The 1200 families were chosen equally from four areas in California: two rural counties; San Jose; Los Angeles; and San Francisco.

Method: Two-hour interviews with the husbands of each family; and 300 additional interviews with wives. For analysis, the sample was broken into three groups: 392 families who had never received aid; 571 families who had received aid for a median time of four months; and 237 long-time assistance families (median twenty-six months).

Conclusions: An over-all similarity in life styles of the three categories was found, especially in family relationships. Most differences related to ethnicity rather than assistance experience. Very few households included more than nuclear family. A major difference between welfare categories was that the never-on-aid group had more relationships with kin than the long-time assistance group. The three categories were similar with respect to education, work history, job mobility. The never-on-aid group had more debts than others; relied more on friends and less on formal channels to find work; reported better health; scored lower on scales of psychological dependency.

Straus, Murray A.
"Deferred Gratification, Social Class, and the
   Achievement Syndrome"
American Sociological Review: 27 (June 1962), 326–335

Purpose: To study deferred gratification phenomenon by testing the following three interrelated hypotheses: (1) there is a general tendency to defer gratification that can be expressed as a unidimensional variable within and across five types of adolescent needs; (2) the higher the socioeconomic level, the greater the tendency to defer gratification; (3) the greater the tendency to defer gratification, the higher the performance on two measures of the "achievement syndrome."

Sample: 338 boys attending the junior and senior classes of the four high schools of one Wisconsin county in the last week of March 1950.

Method: Data were obtained from school records and by questionnaires. Five adolescent needs were chosen for study: need for affiliation, aggression, consumption, economic independence, and sexual expression.

Conclusions:

> . . . the results of this study provide at least some evidence in support of a general deferred gratification pattern, but fail to support the view that this is a peculiarly middle-class normative pattern. Learning to defer need gratification seems to be associated with achievement at all levels of the status hierarchy represented in this sample, and hence can probably best be interpreted as one of the personality prerequisites for achievement roles in contemporary American society. [p. 335]

Turner, Ralph
"Some Family Determinants of Ambition"
Sociology and Social Research: 46 (July 1962), 397–411

Purpose: To test several hypotheses regarding family determinants of ambition.

Sample: 2175 nonethnic seniors in ten Los Angeles high schools selected to represent the range from high to low socioeconomic neighborhoods.

Method: Questionnaire administered in required classes.

Conclusions:

> High ambition and a relative emphasis on the educational rather than material component of ambition were found to be associated with high breadwinner's education relative to occupation, higher mother's than father's education, and a small family. Level but not emphasis on ambition may be related to family stability. Position and sex of siblings were unrelated to ambition when controls were introduced for family size. [p. 397]

White, Martha Sturn
"Social Class, Child Rearing Practices, and Child Behavior"
American Sociology Review: 22 (December 1957), 704–712

Purpose: To investigate the degree to which child-rearing practices may have changed since the decade when the studies of Davis and Havighurst were reported and to determine whether these changes are a result of the different reference groups used by middle- and working-class mothers.

Sample: 74 mothers and 74 children, San Francisco residents. This was part of a larger investigation on stress caused by the arrival of a second child in the family.

Method: Standard questions, many identical with those of the Boston study, were used in the interview with the mother with follow-up probes. Social class was measured according to the Warner scale. The coding areas were similar to those of the Boston study: oral and feeding, toilet training, dependency, obedience, mother's responsiveness to child, aggression, sources of ideas about child rearing.

Conclusions: Child-rearing practices have changed in the middle-class family. Middle-class children are now reared in an equally permissive and sometimes more indulgent atmosphere than lower-class children. Available evidence suggests that this change is due to the different reference groups used by the two classes. The middle-class mother gets her ideas from friends or relatives and specific experts (Spock and Gesell), while the lower-class mother obtains her ideas in a more diffuse manner, relying on tradition or common sense.

Whyte, William F.
Street Corner Society: The Social Structure of an
   Italian Slum
Chicago: University of Chicago Press, 1943

This classic study describes the life of two kinds of boys growing up in a lower-class neighborhood. They are the "corner boys" and the "college boys," distinguished by different patterns of behavior, values, and activities. The data were gathered primarily by participant observation.

In the street corner society, kin ties play an important role. Although the groups studied were all Italian in origin, it was found that there was stratification on the basis of region of origin. Whyte examines the relations within the group as well as those between the group and such social structures as the rackets and the political system.

Williams, J. R., and R. B. Scott
"Growth of Negro Infants: IV. Motor Development and Its
   Relationship to Child Rearing Practices in Two Groups
   of Negro Infants"
Child Development: 24 (June 1953), 103–121

Purpose: To determine whether gross motor acceleration is related to the manner in which an infant is handled and cared for, whether it is a "racial" characteristic.

Sample: 104 Negro babies, four to eighteen months of age, divided equally as to sex, in Washington, D.C. The subjects were divided into an upper group (receiving their medical care from a private pediatrician) and a lower group attending one of two public clinics.

Method: There was a preliminary interview with the adult who brought the baby for medical care, an examination of the child limited to the gross motor items on the Gesell Developmental Schedules, and a visit to the child's home three to six months after the initial contact for observation and further interviewing.

Conclusions: "The infants from the low socio-economic group showed significant gross motor acceleration when compared to those from the high socioeconomic group." The groups differed significantly in their handling of the infants, the over-all atmosphere being more permissive among low socioeconomic families. Children from this more accepting environment scored higher on the Gesell Developmental Schedules. "The findings suggest that motor acceleration is not a 'racial' characteristic."

Wolf, Richard M.
"The Identification and Measurement of Environmental Process
   Variables Related to Intelligence"
Ph.D. Dissertation, University of Chicago, 1964

Purpose: To investigate the relationship between intelligence and certain process variables in individuals' family environments, measured concurrently.

Sample: 60 fifth-grade students were selected on a stratified random basis from among all fifth-grade students in one school system; seventeen with fathers from "High" occupational levels (Department of Labor classifications); twenty from "Middle" levels; and twenty-three from "Low" levels. Urban, suburban, and rural schools were represented. "Lower lower" class students were under-represented.

Method: Henman-Nelson intelligence test scores obtained one year earlier were taken from school records. Ratings, on the basis of interviews with mother, were made of four scales of familial "Press for Achievement Motivation"; four scales of "Press for Language Development"; and five scales of "Provision for General Learning" in the home. Each environment was rated on a seven-point scale for the thirteen dimensions. Correlations were calculated between ratings and IQ scores.

Conclusions: The simple correlation between the total environmental process rating (sum of all thirteen scores) and IQ was 0.690; the multiple correlation between the three variables and IQ was 0.700; the multiple correlation between the 13 characteristics and IQ was 0.756. Very low correlations were found between class and IQ: 0.024 for an over-all index of social class; 0.064 for father's occupation; and 0.172 for combined parents' education. Correlations between total environmental process scores and IQ for the three classes separately were: upper and middle, 0.942; lower middle, 0.737; upper lower, 0.646. Differences are not significant. There was no relationship between environmental process ratings and social class.

Wortis, H., J. L. Bardach, R. Cutler, R. Rue, and A. Freedman
"Child Rearing Practices in a Low Socio-Economic Group"
Pediatrics: 32 (August 1963), 298–307

Purpose: To examine the view "that there are characteristics in child rearing practices which are related to class status, and that these differences become more pronounced with the extremes of class." [p. 306]

Sample: 250 Negro mothers of premature children of low social class (rated on Warner's Occupational Scale). This was part of a larger five-year study of premature births in a municipal hospital in Brooklyn, New York.

Method: There were two interviews, the first given when the child was two-and-one-half years old, the second when the child was five. Interviews were conducted by two social workers using a questionnaire pertaining to child-rearing practices and measures of the child's behavior selected from the Vineland Social Maturity Scale.

Conclusions: The first interview showed evidence of maternal rejection, coldness, and reliance on physical punishment:

> There was a lack of restrictiveness in regard to toilet training and training for manners. At five years there was much restrictiveness in regard to aggression against parents and against sex play. There was great concern for education for the child and a strong feeling that the child should fight back if molested. [p. 306]

These attitudes and practices were considered definitely class related. Positive elements in the child's development were permission to grow at his own speed, lack of pressure to do better when he was unable to perform.

> The inadequate incomes, crowded homes, lack of consistent familial ties, the mother's depression, and helplessness in her own situation, were as important as the child-rearing practices in influencing the child's development and preparing him for an adult role. [p. 306]

Annotated References for Chapter Two

Abrahamson, Stephen
"Our Status System and Scholastic Rewards"
Journal of Educational Sociology: 25 (April 1952), 441–450

Purpose: To test the hypothesis that there is a relationship between the social-class status positions of students in a community and the rewards and punishments they receive.

Sample: 705 students in six communities—two urban, two suburban, and two away from large centers. At least three homeroom groups from each school were included, one each of grades seven, eight, and nine.

Method: There is no indication of how the data were collected.

Conclusions: Students from upper-middle- and lower-middle-class homes (1) received more than their share of high grades; (2) were chosen more often for favor-running errands, monitoring, committee chairman, and the like; (3) tended to participate more in extracurricular activities; (4) won most of the prizes and awards; (5) tended to receive higher social acceptance scores; (6) held almost all student government offices.

Alexander, C. Norman, Jr., and Ernest Q. Campbell
"Peer Influence on Adolescent Educational Aspirations and Attainment"
American Sociology Review: 22 (December 1957), 704–712

Purpose: To examine high school senior's educational goals and their attainment as these are influenced by peers within a framework of theories of interpersonal balance.

Sample: 1410 male seniors in thirty high schools in the Eastern and Piedmont sections of North Carolina; 653 of the 707 respondents who said that they expected to go to college were subsequently located.

Method: Administration of a questionnaire by which was obtained data concerning best friend, status as measured by parental educational attainment, college plans, and expectations of self and friend.

Conclusions: It was found that the plans and expectations of a best friend influenced a student's plans and expectations at a given status level, from increasing his desire to attend to increasing the likelihood that he would attend. "Our findings suggest that communication among male high school seniors affects both college plans and attendance."

Antonovsky, Aaron, and Melvin J. Lerner
"Negro and White Youth in Elmira," in
    Aaron Antonovsky and Lewis L. Lorwin, eds.
    Discrimination and Low Incomes
New York: New School for Social Research, 1959, pp. 103–145

Purpose: To inquire into the Negro youth's view of his future, with particular stress on vocational orientation. The general hypothesis was that Negro youth would have aspirations and orientations different from those of white peers because of specific factors in the environment with which they are confronted.

Sample: Consisted of sixty-nine Negroes and ninety-nine whites who entered the high school in 1951–1954 and who attended the two junior high schools in the most depressed areas of the community. Usable data were collected from sixty-one Negroes and fifty-four whites, about equally balanced for sex.

Method: Interviews were conducted with all but eleven respondents, from whom data were collected by mail questionnaire. The small sample size, the high proportion of white nonrespondents, and the lack of controls over relevant variables are recognized as limiting factors in the study.

Conclusions: There is a tendency for the Negroes in this study to have a higher level of occupational aspirations than comparable white youth. They appear to have a more positive and constructive attitude toward school than whites, and view school as a channel for mobility. This in spite of the fact that parents of Negro respondents tended to have less education and to be less successful occupationally. Authors suggest that in addition to accepting general value of mobility, Negro youth recognize their fathers as unsuccessful and want to escape their fate. The white youth accept their fathers, and are satisfied with a modicum of upward movement compared to them.

Baeumler, Walter L.
"The Correlates of Formal Participation among High School Students"
Sociological Inquiry: 35 (Spring 1965), 235–240

Purpose: To examine (1) the extent to which middle- and working-class adolescents are affiliated with and involved in informal organizations, (2) affiliation as a family-linked characteristic, and (3) whether early involvement is related to subsequent membership in formal groups.

Sample: 105 high school students out of a total of 456 and 105 of their parents in a city of 5000 in Nebraska. Eighty families were classified as middle class (white-collar occupations and at least high school graduation) and twenty-five as working class.

Method: A structured questionnaire was administered to all students and interviews were conducted with one parent of each case in the sample.

Conclusions: There were no significant class differences in affiliation or attendance at meetings. However, middle-class students were more likely to be officers of groups. Adolescents whose parents were affiliated were more likely to be members of groups. Membership in adolescent groups was associated with prior membership in childhood groups only for working-class students. Participation by middle-class youth was high during both childhood and adolescence.

Becker, Howard S.
"The Career of the Chicago Public School Teacher"
American Journal of Sociology: 57 (March 1952), 470–477

Purpose: To examine the "horizontal" aspects of career, movement among positions at one level of the school-work hierarchy.

Sample: 60 teachers in the Chicago public school system.

Method: Largely unstructured interviews.

Conclusions: There being little opportunity for upward movement, the teacher's career tends to consist of moves in search of a school where the occupation's basic work problems are least aggravated and most susceptible of solution. Since the greatest work problems are found in lower-class schools, most movement tends to be out from the "slums" to the "better" neighborhoods. Thus there is a tendency for replacement in slum schools to be made from among beginning teachers. The alternative for teachers who do not move out is adjustment to the "slum" work situation, which usually involves a downward revision of what can be expected from the students and satisfaction with smaller accomplishments.

Becker, Howard S.
"The Teacher in the Authority System of the Public School"
Journal of Educational Sociology: 27 (October 1953), 128–139

Purpose: Analysis of the authority problems of the metropolitan public school teacher.

Sample: 60 teachers in the Chicago public school system.

Method: Largely unstructured interviews.

Conclusions: The problem for the teacher is to maintain what she regards as her legitimate sphere of authority in the face of possible challenge by others. The parent is viewed as a person who lacks professional background, is unable to understand the teacher's problems, and as a threat to the authority system of the school. The principal and colleagues are expected to support the teacher over the parent and the students. Parents in higher-income areas are considered more of a threat than those in lower-income areas, and this is one of the advantages of teaching in the latter type of school.

Bell, Gerald D.
"Processes in the Formation of Adolescents' Aspirations"
Social Forces: 42 (December 1963), 179–186

Purpose: To test the following hypotheses: (1) adolescents who receive high aspirational encouragement from parents will possess higher levels of ambition; (2) individuals who interact more frequently in upper-status reference groups will develop higher aspirational levels; (3) in the academic clime, authoritarian individuals will tend to follow the motivational directive of their parents more frequently than the nonauthoritarian; (4) conforming individuals will tend to follow aspirational motivations provided by their parents more frequently than will nonconforming individuals.

Sample: 88 male students with an IQ of 115 or above attending Boulder High School, Boulder, Colorado, in the spring semester, 1961, whose fathers could be put into Class II, III, or IV according to the Hollingshead scale.

Method: A questionnaire including scales for dogmatism, conformity, and interaction, as well as questions from which a scale of parent's aspirations was conducted.

Conclusions: Aspiration levels were found to be positively associated with motivational directives of parents and students' interaction in higher-status groups. Authoritarian and conforming respondents tended to follow the motivational directives more frequently than the nonauthoritarian and nonconforming respondents.

Bertrand, Alvin L.
"School Attendance and Attainment: Function and Dysfunction of School and
   Family Social Systems"
Social Forces: 40 (March 1962), 228–233

Purpose: To investigate the relationship between family and school as social systems, and to explore the basis of dysfunction between these systems. Hypothesis was that sociocultural factors hold the key to the school drop-out problem.

Sample: 369 juniors and seniors from four schools in each of two parishes in Louisiana; 68 drop outs ages sixteen to nineteen; 125 parents of youth in school and 68 parents of drop outs.

Method: Interviews with students and parents; conferences with principals and some teachers.

Conclusions: With reference to the family, (1) farm fathers of drop outs were more likely to be employees than owners or operators; (2) parents of drop outs had less completed education, participated less actively in school affairs, and placed a relatively low value on dropping out; (3) families of drop outs tended to be lower in socioeconomic status.

With reference to school, dropouts tended (1) to live further from school and have less opportunity for participation in school activities; (2) to have lower grade averages; and (3) were less likely to be officers or leaders in school organizations.

Bordua, David J.
"Educational Aspirations and Parental Stress on College"
Social Forces: 38 (March 1960), 262–269

Purpose: To determine the differences in college aspirations of boys and girls and the extent to which differences can be accounted for by parental stress.

Sample: 1529 ninth through twelfth grades in two cities in Massachusetts.

Method: A questionnaire administered in class, in 1955.

Conclusions: Sex, religious affiliation, and socioeconomic status were all related to a measure of college plans, with males having a higher college-planning score under all conditions. Parental stress was also related to college plans and reduced the effect of religion and class. As the parental stress level became higher, girls showed a larger college-planning score than boys.

Bowman, Paul H., and Charles V. Matthews
Motivations of Youth for Leaving School
Chicago: University of Chicago Quincy Youth Development Project,
Cooperative Research Project #200, U.S. Office of Education, 1960

Purpose: To answer the following questions: (1) What children drop out of school? (2) What characteristics of these children distinguish them from those who remain? (3) What experiences lead them to leave? (4) How are drop outs seen by their peers, their teachers, and themselves? (5) What do they think of their school experience? (6) What do they do after leaving school, and how well do they do it?

Hypotheses: (1) more boys than girls will drop out; (2) drop outs will have lower intellectual ability than stay ins; (3) family socioeconomic status will be lower for drop outs than for stay ins; (4) drop outs will be inferior to a control group matched on age, sex, intelligence, and social status with regard to (a) personal and social adjustments, (b) school adjustment, (c) work adjustment, (d) marital adjustment, and (e) achievement values and aspirations; and (5) those students dropping out at an early age will be lower on ability, personality, and social-status measures than those dropping out at later ages.

Sample: Population consisted of 487 children in the potential graduating class of 1958 in the Quincy, Illinois, public schools. Of 432 who could be followed, 138 dropped out.

Method: Data were collected over an eight-year period by the project. Drop outs were interviewed six months after leaving school. Additional data were obtained from project case records, school records, a survey of church affiliations, questionnaires, and employer interviews. The variables studied included intelligence, social status, personal and social adjustment, school adjustment, work adjustment, marital adjustment, and achievement values. The drop out group was matched with two control groups of stay ins separately for intelligence and social status.

Conclusions: All of the hypotheses were accepted except (1), which was rejected for this population, and (5), which was rejected for all groups in this population except the early drop out boys.

Boyd, George F.
"The Levels of Aspiration of White and Negro Children in a Non-Segregated
    Elementary School
Journal of Social Psychology: 36 (November 1952), 191-196

Purpose: To determine whether or not there is a measurable difference in level of aspiration between white and Negro children of the same intelligence level in a nonsegregated elementary school.

Sample: 25 white and 25 Negro children in Oregon, matched for socioeconomic status and intelligence.

Method: Children were given a target test and an arithmetic test, as well as a questionnaire designed to obtain verbalizations of future hopes and plans.

Conclusions: Negro children had a significantly higher level of aspiration. They also seemed to have a good deal of race pride as evidenced by their selection of predominantly Negro figures as the greatest people in the world and of being Negro as the reason to be liked.

Brookover, Wilbur B., Ann Paterson, and Shailer Thomas
"Self-Concept of Ability and School Achievement"
East Lansing, Mich.: Office of Research and Publications, Michigan State University, 1962,
    Cooperative Research Project No. 845

Purpose: To determine the relationship between self-concept of ability and actual school achievement.

Sample: The sample varied according to the hypothesis being tested. To determine the relationship between general self-concept of ability to high and low achievement, as well as students' self-concept of ability in specific school subjects, 1050 seventh-grade white students in four public junior high schools were interviewed. To determine how the expectations of others perceived significant by students correlated with the students' self-concepts as learners, 112 interviews with over- and underachieving students were conducted.

Method: Standard measures of intelligence, the California Test of Mental Maturity, and interviews were used to collect data.

Conclusions: The data indicate that self-concept of ability is significantly related to achievement at the 0.57 level. Self-concept in particular subjects is also related to achievement in these subjects and may differ from one subject to another. Student's self-concept of ability is positively related to the image he perceives others to have of him, and parents were rated by nearly all subjects as important in their lives and concerned about how well they do in school. Finally, students who aspire or expect to go to college have significantly higher mean self-concepts of ability than students with low educational aspirations.

Buswell, Margaret M.
"Relationship between the Social Structure of the Classroom and the
   Academic Success of the Pupils"
Journal of Experimental Education: 22 (September 1953), 37–52

Purpose: To determine whether or not those children who are accepted by their peers differ in certain achievements from those who are rejected.

Sample: Random sample of 321 fifth graders and 286 kindergarteners from eight schools in St. Paul, Minnesota.

Method: The older group was tested, toward the end of the fifth grade and again at the beginning of the sixth grade, using the Iowa Every Pupil Test of Basic Skills, Revised Stanford Binet, and three measures of social acceptability. The younger group was tested, near the end of kindergarten, and at the beginning of first grade, using the Detroit Beginning First-Grade Intelligence Test, and the Gates Reading Readiness Test, and an interview to obtain sociometric measures. Sims Score Card for Determining Socio-Economic Status was used. On the basis of sociometric data, two groups of children were selected at each level, one group well-liked by others, the other group not well-liked.

Conclusions: At both grade levels, there was a significant difference in the achievement levels, in favor of the accepted group. When the data were manipulated, the author concluded that in only one instance, arithmetic achievement in the sixth grade, was the difference attributable to social status. It appeared that the intelligence factor associated with achievement was the basic component in relating achievement to acceptability. The author points to the change between kindergarten and first grade for a test of this hypothesis:

> In kindergarten, before academic success is evident, the future achiever is not chosen in social relationships any more frequently than the future non-achiever. Early in the first grade, when a different kind of achievement

than occurred in kindergarten is becoming evident, those who are successful in this achievement are also the socially most accepted. [p. 51]

The author goes on to note, however, that:

> Even if the first step in the process of becoming rejected in school is a matter of non-achievement, it seems possible that a circular reaction might be set in motion so that once a child is unaccepted he becomes insecure and finds it more difficult than ever to succeed. [p. 51]

Caro, Francis G.
"College and Occupational Goals: A Social Class Comparison of Attitudes of Male High School Students"
Minneapolis, Minn.: Abstract, Ph.D. Dissertation, University of Minnesota, 1963 (ditto)

Purpose: To investigate the male high school student's perception of a possible means-end relationship between immediate posthigh school activity and the more distant world of work. The basic proposition examined is that to understand a young person's occupational ambitions it is necessary to consider his views of the means by which he might achieve those objectives.

Sample: 144 male juniors in four St. Paul high schools, stratified by class: (1) middle class—fathers held professional, semiprofessional, or managerial positions and had at least completed high school; (2) working class—fathers were employed in unskilled or semiskilled occupations and had not completed high school.

Method: Highly structured interviews providing data on student attitudes in five areas: (1) occupational goals; (2) beliefs regarding the means by which occupational objectives might be obtained, (3) evaluation of possible posthigh school activities apart from their likely long-term objectives, (4) accessibility to means by which occupational objectives might be attained, and (5) time orientations.

Conclusions: Some 90 percent of the middle-class sample indicated that if they were free to do what they wanted after high school, they would go to college; only about 20 percent of the working-class youth so responded. About the same proportions of each group reported that most of their best friends would attend college. Ninety-six percent of the middle-class boys and 50 percent of the working-class boys reported that their parents hoped they would go to college, and the middle-class boys reported that their parents were more concerned about what they would do after finishing high school than was reported by the working-class students.

> On the indices of time orientation of willingness to defer gratification, both middle and lower class boys responded that given complete foreknowledge and freedom, they would tend to spread satisfaction evenly over their entire life. . . . Since the great majority of both middle and lower class students who planned to attend college indicated that college was their

preferred post-high school activity apart from possible long-term consequences, it is clear that college attendance by itself cannot be interpreted as
behavior involving deferment. [pp. 6–7]

Lower-class boys at a school with a predominantly middle-class orientation
tended to be closer in their plans and general orientation to the middle class
than to other working-class boys.

Cloward, Richard A., and James A. Jones
"Social Class: Educational Attitudes and Participation," in
   A. Harry Passow, ed.
   Education in Depressed Areas
New York: Bureau of Publications, Teachers College, Columbia University, 1963,
   pp. 190–216

Purpose: To examine the problem of differences in attitudes toward education by social class and to see whether involvement in educational activities
influences these attitudes.

Sample: Random selection of 1250 households in the lower East Side of
Manhattan. Within each household, random selection of one person twenty
years or older as respondent.

Method: Interviews were conducted with 988 of the 1,250 potential respondents. Social class was measured on the basis of the education and occupation of the head of the household, and total family income, adjusted for the
number of persons living on that income. Measure of school involvement was
developed for those with children in school, based on PTA activity and school
visits.

Conclusions: Two tentative findings emerge:

> The first is that evaluations of the importance of education in the lower
> and working classes appear to be influenced by occupational aspirations.
> The point is not, as has often been suggested, that low income people fail
> to perceive the importance of education as a channel of mobility, but
> rather that their level of occupational aspiration influences their evaluation
> of education much more than is characteristic of the middle-class person. . . .

> Second, our data suggest that participation in educational activities does
> influence evaluations of the importance of education, and attitudes toward
> the school as an institution. The tendency of participation to heighten the
> emphasis on education is especially pronounced in the lower class. [p. 215]

Cohen, Elizabeth G.
"Parental Factors in Educational Mobility"
Sociology of Education: 38 (Fall 1965), 404–425

Purpose: To test the hypothesis that working-class parents are a major
source of college aspirations in high school boys. It was hypothesized that

parents of mobile boys should be distinguishable from parents of nonmobile boys in their attitudes toward a college education, in their encouragement of high aspirations and good school performance, and in certain background characteristics leading to a high degree of parental ambition.

Sample: A matched-pair design in which a junior or senior high school boy of working-class background who was definitely planning on attending a four-year college was matched on IQ and community with a boy of working-class background who was definitely planning on not attending college. The sample of 100 boys as selected by means of a written questionnaire given in four communities around Boston, and was characterized as white, from stable homes where both parents were present, whose fathers were more likely to be in semi-skilled or skilled occupations than unskilled ones. Subjects were between the sixtieth and ninetieth percentile range on IQ scores.

Method: A standardized interview was administered to the mother and father of each subject, in their home. The interview included questions on paternal, maternal, and grandparental occupations, measures of subjective class identification, attitude toward college, and parental encouragement of mobility.

Conclusions: Three principal sources of parental aspirations were hypothesized: (1) closeness to middle-class position on socioeconomic variables, (2) paternal job dissatisfaction, and (3) maternal downward mobility. The latter two sources were confirmed, but mixed results were obtained concerning closeness to middle-class position.

Four parental indicators significantly related to mobility were: (1) an index of pressure for a middle-class occupation starting in childhood, (2) a score representing the saliency of the idea of college in the parents' minds, (3) a tendency to find few if any working-class jobs acceptable for any child of the family, and (4) a specific choice of a middle-class job requiring a college education for the son in question.

Responses to questions dealing with reaction to a peer high school report card were quite unrelated to mobility. "The crucial role of the parents may be to send the child to school with a receptive attitude toward the values and norms advocated by school personnel." [p. 422]

Two independent types of parental motivation were isolated from an examination of background characteristics: (1) a vocational orientation emphasizing the desirability of certain jobs requiring a college education; and (2) a status orientation, emphasizing the college degree as a key to middle-class status. A second type of influence was concrete pressure and encouragement. Parents of mobile sons reported more deliberate encouragement of college from an early date, and were more likely to want their sons to have middle-class occupations. Finally, parental favorability toward college was closely related to a son's mobility.

In review, we see the origin of mobility aspiration in a long-term socialization process involving alternative patterns of motivational sources, general attitudes and timing and techniques of encouragement by the parent. [p. 425]

Coleman, Hubert A.
"The Relationship of Socio-economic Status to the Performance
    of Junior High School Students"
Journal of Experimental Education: 9 (September 1940), 61–63

Purpose: To analyze the relationship between socioeconomic status and: age, intelligence, school achievement, and personality and interest manifestations.

Sample: A national sample of 4784 junior high school students representing 5 percent in each of grades 7, 8, and 9. Sample stratified into four levels on basis of Sims Socio-Economic Score Card.

Method: Data made available by the Advisory Committee of the Coordinated Studies in Education, Inc. IQ's were determined by Kuhlman-Anderson tests; achievement scores, by the Unit Scale of Attainment Battery. Personality adjustment scores were based on BPC Personal Inventory. Teachers supplied data on extracurricular activities and hobbies.

Conclusions: Children from the higher SES group are consistently younger and have consistently higher median IQ. The differences are reliable. Poor readers, as a group, come from low class levels and the differences here are reliable. High-SES children score better in geography and history and rank higher in problem solving. It was found that maladjustment increases consistently from the high to the low classes. High groups have the greatest number of hobbies and participate in extracurricular activities to a greater extent.

Cook, Edward S., Jr.
"An Analysis of Factors Related to Withdrawal from High School Prior to Graduation"
Journal of Educational Research: 50 (November 1956), 191–196

Purpose: To test two hypotheses: (1) there are measurable differences between withdrawing and nonwithdrawing students, (2) the reasons students give for withdrawal at the time they leave school are basically unreliable in that they fail to reveal the actual causes of withdrawal.

Sample: 95 students who withdrew from a public metropolitan high school and 200 nonwithdrawing students at the same school, selected at random but proportionate as to sex and grade to the total student body.

Method: A battery of standardized tests was administered to all nonwithdrawals and to an unstated number of "cooperative" withdrawals. Tests included measures of adjustment, ability, aptitude, and mental maturity. Family and school data were also collected, as well as the reason for withdrawing from the relevant groups.

Conclusions: The withdrawals contained a higher proportion of males than was found among the nonwithdrawals in the ninth grade; and in the eighth, ninth, and tenth grades, the withdrawals were older. In addition, they transferred more often in high school; were more retarded educationally, had lower scholastic marks; failed more courses; attended less frequently; had a lower measured IQ; were more poorly adjusted to school, home and family, and were in poorer health.

The author shows that the reasons given by students for their withdrawals differed from the judgments of counselors about the causes of their withdrawals.

Coster, John K.
"Attitudes toward School of High School Pupils from Three Income Levels"
Journal of Educational Psychology: 49 (April 1958), 61–66

Purpose: To study the relationship of specific attitudes toward school and income level.

Sample: 3000 students in nine Indiana high schools.

Method: Administration of questionnaire containing a morale scale, and Remmer's "house and home scale" as a measure of status.

Conclusions: There was no difference between students of different income levels on items pertaining to attitudes toward school, the school program, and the value of education. Differences were found on items pertaining to interpersonal relationships; that is, social life, being liked by other pupils, opinions of other pupils, feelings of parental interest in school work, and personal interest of teacher. Variations were also found in the over-all impression of school, and in estimates of being able to get the kinds of jobs they wanted after school. These differences were positively related to income.

Curry, Robert L.
"The Effect of Socio-economic Status on the Scholastic Achievement
     of Sixth Grade Children"
British Journal of Educational Psychology: 32 (February 1962), 46–49

Purpose: To determine whether the differences in scholastic achievement were significant between groups of sixth-grade children when the groups were of comparable intellectual ability but differed in socioeconomic status.

Sample: 360 sixth-grade students randomly selected from 2623 subjects in thirty-three elementary schools in a large city in the Southwest. Subjects were Caucasion with American-born parents, had no school record of serious emotional-adjustment problems, and had attended the same elementary school the previous academic year.

Method: Three intellectual ability groups (high, medium, low) were formed on the basis of the California Test of Mental Ability; the California Achievement Test was used as a measure of achievement in reading, arithmetic, language, and total achievement; and a questionnaire was used to obtain social status.

Conclusions: The lower the intellectual-ability group, the greater the effect of socioeconomic status. Status seemed to have no effect upon achievement for the high-ability students. Upper- and middle-status students achieved better than low-status students in language, while upper-status students did better on total achievement than lower-status students. For the low-ability group, status appeared to have an effect in reading, language, and total achievement. Achievement in arithmetic seemed to be unaffected by status.

David, Martin, Harvey Brazer, James Morgan, and Wilber Cohen
Educational Achievement—Its Causes and Effects
Ann Arbor, Mich.: Survey Research Center, Monograph 123, 1961

Purpose: To learn what determines how much education an individual gets, and the extent to which education depends upon the parent's education and income.

Sample: Part of a larger investigation of income and welfare in the U.S., data are based on a national sample representative of the noninstitutional population of the U.S.

Method: Personal interview, which included questions pertaining to the education of the spending-unit heads, their wives, and their fathers, about the completed education of their children, and plans for the education of their children who had not finished school. There were also some general questions about how much schooling children should get and attitudes toward government aid to higher education.

Conclusions: Education of the father is the most powerful predictor of children's education. Occupation of the father was another important factor, mitigated somewhat by income. Other important influences were number of children, father's achievement motivation; father's attitude toward hard work; and age of father at time when first child was born.

The overwhelming majority plan to send their children to a state college and expect their children to finance their own college education, in whole or part. A surprisingly large number of people favored tax support for all college students rather than only for those with need or ability.

Davidson, Helen H., Judith W. Greenberg, and Joan M. Gerver
"Characteristics of Successful School Achievers from a Severely
   Deprived Environment"
New York: The City University of New York, 1962 (mimeo)

Purpose: To ascertain some of the cognitive and affective traits that characterize successful school achievers from an underprivileged environment.

Sample: 20 Negro children, ten "good" and ten "poor" school achievers, selected from five fourth-grade classes in one school location in a severely depressed urban area. They were approximately nine years of age, with five boys and five girls in each subgroup.

Method: Subjects were chosen chiefly on the basis of third-grade standardized achievement tests, plus teacher ratings. A battery of eight instruments was chosen to assess a broad spectrum of cognitive and affective factors. All tests but the Semantic Differential and two Free Drawings were administered individually.

Conclusions:

The hypothetical good achiever emerges as a child who is relatively controlled and cautious, often stereotyped and constricted, but who still retains a degree of originality and creativity. He seems more willing than his less successful classmates to conform to adult demands, has a more positive view of authority figures and greater self-confidence. In cognitive functioning he excels chiefly in tasks requiring memory, attention, and verbal abilities. He is also superior in analytical and organizational abilities and generally in processes that require convergent thinking.

In contrast, the composite picture of the poor achiever is that of a child burdened by anxiety, fearful of the world and authority figures, and lacking in self-confidence. He is more apt to be impulsive and labile with relatively poor controlling mechanisms. His defenses against anxiety and feelings of inadequacy may be expressed in excessive talking and uncritically favorable surface attitudes toward self and others. Nevertheless, the poor achiever still seems to have sufficient potential for adaptive behavior which the school could build upon. His cognitive activities are often quite similar in content, approach, and process to those of the good achiever and in fact, he demonstrates greater facility in divergent production. Many of his reactions give evidence of creative capacity which might be directed and controlled. From his behavior in the testing situations and in tasks requiring social comprehension, the poor achiever seems to possess substantial understanding of the world around him, although he seems less able to act upon his understanding than the good achiever. [p. 18]

Davidson, Helen H., and Gerhard Lang
"Children's Perceptions of Their Teachers' Feelings toward Them Related to
   Self-perception, School Achievement and Behavior"
Journal of Experimental Education: 29 (December 1960), 107–118

Purpose: To relate children's perception of their teacher's feelings toward them to self-perception, academic achievement, and classroom behavior.

Sample: 89 boys and 114 girls in grades four, five, and seven in a New York City public school.

Method: A check list of Trait Names consisting of thirty-five descriptive terms was administered. The children were also rated by their teachers for achievement and on a number of behavioral characteristics.

Conclusions: (1) The children's perception of their teacher's feelings toward them correlated positively and significantly with self-perception. The child with the more favorable self-image was the one who more likely than not perceived his teacher's feelings toward him more favorably. (2) A positive perception of the teacher's feelings correlated positively with academic achievement and desirable classroom behavior. (3) Children of upper and middle social classes perceived their teacher's feelings toward them more favorably than did those in the lower social-class group. (4) Social-class position was also related to achievement in school. (5) Girls generally perceived their teachers feelings more favorably than did boys. (6) There were some significant classroom differences in the favorability of the children's perception of their teacher's feelings.

Davie, James S.
"Social Class Factors and School Attendance"
Harvard Educational Review: 23 (Summer 1953), 175–186

Purpose: To study the influence of social-class factors on: (1) the amount of schooling received; and (2) the type of schooling, or the different kinds of schools attended.

Sample: All children sixteen or seventeen years of age as of September 1949, legally resident in New Haven, Connecticut. Children were classified into six educational groups: nonattendant, trade school, high school, private secondary school, liberal arts college and university, and post-secondary vocational school. Parents were classified into six social strata on the basis of ecological area of residence.

Method: Data were collected from school records and from interviews with families in "key spots in the class structure."

Conclusions: Differences existed in both the type and amount of schooling received in different classes. The lowest class was overrepresented among nonattendants and in trade school and underrepresented in private school, college, and higher vocational school.

> Viewing the class structure as a whole, one notes a decided shift away from the public high school as one moves from the middle of the class structure toward the extremes. As one approaches Class I, the shift is in the direction of the private school followed by a liberal arts college or university. As one approaches Class VI the shift is in the direction of trade school and nonattendance. [p. 180]

With reference to attendance at school, the lower one went in the social structure, the greater was the population of children not attending school.

Davis, Allison
"Social-Class Influences upon Learning"
Cambridge, Mass.: Harvard University Press, 1948

In the Inglis Lectures, Davis discusses the basic socialization of the human character and intellect as it is affected by class culture. The topics covered include (1) the nature of social classes in the United States; (2) the effect of social-class culture in differentiating the basic early training of children; (3) the cultural definition by each class of what is pleasant and desirable and of what is unpleasant and dangerous; (4) the influence of the social-class environment in defining the types of mental problems regarded important by children in each social class, and teaching skills for dealing with such problems; and (5) the effects of social-class culture upon teachers and curricula.

In his review of the problem of cultural bias in testing (reported fully in Kenneth Eells, Allison Davis, and Robert J. Havighurst, *Intelligence and Cultural Differences*, Chicago: University of Chicago Press, 1950), and in education generally, Davis anticipated much of the concern that has developed in the 1960s.

DeGroat, Albert F., and George D. Thompson
"A Study of the Distribution of Teacher Approval in the 6th Grade"
Journal of Experimental Education: 18 (September 1949), 57–75

Purpose: To develop scales of teacher approval and disapproval of the "Guess Who?" type and to determine some of the psychological characteristics of children living under more or less clear-cut patterns of teacher approval-disapproval.

Sample: For the latter purpose, the sample consisted of 133 elementary school pupils from four classrooms in a small upstate New York city.

Method: The following tests were administered: Teacher Approval-Disapproval Scales developed by the authors; California Test of Mental Maturity, Short Form; Progressive Achievement Test; and California Test of Personality. Children were organized into five categories: high approval-low disapproval; high approval-medium disapproval; low approval-low disapproval; high disapproval-medium approval; and high disapproval-low approval.

Conclusions: While there were some differences in the behavior of individual teachers, a small percentage of pupils received most of the approval and disapproval. "It may be stated, as a first approximation, that children who are considered by their classmates to be experiencing a high degree of teacher approval coupled with a low or moderate degree of disapproval are more intelligent, are better students, and are better adjusted than their less favored classmates."

The authors note that the cause and effect relationship between approval-disapproval and "adjustment" is not directly tested in this study. "However, one gets some hints that children experiencing a high degree of teacher approval have a better opinion of themselves, are more 'out-going,' and have more confidence in their ability to adjust to social situations."

Deutsch, Martin
"The Disadvantaged Child and the Learning Process," in
    A. Harry Passow, ed.
    Education in Depressed Areas
New York: Bureau of Publications, Teachers College, Columbia
    University, 1963, pp. 163–179

See Appendix, Chapter One.

Deutsch, Martin
"The Role of Social Class in Language Development and Cognition"
American Journal of Orthopsychiatry: (January 1965), 78–88

Purpose: To study the use of language in impoverished families.

Sample: 292 children from an extended population of about 2500 children of various racial and social class groupings.

Method: Assessment of fifty-two identifiable variables (drawn from a group of over 100) concerned with a range of cognitive functions with a few demographic measures, with language variables at the core.

Conclusions: The most impoverished area of activity of impoverished families is that of language feedback in adult-child interactions. There are significant socioeconomic and race differences seen in measured variables at the first-grade level, which become more marked as the child progresses through school. This process, which takes place between the first and fifth grades, was labeled a "cumulative deficit phenomenon" and seemed more pronounced for Negro children. While some cumulative deficiency is associated with poor early environment, the adequacy of the schools must be questioned.

Deutsch, Martin, and Bert Brown
"Social Influences in Negro-White Intelligence Differences"
Journal of Social Issues: 20 (April 1964), 24–35

Purpose: To explore the intellectual test differences between Negro and white first and fifth graders of different social classes, with particular focus on the lower class. Two specific independent variables were examined, the presence or absence of father in the home, and whether the child had an organized preschool experience.

Sample: 543 public school children, stratified by race, grade level, and social class; measured by a scale derived from prestige ratings of occupation as well as education of main breadwinners.

Method: IQ measured by the Lorge-Thorndike test, Level 1, Primary Battery for first graders, and Level 3 for fifth graders. Social-status data were collected by mail questionnaires and home interviews.

Conclusions: Fifth grade IQ scores do not differ significantly from scores by first graders. Differences between scores of Negro and white children are highly significant and are equally strong between class levels. Inspection of the means shows: (1) Negro children at each SES level score lower than white children; and (2) Negro-white differences increase at each higher SES level. The gain associated with social status is greater for the white group. This suggests that the influence of racial membership tends to become increasingly crucial as the social-class level increases.

Support was found for the participation hypothesis in that there were fewer family activities in the Negro group, especially at the lower SES levels. Significant differences were also found for the race and presence of father variables, with white children scoring higher than Negro, and children coming from homes where fathers are present having significantly higher scores than children from fatherless homes. The authors recognize "that there is no reliable way of knowing how long the fifth grade children have lived in homes without fathers, or whether this has been a recurrent or a consistent condition."

For the fifth-grade children, race and preschool experience differences were significant, with children having preschool experience having higher IQ scores. Among first-grade children, while the significant race difference prevailed, the differences with regard to preschool experience did not. This finding supports the cumulative deficit hypothesis of the authors: "deprivational influences have a greater impact at later developmental stages than at earlier ones."

Dillon, Harold J.
Early School Leavers
New York: National Child Labor Committee, 1949

Purpose: To analyze the process of early school leaving, the characteristics of those who leave early, and the role of counseling.

Sample: A 10 percent sample (N = 1360) of all students leaving school voluntarily (excluding those who left for military service) in the year 1944–1945 in the cities of Jackson County and Lansing, Michigan, Cleveland and Cincinnati, Ohio, and Indianapolis, Indiana.

Method: Data were obtained from school records, from two or three teachers acquainted with each student, and from interviews. Comparisons were made with the total population from census data where available.

Conclusions: (1) There were no significant differences from the normal population in terms of (a) stability of the family, (b) family size, (c) language spoken in the home, (d) economic conditions, (e) place of birth, and (f) length of time in the school system. (2) The great majority terminated in the ninth grade, indicating they tended to be behind their age grade. (3) They experienced frequent school transfers. (4) They showed a decline in attendance from elementary school on, which became marked in junior high school. (5) Almost half had intelligence scores sufficient to enable them to complete high school at least. (6) They experienced failures of subjects and repetition of grades. (7) With regard to jobs, few used school placement facilities; about 80 percent stated that school did not prepare them for jobs, and nearly 40 percent indicated that none of the subjects studied in school were helpful in their work.

Dreger, Ralph Mason, and Kent S. Miller
"Comparative Psychological Studies of Negroes and Whites in the United States"
Psychological Bulletin: 57 (September 1960), 361–402

A review of published psychological studies involving the comparison of Negroes and whites during the period, in the main, from 1943 to 1958, largely confined to the experimental literature. The literature is reviewed under the following headings: Physical and Motor Development, Psychophysical Functions, Educational and Post-Educational Attainment, Values and Attitudes, Social Structure, Emotional Disturbances and Mental Illness, Crime and Delinquency.

Eckert, Ruth E., and Thomas O. Marshall
When Youth Leave School
New York: McGraw-Hill, Inc., 1938

Purpose: To outline the characteristics of pupils leaving the secondary schools, and to find out how the school personnel views its leaving pupils.

Sample: Basic sample consisted of some 23,000 boys and girls in sixty-two selected high schools located in fifty-one New York State communities chosen to be representative of social and educational conditions in the state. Additional data were obtained from 350 secondary schools, which participated on a voluntary basis.

Method: Students in the basic sample were tested for aptitudes, ability, knowledge, and interest. Also employed were an inventory of general interests and a questionnaire that probed future educational and vocational plans.

Conclusions: The withdrawing pupil tended not to complete the tenth grade, and many left before then. Withdrawal from school was more prevalent for boys, in small communities, and in the vocational curriculum. Drop outs are more likely to come from poor families and to be more seriously handicapped in basic information and social and vocational skills than those who stay in school. Both leavers and nonleavers were found to do little planning for the future.

Elder, Glenn H., Jr.
Adolescent Achievement and Mobility Aspirations
Chapel Hill, N.C.: University of North Carolina, Institute for
   Research in Social Science, 1962

Purpose: To provide a more complete picture of mobility potential among adolescents by systematically categorizing and investigating the effects of theoretically relevant independent variables on educational and occupational motivation, aspirations, and achievement.

Sample: This report is based on data collected for the adolescent study. Approximately 25,000 junior and senior high school students in North Carolina were included in the original study, and a random subsample of 40 percent of the seventh- and ninth-grade students and 61 percent of the tenth- and twelfth-grade students was used here.

Method: Administered questionnaire.
Conclusions:

1. Social class, parental education, religion, size of family, and ordinal position are all related to how much adolescents try to achieve in school.

Social class and amount of parental education are positively related to academic motivation and achievement, with father's education apparently having a stronger effect on academic motivation than mother's education.

2. Adolescent academic motivation is positively related to the involvement of both parents in independence training, and this holds within social classes. Academic achievement likewise was found to be related to independence training. For given levels of independence training, parental education has a greater influence on academic motivation than social class.

3. Low achievers are more apt to report strong achievement demands from their parents than are high achievers. Middle- and lower-class parents are equally likely to put pressure on high-achieving children; middle-class parents are much more likely to pressure low achievers.

4. The desire and effort to achieve in high school are strongly related to plans to attend college. Parental goals appear to have little effect on adolescent motivation to achieve in high school.

5. "For the most part, the relationship between educational goals and motivation in school is similar within each social class. This result suggests that the previously observed large social class differences in academic motivation may be to a significant extent accounted for by differential acceptance of middle class values and goals between the classes." [p. 130]

The author summarizes as follows:

Which independent variable has the greatest effect on mobility behavior? Our data indicate that the three basic independent variables may be ranked in terms of effect as follows: motivation and ability, values, and the structure of opportunities. Without motivation and ability, even the most favorable conditions are unlikely to improve the chances of upward mobility. Given the capacity to achieve, the values of parent and child are most crucial in that they specify the direction in which this potential may be expressed. And lastly, given the capacity to achieve and high educational and occupational goals, the availability of advancement opportunities, such as financial support, may either facilitate, hinder, or completely frustrate the expression of achievement motivation in the direction of traditional success goals. [p. 232]

Fox, Robert S., Ronald O. Lippitt and Richard A. Schmuck
Pupil-Teacher Adjustment and Mutual Adaptation in Creating
Classroom Learning Environments
Ann Arbor, Mich.: Institute for Social Research, University of Michigan, 1964

Purpose: To examine the social-psychological factors linking peers, parents, teachers, and individual pupils in creating productive classroom learning atmospheres.

Sample: Selected from a group of teachers in southwestern Michigan, who volunteered to participate, to provide a diverse representation of types of communities and grade levels. A subject pool of 727 children was drawn from twenty-seven public school classrooms.

Method: Data from each classroom were obtained from three sources: questionnaires and group interviews with pupils, questionnaires and interviews with teachers, and a brief period of classroom participation. All questionnaires were administered by the research team in the spring of 1960 and again in 1961. A short family-background information form and a sentence-completion test were administered by the regular classroom teacher. To obtain a measure of "utilization of abilities," each class was split at the median into a high-intelligence and a low-intelligence group on the basis of test scores, and by the teacher into high and low achieving subgroups, thus creating four ability-achievement groups.

Conclusions:

> . . . when the influences of familial social class, perceived parental support, perceived peer status, and satisfaction with the teacher are compared for the relative impact on the utilization of intelligence, pupil satisfaction with the teacher and utilization are associated when the other three variables are controlled. . . . The teacher, as a social-emotional leader, has an effect on achievement for both boys and girls . . . which is independent to a significant degree from the effects of parents and peers.

> In contrast to the relative importance of satisfaction with the teacher, . . . familial social class is a minor factor in influencing pupil utilization in our population. Particularly for the boys, familial socal class and parental support are less important than the factors of peer group status and satisfaction with the teacher in influencing utilization. [pp. 130–131]

The authors sum up by saying, "The results indicate that pupil perceptions of the teacher far outweigh all other influences on the level of utilization of intelligence for both sexes." [p. 131]

Gist, Noel P., and William S. Bennett, Jr.
"Aspirations of Negro and White Students"
Social Forces: 42 (October 1963), 40–48

Purpose: To compare the occupational and educational aspirations and expectations of Negro and white high school students.

Sample: 873 ninth- and twelfth-grade students from four large Kansas City high schools, representing neither the wealthiest nor the most impoverished school districts.

Method: Respondents completed a questionnaire during one fifty-minute period, providing data on their own aspirations and expectations as well as those of their father, mother, and most influential nonfamily member.

Conclusions: No significant difference was found in occupational aspirations even when socioeconomic status and IQ were held constant. However, Negro educational aspirations exceeded those of whites. In addition, the mobility aspirations of Negro students exceeded those of whites, as did the mobility aspirations of Negro fathers and mothers for their children, as compared to white fathers and mothers. Finally, while, in general, females were more likely to influence Negroes, male or female, than was true for whites, there was also evidence of profound maternal influence in the white group. In the same way, while Negro and white girls tended to aspire higher for future husbands than males aspire for themselves, the gap is greater for Negroes.

Goldberg, Miriam L.
"Factors Affecting Educational Attainment in Depressed Urban Areas," in
  A. Harry Passow, ed.
  Education in Depressed Areas
New York: Bureau of Publications, Teachers College, Columbia
  University, 1963, pp. 68–99

The author reviews significant changes in recent decades that have created urgent problems for urban school systems:

1. The changing nature of the city population resulting from the out-migration . . . of middle-class families and the in-migration of low-income groups.
2. The raised school-leaving age and the need for adequate secondary school provisions for presently unmotivated and uninterested pupils.
3. The ethnic and racial membership of the present in-migrants, which create problems of caste as well as class that affect both educational aspirations and employment opportunities.
4. The changing job market with its decreasing demand for unskilled and semi-skilled labor and its increasing need for people who can fill occupations which require higher levels of educational training. [pp. 79–80]

She also discusses the findings concerning achievement and motivation, with particular reference to Negro and Puerto Rican pupils. The article ends with several excellent suggestions for needed research and for educational experiments.

Gottlieb, David
"Goal Aspirations and Goal Fulfillments: Differences between Deprived
  and Affluent American Adolescents"
American Journal of Orthopsychiatry: 34 (October 1964), 934–941

Purpose: To identify differences and similarities in the social systems of different groups of adolescents. This paper focuses on findings relating to the perceptions, aspirations, and values of these youth.
Sample: Four groups: (1) all students from two Negro segregated Southern

high schools, one in a rural community, one in an urban community; (2) all students from a white segregated high school from each of the above two communities; (3) a 25 percent random sample of Negro and white students in an interracial high school in a newly industrialized Midwestern community; (4) a 25 percent sample of Negro students in an all Negro high school in a Northern metropolis.

Method: Administration of paper-and-pencil questionnaire.

Conclusions: There was an inverse relationship between class (based on father's education) and parental education and family disorganization. For each class level, the relationship was stronger for Negroes.

Among white youth, the lower the class level, the lower his mobility aspirations, with girls less likely than boys to indicate a desire for higher education at each class level. Among Negroes, at each class level, more than 80 percent expressed a desire for college, with girls more likely than boys to want a college education. A higher proportion of Southern than of Northern Negroes were college oriented. However, Negro youth from each social class and type of school were less likely than their white counterparts to select an occupational field requiring advanced education.

Among white students, as has been found in other studies, the discrepancy between college-going aspirations and expectations declined with higher status. Among Negro students, however,

> For each stratum at least 20 percent of the students who express a desire for college indicate that they do not actually expect to go on to college. . . . The greatest discrepancy is found among Negro youth in the northern interracial high schools. [p. 936]

The higher the class background, the greater the belief that the teacher is aware of and understands the goals of the students. At each class level, however, Negro students see a greater discrepancy than do white students. There is little difference between the groups in perceptions of the teachers' ability to help the student attain certain goals. But there are differences, by class and race, in perceptions of the teachers' desire to help the student attain those goals.

Haller, Archibald O., and C. E. Butterworth
"Peer Influences on Levels of Occupational and Educational Aspiration"
Social Forces: 38 (May 1960), 289–295

Purpose: To test the general hypothesis that interaction with peers influences levels of occupational and educational aspiration of American adolescent boys.

Sample: All seventeen-year-old boys in one Michigan county in Spring 1957.

Method: The 442 boys were interviewed by trained social psychologists. The unit of analysis was the peer-pair—a pair of subjects who named each other when asked to list all those they considered to be their good friends. Control variables included (1) social class, using prestige ratings of father's occupation based on the NORC scale; (2) the degree to which the parents desired high-level social achievement for the respondent; (3) general intelligence as measured by Cattell's Test of G: Culture Free.

Conclusions: The results were not conclusive. There was a small degree of support for that aspect of the hypothesis concerning levels of occupational aspiration, but little or no support for the relationship of peer influence to educational aspiration.

Health and Welfare Association of Allegheny County
Survey of Westinghouse High School Dropouts, 1959–1961
Pittsburgh: The Association, 1962

Purpose: To obtain information on a number of characteristics of the drop outs, their interest in a work-training program, and the kinds of occupations in which they might like to receive training.

Sample: Data were collected on 475 students who dropped out between January 1, 1959 and December 31, 1961. A 50 percent sample was selected for interviews, and a total of 112 were completed.

Method: Data were collected from permanent school records, from personal interviews, and from the Social Service Exchange. Respondents were interviewed about their current marital status, their work experience, their desired occupations, and their attitudes toward possible participation in a work-training project.

Conclusions: The major characteristics of the drop outs were as follows:

1. Most of the dropouts had below average I.Q.
2. Most had failed at least one semester in school.
3. Nearly half of them were not living with their fathers at the time they were enrolled at Westinghouse.
4. Most were not employed at the time of the interview, and most of those employed had low-paying, unskilled jobs.
5. Most were interested in participating in an employment training program. [p. 3]

Heimann, Robert A., and Quentin F. Schenk
"Relation of Social-Class and Sex Differences to High-School Achievement"
School Review: 62 (April 1954), 213–221

Purpose: To test two hypotheses: (1) there are no mean differences in the marks and test performances of students from higher and lower socioeconomic classes; and (2) there are no mean differences in the marks and test performances of boys and girls.

Sample: 120 cases drawn by random from a previous study population of 869 sophomores in two large and two small Wisconsin high schools. Reduced to 114 (forty-four in Class III, seventy in Class IV) after social-class categorizations were made, using the Hollingshead scale.

Method: School marks accumulated for the four years of high school were averaged for each student. Henmon-Nelson Test of Mental Maturity was administered to almost all.

Conclusions: With regard to class differences, they were significant both for school marks and mental ability, in favor of the higher class (III). With regard to sex differences, girls showed significantly higher school marks, but did not score significantly higher in mental ability. Within each social class, girls accumulated higher marks.

Hoehn, Arthur J.
"A Study of Social Status Differentiation in the Classroom Behavior of
    Nineteen Third Grade Teachers," in
    W. W. Charters and N. C. Gage, eds.
    Readings in the Social Psychology of Education
Boston: Allyn and Bacon, Inc., 1963, pp. 181–189

Purpose: To correlate teacher's interaction and responsiveness to children as directly related to children's social status. Hypothesis: (1) the amount of attention a pupil receives from the teacher varies directly with pupil social status; (2) the proportion of teacher conflict contacts varies inversely with pupil social status; (3) the proportion of teacher contacts showing a high degree of respect for pupil goals varies directly with pupil social status; (4) the "mental hygiene" value of teacher contact varied directly with pupil social status.

Sample: 19 third-grade teachers in two central Illinois communities. The teachers were all women, clearly middle class in status, who expressed middle-class values.

Method: The social status of pupils was measured by Warner's ISC; achievement was measured by reading achievement scores; each teacher was observed for five hours, using the Anderson-Clifton simplification of the Anderson-Brewer scheme, recording only individual contacts.

Conclusions: Only the fourth hypothesis was supported. In only ten classrooms did the mean frequency of contacts involving middle-class pupils exceed that for lower-class pupils, a difference not significant. The author tentatively suggests that teachers have more contacts with low achievers, though high achievers are more "favored." The differentiation, however, is basically a function of achievement rather than one of status.

Hollingshead, August B.
Elmtown's Youth: The Impact of Social Classes on Adolescents
New York: John Wiley & Sons, Inc. (Science Editions), 1949

This volume is an analysis of the way the social system of a Middle Western Corn Belt community (Elmtown, Home State, U.S.A.) organizes and controls the social behavior of high-school-aged adolescents reared in it. It describes the relationships existing between the behavior patterns of the 735 adolescent boys and girls in the study and the positions occupied by their families in the community's class structure. Seven major areas of social behavior are covered—the school, the job, the church, recreation, cliques, dates, and sex.

The presentation of the material is divided into five parts. Part I discusses the problem on which the research was focused and discusses in some detail when, where, and how the data were obtained. Part II gives the communal, family, and social setting of the study. Part III tells the story of the 390 boys and girls who were in high school. Part IV traces the impact of the class system on the 345 young people who had left school prematurely. Part V is a brief summary and conclusion. It asks the question: What can we do to mitigate the problem this study poses? [p. vii]

The fieldwork for this classic study was conducted between May 1941 and December 1942. Despite the fact that the community was small (about 6000 people), 93 percent native born, and almost 100 percent white, findings remain largely applicable to current problems in larger urban areas.

Holloway, Robert G., and Joel V. Berreman
"The Educational and Occupational Aspirations and Plans of Negro and
   White Male Elementary School Students"
Pacific Sociology Review: 2 (Fall 1959), 56–60

Purpose: To test two sets of hypotheses:

1. On the basis of the theory that aspirational level reflects class subcultural values: (a) aspiration levels vary with class; (b) aspiration level does not differ significantly between Negroes and whites of the same class.
2. On the basis of theory derived from Stephenson ("Mobility Orientation and Stratification of 1000 Ninth Graders," *American Sociological Review:* 22 (April 1957), 204–212: (a) aspirations, when measured independently of plans, do not differ by race and class position; (b) the white middle class shows no difference between aspirations and plans; (c) the Negro middle class and the lower class of both races show plans significantly lower than aspirations; (d) the Negro lower class shows a greater difference between aspirations and plans than either the Negro middle class or the white lower class.

Sample: 313 Negro and white male pupils of grades six, seven, and eight in three elementary schools in a Pacific Northwest city. Only fifteen (8 percent) of the Negro pupils were rated middle class.

Method: An open-ended questionnaire was administered, designed to elicit biographical data as well as both realistic aspirations and practical plans in education and work. Social status was derived by a rating procedure carried out by classroom teachers.

Conclusions: With regard to the first hypothesis, occupational aspirations of lower-class pupils were significantly lower, but there was no class difference in educational aspirations, these being predominantly high for all race-class categories. Both educational and occupational aspiration levels were similar for Negroes and whites of the same class.

With regard to the second set of hypotheses, educational aspirations, independent of plans, did not differ by race or class, but occupational aspirations did. The white middle class showed no difference between aspirations and plans. The educational plans of the lower classes of both races were significantly below aspirations, as hypothesized; but the occupational plans of lower-class pupils of both races remained as high as aspirations, as did both educational and occupational plans of Negro middle-class students. Finally, contrary to the hypothesis, Negro lower-class pupils scaled down their educational plans, but no more than did the lower-class whites, and, like lower class whites, their occupational plans were as high as their aspirations.

Jaffe, A. J., and Walter Adams
"College Education for U.S. Youth: The Attitudes of Parents and Children"
American Journal of Economic Sociology: 23 (July 1964), 269–283

Purpose: To compare the attitudes of parents and children on children's college attendance around 1960 with the attitudes held just prior to World War II, and by class.

Method: Analysis of public opinion surveys at the Roper Public Opinion Research Center, Williams College, Williamstown, Massachusetts.
Conclusions:

1. Virtually all parents want their children to go to college.
2. Between 1939 and 1959, the proportion of parents wanting their children to go to college rose from 57 to 72 percent; the proportion of children expressing this desire rose from 40 to 49 percent.
3. Class differences of children and their parents remained about the same. About two thirds of high school students of professional and managerial families planned to go to college in 1939 and 1959, as compared to about two fifths of children of manual workers at both times.

Jones, Mary Cover
"A Study of Socialization Patterns at the High School Level"
Journal of Genetic Psychology: 93 (September 1958), 87–111

Purpose: To explore some of the factors that make individuals psychologically more or less accessible to the molding influences of the school through its program of social participation, and to attempt to determine criteria that can be used to ascertain which students are responding to and which are evading efforts at socialization.

Sample: Two groups of high school students (N = 122), members of the Adolescent Growth Study of the Institute of Child Welfare, who fall at opposed extremes of a sample distributed on the basis of frequency of mentions in the daily newspaper of the high school they attended for three years.

Method: Five hundred and forty issues of the newspaper were read and all mentions were tabulated for the study members. Mentions per individual ranged from 0 to 112. The 0 or low-prominence group consisted of nine boys and nine girls. In selecting a high-prominence group, twelve cases in each sex who were in the top 20 percent of the distribution, ratings were weighted according to the prestige of the areas in which mentions were made. The two groups were compared on the following factors, with sources as indicated: (1) age; (2) behavior, measured by staff members' observation in playgrounds, school halls, excursions, club meetings, and social gatherings; (3) reputation measure, derived from a "Guess Who?" reputation test; (4) drive ratings, measured by the Murray needs test; (5) intelligence; (6) physical abilities, based on strength indices; (7) socioeconomic status based on Census Tract data and home ratings; (8) attitudes, based on a reputation score; and (9) self-concept, from a self-report inventory.

Conclusions: The following significant differences were found, with the high-prominence group showing: (1) early maturation for boys, late maturation for girls; (2) a rating as making a good impression for boys and girls, with girls having more expressive behavior; (3) above-average score in prestige traits such as popularity, friendliness, sense of humor, niceness; (4) relatively strong drives, and, for boys, a need for recognition and for control; (5) a more friendly attitude.

Differences were not significant with reference to (1) intelligence; (2) strength, for boys; (3) social status; (4) prejudice toward outgroups; and (5) self-concept.

Kahl, Joseph
"Educational and Occupational Aspirations of Common Man's Boys"
Harvard Educational Review: 23 (Summer 1953), 186–203

See Appendix, Chapter One.

Karpinos, Bernard D.
"School Attendance as Affected by Prevailing Socio-Economic Factors"
School Review: 51 (January 1943), 39–49

Purpose: To examine the relationship between socioeconomic factors and school attendance.

Sample: That used by the National Health Survey conducted in midwinter 1935–1936.

Method: School attendance—the proportion of persons in school, excluding any working full time but also in school regularly—examined in terms of age, sex, color, and income, for age groupings between seven and twenty-four.

Conclusions: For the white male, there is a direct relation between school attendance and family income, particularly in the older age groups. Differences become noticeable in the fourteen to fifteen-year age group, and become progressively sharper. The pattern is the same for white girls, but the differential becomes marked earlier.

Attendance of nonwhites (includes Negroes, Mexicans, and others) varies materially with income, sex, and region. The differences become sharp at an earlier age than for whites, the sex difference is not as large as among whites, and attendance is generally lower than for white groups.

Karpinos, Bernard D., and Herbert J. Sommers
"Educational Attainment of Urban Youth in Various Income Classes. I"
Elementary School Journal: 42 (May 1942), 677–687

"Educational Attainment of Urban Youth in Various Income Classes. II"
Elementary School Journal: 42 (June 1942), 766–774

Purpose: To examine the relationship between economic status, as measured by family income, and educational attainment.

Sample: That used by the National Health Survey conducted during winter 1935–1936. Included 423,000 youth, of whom 381,000 were white, aged fifteen to nineteen and twenty to twenty-four in 1936.

Method: Educational attainment was defined as highest grade achieved, for elementary schools; for high schools and college, it was the type of school that an individual entered, but did not necessarily complete.

Conclusions: Progression in educational attainment is noted, for white youth, as income increases, in all age and sex groups. It is recognized that the measure employed underestimates drop outs. The same pattern is found for nonwhites, but attainment in general is lower.

The second part of the article continues the above analysis, by region.

Kennedy, Wallace A., Vernon Van De Riet, and James C. White, Jr.
"A Normative Sample of Intelligence and Achievement of Negro
   Elementary School Children in the Southeastern United States"
Monographs of the Society for Research in Child Development:
   V. 28, No. 6 (1963)

Purpose: To provide normative data on intellectual and achievement variables for Negro elementary school children in the Southeastern United States.

Sample: The study included the states of Florida, Georgia, Alabama, Tennessee, and South Carolina. Based on 1950 and postcensus trends, a one-third sample was drawn from large metropolitan counties, urban counties, and rural counties. The sample totaled 1800 children, twenty at each grade level in each of fifteen county systems sampled, restricted to those in attendance at school at the time of the study.

Method: The Binet was used to measure IQ, the California Achievement Test to measure achievement, and demographic data (not specified) to measure socioeconomic level.

Conclusions:

1. With regard to intelligence, the Negro children had a mean IQ of 80.7; there was no significant trend from grades one to six, but IQ was negatively correlated with age. IQ was highly correlated with socioeconomic level, and, though the differences were small, with urban and rural residence.

2. There was a significant difference in the mean levels of achievement between the sample and the scores of the standardizing group, and this difference increased with grade. Achievement also correlated with socioeconomic level, and there was a tendency for girls to score higher than boys at each socioeconomic level.

Krauss, Irving
"Sources of Educational Aspirations among Working-Class Youth"
American Sociological Review: 29 (December 1964), 867–879

Purpose: To locate the sources of educational aspirations among working-class youngsters, concentrating on five areas: (1) discrepant situations in the family of orientation; (2) the experience of family members and friends; (3) the relative status of the working-class family; (4) the influence of peers and participation in the school culture; and (5) working-class students' attitudes and middle-class values.

Sample: 706 high school seniors in four San Francisco Bay Area high schools approximately three weeks prior to their graduation in June 1959. No indication was given of racial or ethnic composition of the sample.

Method: Precoded questionnaires were administered, and 654 usable ones were obtained. Students were characterized for potential mobility depending on their plans for college, technical school, or no further education. They were assigned to middle class or lower class on the basis of U.S. Census classifications of blue-collar and white-collar occupations.

Conclusions: Sixty-four percent from middle-class homes and 41 percent from working-class homes planned to attend college. The similarities between college-oriented working-class and middle-class students was found to be striking "in regard to occupational preference, income expectations, belief in the existence of opportunity, interest in national and international affairs, interest in classical or serious music, and the number of books recently read." In their attitude towards labor, the college-oriented working-class students fall between other working-class students and the college-oriented middle-class youth. In their attitude toward the role of government, they were somewhat closer to the college-oriented middle-class students.

Two major sources of educational aspiration were found: (1) certain conditions in the family, and (2) the nature of the student's peer associations and his participation in school activities. Within the family, such factors as (1) status discrepancies indicative of downward mobility; (2) college-going experience; (3) high occupational status of the father, within the working class, particularly when the father had completed high school.

With reference to the second set of factors:

> (a) College-oriented working-class students were very likely to have acquaintences who also have college aspirations. (b) They tend to be extremely active in extracurricular activities. (c) They were more likely to be attending a predominantly middle-class than a predominantly working-class school. [p. 877]

Krippner, Stanley
"The Educational Plans and Preferences of Upper-Middle Class
   Junior High School Students"
Vocational Guidance Quarterly: 13 (Summer 1965), 257–260

Sample: 189 boys and 162 girls in the seventh and eighth grade of a suburban Chicago school system. A "large proportion" of fathers held professional, semiprofessional, and managerial positions.

Method: The Iowa Every-Pupil Test of Basic Skills was administered, as well as an educational interest questionnaire. High and low achievement groups were obtained by including those who scored one standard deviation above and below the mean score for each sex.

Conclusions: Significantly more girls (83 percent) than boys (60 percent) said they liked school, but only an insignificant proportion of the boys (4 percent) did not plan to attend college. There was no significant difference in reported educational wishes of parents for the respondents between the high and low achieving groups. Seventy-nine percent of the low achieving boys and 77 percent of the low achieving girls planned to go to college. A significantly higher proportion of the higher achieving boys and girls claimed to like school.

Livingstone, A. Hugh
"High School Graduates and Drop-Outs: A New Look at a Persistent Problem"
School Review: 66 (June 1958), 195–203

Purpose: To review previous research to develop a list of possible relevant characteristics or indices; to examine the degree of the relationship of each to the persistence of students in school; and to examine seemingly plausible and reasonable combinations of such significant indices or characteristics to secure a basis for improved predictions of proneness to early school leaving and an improved understanding of the pattern of drop out behavior.

Sample: 309 subjects who entered the first grade in an Illinois city during the 1944–1945 school year and remained in the schools of the community until they graduated (193) or voluntarily dropped out of school (176).

Method: Twenty-four characteristics were drawn from the literature and tested for their relationship to persistence in school. There is no indication of data collection methods.

Conclusions: Eighteen characteristics were found to be significantly related to persistence in school: marital status of parents; area of residence; those with whom student resided; attendance record in grades six, seven, and eight; scholarship record in elementary school; reading level; participation in both formal and informal activities in elementary school; mental ability; number of grades detained; area of curricular emphasis; average high school marks in all subjects; number of subject failures; high school attendance record; leadership positions held in secondary school; number of years retarded at entry to high school; extent of participation in activities in high school. Only one, however, participation in extracurricular activities at the secondary school level, accounted for more than one third of the variance between the two groups.

Lott, Albert J., and Bernice E. Lott
Negro and White Youth: A Psychological Study in a Border-State Community
New York: Holt, Rinehart and Winston, Inc., 1963

Purpose: To explore the values and goals of Negro and white youth in areas most relevant to their educational and vocational choices and plans.

Sample: The sample was selected from two high schools in Fayette County and two in Lexington, Kentucky, one of each pair being predominantly Negro and consisting of 116 Negroes and 185 whites. In addition, within each school, fifteen seniors considered to be potential sources of community leadership were selected for more intensive study. Because of significant differences in background characteristics, two small matched groups of Negro and white seniors who fell within the same range on both parent's occupation and IQ were selected. A second pair of groups was selected for comparison, made up of Negro and white students who planned to attend college.

Method: Test materials included Goal Preference Inventory, a modified form of the Study of Values, a background and outlook questionnaire, a leadership poll, and a test of insight.

Conclusions:

1. Values. Negroes scored higher on the theoretical scale, whites on the economic scale, and there were no differences with reference to religious, political, social, and esthetic values. The results were the same for the matched groups.
2. Goal Preference Inventory. The white group scored significantly higher on the need for social recognition, the need for love and affection; and the Negro group scored higher on the need for academic recognition. The Negro matched group scored higher on the need for academic recognition, but differences on the other two measures disappeared.
3. Test of insight. The white group scored significantly higher on achievement motivation but there was no significant difference on affiliation motivation. The white matched group scored higher on achievement motivation, but the difference was not significant.

4. Outlook. For the total group, the matched groups and the college-bound groups, Negroes were significantly more likely to want to leave Kentucky for non-Southern states. There were no significant differences between the matched groups with reference to occupational desires and expectations, although there were differences based on the total sample. A larger proportion of white males were planning either to go to college or directly to work rather than to vocational training or the armed forces, for both the total and the matched groups.

McDill, Edward L., and James Coleman
"Family and Peer Influences in College Plans of High School Students"
Sociology of Education: 38 (Winter 1965), 112–126

This article continues the analysis first reported in McDill and Coleman, "High School Social Status, College Plans, and Interest in Academic Achievement: A Panel Analysis," *American Sociological Review:* 28 (December 1963), 905–918. (See entry below for annotation.)

Conclusions:

> The results of this investigation seriously challenge the generally accepted position that the socio-economic background of the child is a more important source of variation in his educational aspirations than are peer group influences. Using students from a limited number of high schools, it has been shown that by the end of the senior year of high school, the prestige of the adolescents in the school social system contributes more to variation in their stated college plans than does their father's or mother's education. Even more importantly, the data reveal that their high school status assumes an importance, by the end of the senior year, only slightly lower than the desires of their parents in the freshman year. Finally, it has been shown that the importance of social status in explaining variation in college plans varies according to the social climate of the school: in those high schools where college attendance is highly valued, social status in school is a more important source of variation in such plans than in those schools in which college-going is not highly valued. [p. 125]

It should be noted that the authors do not deal with the issue of the extent to which social status in school is affected by social-class origins.

McDill, Edward L., and James Coleman
"High School Social Status, College Plans, and Interest in Academic Achievement:
  A Panel Analysis"
American Sociological Review: 28 (December 1963), 905–918

Purpose: Previous research has shown that high status in school appeared to lead both to a greater interest in college and to a lesser interest in scholarly achievement. This paper reports on further exploration of the relations between status in adolescent social systems, college intentions, and academic achievement.

Sample: 612 seniors from six schools out of approximately 8900 students in ten schools in northern Illinois who had participated in an earlier study.

Method: Data for the first wave of the panel was obtained in the fall of 1957; and by means of the same questionnaire, in the second wave, in the spring of 1961. For the schools involved, there was a loss of 26 percent mainly because of drop outs, geographic mobility, and absenteeism.

Conclusions: The relationship between college plans and status probably involves two processes. Those in the high-status group are in a group in which the majority are probably going to college. Entry into the group therefore involves socialization to college intentions. Socialization outside the leading crowd is probably towards noncollege activities. The second process involves the association and communication around common curriculum, which facilitates movement in and out of the leading crowd.

Socialization to college going, however, does not involve socialization to scholastic achievement within the leading crowd. That these two values are more highly associated among other groups "suggests that the path to college is somewhat different for the two groups. For those outside the leading crowd, college plans more often stem from (and lead to) achievement orientation than is true for those inside the leading crowd." [p. 915].

Orientation to adult activities may hold the clue for the paradoxical combination of values.

> For a teen-ager in a generally middle class environment, college holds promise of such [sophisticated, adult] activities—campus social life, freedom from parental control, a shift to new friends, and all the other social attributes of college. But being a brilliant student promises none of these. Rather, it is associated with childhood, with good grades and gold stars dispensed by teachers.

> In short, to teen-agers the image of scholastic achievement is largely an image of a subordinate status relative to adults that they are trying to escape. The source of this may well be that scholastic achievement in elementary and high school is largely gained by conformity and not by intellectual ferment. [p. 918]

Michael, John A.
"High School Climates and Plans for Entering College"
Public Opinion Quarterly: 25 (Winter 1961), 585–595

Purpose: To show that the varying college-entrance rates from school to school is related to the high school's characteristics, which are independent of the attributes of any senior attending that school.

Sample: 35,000 seniors from a nationally representative sample of over 500 public high schools.

Method: In 1955, Educational Testing Service conducted a survey on the careers and college plans of these seniors, administered a twenty-item aptitude test, and collected background information. Descriptive material concerning the schools was also gathered from the principals, and additional data were abstracted from national and state school directories, other published surveys, and census sources. An index of family socioeducational status was constructed, and a typology of five school climates was established, using the proportion of the senior class in the top two family-status quintiles as an index of educational milieu, with Type I having the lowest proportion.

Conclusions:

1. Family background and ability. Within each school climate, a larger proportion of high status seniors score above the median on aptitude. For every family-status level, a larger proportion of seniors in Type V climates score above the median. The proportionate increase is greater for high-status than for low-status seniors, but low-status seniors in the Type V climate do better than high-status seniors in the Type I climate. For all students, family background is as important as high school climate in explaining variations in ability, but for seniors in the top quartile on ability, family background is more important.

2. Family background, ability, and college plans. Based on an analysis of students in the top quartile on ability, those in the Type V climate show a greater propensity to go to college, but the differences within climates are more significant. In the first three climates, social class is more predictive of college plans than ability. But in Type IV and V climates, ability is more predictive than class.

Milner, Esther
"A Study of the Relationship between Reading Readiness in Grade One
   School Children and Patterns of Parent-Child Interaction"
Child Development: 22 (June 1951), 95–112

Purpose: To test three hypotheses: (1) that the extent of reading ability in grade one children is related to certain ascertainable patterns of parent-child interaction in the family setting; (2) that these patterns of parent-child interaction found to be associated with high or low reading ability are correspondingly related to higher and lower family social status; (3) that high reading ability in grade one children is related to higher family social status; low reading ability is related to lower family social status.

Sample: 42 grade one children from three elementary schools in a large Southern city.

Method: All children in one first grade of each of the schools were given the California Test of Mental Maturity. Twenty-one obtaining the highest language factor scores were selected as "high scorers," and twenty-one obtaining the lowest scores were selected as "low scorers." Members of the study group were interviewed individually and privately in their respective school settings. Data were also obtained from thirty-three of forty-two sets of parents or parent-surrogates. A modified form of Warner's ISC was used to measure status.

Conclusions: Findings are reported around the analysis of: (1) children's own perception of family interaction, (2) responses of mothers on home routine and personal background, and (3) actual day-to-day instances of parent-child interaction.

> Specifically, the lower-class child of this study seems to lack chiefly two things upon entering school as compared with the middle class child of this study; a warm positive family atmosphere or adult-relationship pattern which is more and more being recognized as a motivational prerequisite for any kind of adult-controlled learning, not only of the verbal skills; an extensive opportunity to interact verbally with adults of high personal value to the child and who possess adequate speech patterns. [p. 111]

Mugge, Robert H.
"Education and AFDC"
Welfare in Review: 2 (January 1964), 1–14

This study is based on a survey of recipients conducted in November and December 1961, and on related data from the 1960 Census of Population.
Conclusions:

1. Attendance at school. For the group age six to seventeen, the attendance rate was 96.3 percent. But the rate drops off, to 91.9 percent for sixteen-year-olds, and 82.2 percent for seventeen-year-olds.
2. Grade placement by age. Median school grade is "normal" for the first four school ages, but drops regularly after that, to a peak difference of 0.7 of a grade for seventeen-year-olds. Over one third of the AFDC children are retarded at age sixteen and seventeen, as compared to 15 percent for all children. At age fourteen, the rate of advanced position for AFDC is half that of other children.
3. These AFDC children are receiving more education than their parents. The median for seventeen-year-olds is 11.2 years of school, as compared to 8.8 years for AFDC mothers, 8.6 years for unemployed fathers, and 6.0 years for incapacitated fathers.

Nam, Charles B., and John K. Folger
"Factors Related to School Retention"
Demography: V. 2 (1965), 456–462

Purpose: To examine some of the demographic and social factors related to the school retention of children and youth in the United States to older ages and higher educational levels.

Method: Analysis of data from decennial censuses and sample surveys of the Bureau of the Census.

Conclusions: The authors conclude that "the relative importance of factors associated with entrance into, and continuation in, school varies along points of the education continuum." With reference to specific factors, they conclude:

1. Sex and ethnic status tend to have a small effect at all ages, with sex more important at higher levels, and ethnicity more important at lower levels.
2. Rural-urban differences are important at the beginning school ages.
3. Socioeconomic status is moderately important, most so at the level of college entrance.
4. Ability is "exceedingly" important, particularly after compulsory school age.
5. A variety of factors, such as advanced planning, motivations, financial means, and the social background are important with reference to college entrance and completion.
6. "However large or small the effects of different factors, these effects are additive in the sense that each increments the probability of persistence in school." [p. 462]

Neugarten, Bernice
"Social Class and Friendship among School Children"
American Journal of Sociology: 51 (January 1956), 305–313

Purpose: To examine the role of social-class position in the determination of a child's choice of friends and the child's reputation among playmates.

Sample: All children (380) enrolled in grades five and six, ten and eleven, in the local schools of a middle Western town.

Method: A modification of Moreno Sociometric Test and an adaptation of the Hartsborne and May "Guess Who?" were administered as a single instrument. Data on friendship status and reputation were also obtained.

Conclusions: By the time children reach the fifth grade, social-class differences in friendship and reputation are well established. Further, the child's desirability as a friend and his reputation are usually related to class position. The child of the lower class finds himself rejected by peers and teachers.

Oppenheim, A. N.
"Social Status and Clique Formation among Grammar School Boys"
British Journal of Sociology: 6 (September 1953), 228–245

Purpose: To determine the extent to which awareness of social-class distinctions and knowledge of the social system in general influence patterns of friendship and hostility at school.

Sample: 321 grammar school boys in the third year at four schools.

Method: A choice-of-friend questionnaire was used to examine the relationship between social-class values and friendship choices; a sociometric questionnaire to determine actual friendship patterns; and an open-ended question to elicit the boys' own characteristics of a "good friend."

Conclusions: There was a significant difference between middle-class and working-class boys in characteristics selected in responding to the choice-of-a-friend questionnaire. However, on the basis of the sociometric data, there was no evidence that either class chose or rejected their own group more often than expected. It turned out, further, that there was almost no relationship between the characteristics chosen on the structured questionnaire, and those listed in response to the open-ended question, nor was there any class difference in those characteristics. Therefore, says the author, "it must be concluded that in the qualities desired in a friend, as well as the actual formation of friendships, no class differences can be detected within the Grammar School." [p. 241]

Palmore, Erdman
"Factors Associated with School Dropouts and Juvenile Delinquency"
Social Security Bulletin: 26 (October 1963), 4–9

Purpose: To explore factors associated with leaving school and delinquency with a lower-class group of youth.

Sample: The sample combined two groups: (1) 56 children from the 1950 New Haven 5 percent sample who belonged to Class V families (the lowest socioeconomic class as measured by occupation, education, and income) and who had been born in 1942–1944; and (2) the remaining 328 children of 362 who in 1950 were receiving ADC and had been born in the same time period as the other group. This permitted a retrospective cohort study.

Method: Data were obtained from welfare records for the assistance cases, from the 1950 survey for the other cases, and from school and police records in all cases. Each child's records were followed through his eighteenth year.

Conclusions:

1. Drop-out rates were significantly higher among those from lower-class neighborhoods, those moving frequently, males, and those with below-average intelligence. Drop-out rates were not related to receipt of assistance.

2. "Delinquency was found to be significantly associated with several individual characteristics (nonwhite, male, lower intelligence, and leaving school) that were considered as indicators of barriers to legitimate opportunity that produce anomie and delinquency. Delinquency was also significantly related to characteristics of deviant families (illegitimacy, absent parents, and delinquent siblings) and to be characteristic of deviant neighborhoods (public housing and high neighborhood delinquency rates). These characteristics were considered to be indicators of access to illegitimate opportunities that increase delinquency." [p. 9]

3. Although children receiving aid had a delinquency rate twice that of those not receiving aid, the association was considered spurious in that the "background characteristics of the assistance recipients are those that tend to produce higher delinquency rates, and when some of these characteristics (class, age, race, and sex) were controlled there was little or no association left between receipt of assistance and delinquency."

Pohlman, Vernon C.
"Relationship between Ability, Socio-economic Status, and Choice
   of Secondary School"
Journal of Educational Sociology: 29 (May 1956), 392–397

Purpose: To test the hypotheses that (1) a basic factor in the choice of a given type of secondary school is the socioeconomic status of the pupil's family, and (2) socioeconomic status is more closely related to school choice than ability of boys and girls.

Sample: (1) 533 students representing a 10 percent sample of white residents in St. Louis who had completed the eighth grade of public and parochial school in June 1953, and (2) 60 students representing nearly all of the white respondents in St. Louis who completed the eighth grade in June 1953 and who enrolled in some private school in September 1953.

Method: Data on each pupil included home address, father's occupation, sex, type of school chosen, IQ, reading ability, age score, and rank in the eighth-grade class, obtained from school records. Socioeconomic status was obtained by averaging standardized scores based on father's occupation and the dwelling area around the child's home.

Conclusions: The expectation was upheld that there would be a relationship between social status and choice of secondary school, when these choices were ranked from no school through trade or technical, parochial general, public general, private parochial, and other private academic high schools. Ability was more important than social status in determining choice in only one instance—the likelihood that girls would choose a general rather than a technical high school. Neither ability nor status were important in determining the choice between parochial and general high schools.

Remmers, H.H., and D. H. Radler
The American Teenager
Indianapolis: The Bobbs-Merrill Company, Inc. 1957

Purpose: To provide a continuous survey of American teen-agers' problems and opinions.

Sample: A typical sample would be 2000 to 3000 boys and girls, drawn from a larger sample of 8000 to 18,000 in grades nine to twelve, from all areas of the United States, stratified in line with the most recent Bureau of Census figures.

Method: Forty-nine polls, by questionnaire, conducted by Purdue Opinion Polls. In addition to questionnaires, material was drawn from 2000 anonymous letters from high school students dealing with adolescent problems.

Conclusions: Teen-agers view lack of popularity as their most important problem. They desire an improved appearance, more dates, more friends, self-assurance, and acceptance by the crowd. The adolescent is in favor of censorship, wiretapping, third degree, judicial pressure on the Fifth Amendment. The values of teen-agers tend in the direction of anti-intellectualism. The authors conclude that lack of reward for independent thinking is the root of the teen-agers emphasis on conformity.

Schultz, Raymond E.
"A Comparison of Negro Pupils Ranking High and Low in Educational Achievement"
Journal of Educational Sociology: 31 (November 1958), 265–270

Purpose: To identify some of the factors, other than school attended, that differentiate a group of Negro pupils who rank high and low in educational achievement.

Sample: From among 354 ninth-grade Negro pupils in one Florida county, 50 who scored highest on a standardized achievement test and 50 who scored low, but whose ability, as measured by the Iowa School Ability Test, placed them above the lowest sixteenth percentile of their peers in twenty Florida counties, were selected.

Method: Pupils were compared, in terms of their scores on the Iowa Test of Educational Development and the School Ability Test, administered late in 1956, as to age, home status, occupation of head of household, occupation of mother, parental education, and consistency of school attendance.

Conclusions: The most significant findings were in the area of parental education and socioeconomic status. Students whose parents had more education were high achievers to a greater extent. In addition, 91 percent of the high achievers as compared to 42 percent of the low achievers came from homes where both parents worked, which was taken as an index of higher socioeconomic status.

Sewell, William H., Archie O. Haller, and Murray A. Strauss
"Social Status and Educational and Occupational Aspiration"
American Sociological Review: 22 (February 1957), 67–73

Purpose: To test the general hypothesis that levels of educational and occupational aspiration of youth are associated with the social status of their families, when the effects of intelligence are controlled.

Sample: One-sixth random sample (4167) of all nonfarm seniors in public and private high schools in Wisconsin in 1947–1948.

Method: Data for educational aspiration were taken from responses to a series of questions concerning future education; for occupational aspiration, from a question concerning the vocation the student planned to enter, responses being assigned actual or interpolated North-Hatt occupational-prestige values. Persons choosing occupations equal to or higher than public school teachers were considered to have high occupational aspirations, and all others, low. Social status of respondents was measured by prestige of parental occupation.

Conclusions:

> . . . four tests have been made of the hypothesis. . . . On the basis of these tests, it must be concluded that the apparent effect of social status on levels of educational and occupational aspiration are not simply due to the common relationship of these variables to intelligence, although intelligence is related to both types of aspirations. [p. 72]

Sexton, Patricia Cayo
Education and Income
New York: The Viking Press, Inc., 1961

This book does for the urban school, in many ways, what Hollingshead's *Elmtown's Youth* did for schools in smaller communities. It explores the relation between income and educational opportunity, the relation between the social class structure of a community and the allocation of resources for the education of its children. The study encompasses the total public school system of the community (excluding trade, vocational, and technical schools), involving almost 300 schools.

Sexton demonstrates that by almost every conceivable measure, schools catering to low-income students are deficient as compared to other schools in the same system, and as compared to relevant objective standards. Not only are the physical facilities inferior, except where urban renewal has resulted in a new school in a low-income project area, but the teachers tend to be less qualified, the curriculum less varied, and though there is greater need for remediation, the variety and quantity of remedial services are less than what is found in schools in higher-income areas. The author examines primary and secondary school separately, and goes on to make suggestions for altering the situation.

Siemans, Leonard B.
"The Influence of Selected Family Factors on the Educational and
  Occupational Aspiration Levels of High School Boys and Girls"
Winnipeg, Canada: The University of Manitoba, 1965

Purpose: To determine the educational and occupational aspirations of high school youth and to relate these aspirations to a wide range of family, peer group, and school-related factors.

Sample: Drawn from three areas in Manitoba: (1) essentially rural and low income, (2) agricultural and prosperous, and (3) two noncontiguous high school areas in suburban municipalities of metropolitan Winnipeg. Sample consisted of all eleventh- and twelfth-grade students present on the day the questionnaire was administered in twenty-eight high schools—an 88 percent response including 987 boys and 857 girls.

Method: A structured questionnaire including measures of educational and occupational aspirations, father's occupational status, socioeconomic status, and ninth-grade IQ was administered during school hours in May and June 1964.

Conclusions:

1. The educational and occupational aspirations of boys and girls were positively related to size of family's community of residence, socio-economic and occupational status of family, level of father's and mother's educational attainment (except for girls with reference to mother's education), strength of father's and mother's encouragement for continuing education, and religious background of family (for boys only); they were not related to normal versus broken homes, or ethnic background of family.

2. The family factors, except for normal versus broken home, were related to social class. When status was controlled, in the low-status group, none of the family factors related significantly to either educational or occupational aspirations, while in the upper-status group, size of community, father's and mother's educational level, and father's occupational level still were related. For the higher-status group, religious background, father's educational level and occupational status continued to relate to occupational aspirations.

3. Within the same IQ category, the family factors failed to relate significantly to differences in aspiration level, except for mother's encouragement of continuing education.

It should be noted that the measures for educational and occupational aspirations were absolute rather than relative, thus biasing the results in favor of a lower level of aspiration among the lower-status youth.

Smith, Henry P.
"A Study in the Selective Character of American Education:
    Participation in School Activities as Conditioned by Socio-Economic Status
    and other Factors"
Journal of Educational Psychology: 36 (April 1945), 229–246

Purpose: To determine the extent to which participation in extracurricular activities was conditioned by socioeconomic status, personality traits, and other factors in a group of high school students.

Sample: 1751 students in grades ten, eleven, and twelve in the only high school of one city.

Method: A questionnaire was administered to obtain information on the extent of student participation, and this was supplemented with information from faculty sponsors and the school newspaper. Social status was obtained by means of the Sims Score Card. The Bell Adjustment Inventory provided data on emotional, home, and social adjustment. A thirty-five-item introversion-extroversion scale was also used.

Conclusions: (1) The mean status scores for persons in twenty-eight of the thirty-one groups studied were higher than that for the general population. (2) Participants showed a tendency to be superior in social-adjustment scores. (3) They were also superior in vocabulary tests and in scores in the Iowa Test of Educational Development. (4) Participants tended to live closer to school. (5) There appeared to be some relationship between social status and scores on tests of emotional, home, and social adjustment as well as extroversion.

Stendler, Celia Burns
Children of Brasstown: Their Awareness of the Symbols of Social Class
Urbana, Ill.: University of Illinois Press, 1949

Purpose: To examine children's awareness of class, the symbols involved, the developmental stages, and the consequences for the child of this awareness.

Sample: Grades one, four, six, and eight in one of four elementary schools, constituting a study sample of 107 students.

Methods: Rating on the social-class position of each participant child was obtained from people in the community. A group intelligence test was given. Individual interviews were held with each subject, during the course of which pictures were presented to be rated. A "Guess Who?" test was given to each group.

Conclusions: Among the conclusions are the following:

1. Awareness of class symbols becomes apparent in the fourth grade, and sixth and eighth graders are very much like adults in awareness.
2. Girls appear to be more conscious of class symbols than boys in the upper grades. In the lower grades, boys show closer agreement with adults in their ratings of pictures.
3. On the basis of picture ratings, upper-middle-class children are most conscious of class symbols, followed by children from white-collar families, with working-class children revealing the least consciousness.
4. In the earlier grades, children tend to identify being rich with everything desirable, being poor with everything undesirable. "Older children of the white-collar and working class appear to develop a stereotyped concept of class character according to which the child who is rich is a not-very-honest, sissy character, and the child who is poor is a friendly, hard-working, honest kind of person whom everybody likes."
5. Out-of-school activities are conditioned by class position, so that, for example, higher-status children join more organizations, take more lessons, and so on.
6. While the pattern of development is different, for the selection of both in-school and out-of-school friends, by the sixth and eighth grades, class bias is sufficiently effective as to almost eliminate interaction between upper-middle and working-class youths.
7. While first graders show little awareness of their social-class position, reporting themselves as rich, by the fourth grade, children show a tendency to rate themselves "in-between" and this continues through the sixth and eighth grades.
8. Likewise, while first graders show little ability to judge the class position of schoolmates, fourth graders are correct over half the time, and sixth and eighth graders show considerable accuracy.
9. Fourth graders occasionally mentioned father's occupation as a factor

in assigning class, and sixth and eighth graders use such factors as father's occupation, clothes, manners, family connections, and area of residence.
10. There is no class influence in the selection of future occupations in the first and fourth grades. As the authors put it:

> Beginning with the sixth grade and very evident in the eighth grade, there is a tendency for all classes to name an upper- or middle-class occupation for first choice. For the third choice, working-class upper-grade children are more likely to name a lower-class occupation, showing that they have some appreciation of what they realize their life chances to be. [pp. 94–95]

Stinchcombe, Arthur L.
Rebellion in a High School
Chicago: Quadrangle Books, 1964

This study of high school rebellion (the flouting of rules rather than their evasion) is based on a high school of some 1600 students in a logging and sawmill town of 4000 located in California. A paper-and-pencil questionnaire was administered by teachers in required social-science classes, and the author observed in the school itself. The index of rebellion is composed of three self-reported "rebellious" acts: skipping school with a gang of peers, receiving a flunk notice in a noncollege-preparatory course, and being sent out of class by a teacher.

According to Stinchcombe, high school rebellion is a part of a complex of attitudes toward psychologically present authority. This complex is labeled "expressive alienation," and is ideal-typically described as being nonutilitarian, malicious and negativistic, involving short-run hedonism, and emphasizing group autonomy from adult inference as a matter of principle. Rebellion and expressive alienation will occur when future status is not clearly related to present performance, when the symbols of formal school culture fail to provide a satisfactory identification with the role of adolescent, and when the goals of success are strongly internalized but inaccessible.

Stinchcombe provides evidence for the argument that "articulation"—that is, a good fit between projected posthigh school status and present academic activity—produces conformity in school, while poor articulation is related to expressive alienation and hence to rebellion. He contends, further, that the fit between image of the future and present academic activity is a better predictor of rebellion than social class. He finds, actually, that the "relation of social class to rebellion is weak and unreliable," though he cautions that the finding may be an artifact of the "small town" setting of the study.

It should be noted that Stinchcombe's use of the term "rebellion" may accord with popular notions that anyone who does not conform is a rebel, but is not consistent with the more traditional use of the term whereby rebellion is seen as an act, not only against the existing structure, but also to construct a new one. This is precisely what Lindner was alluding to when he used the phrase "rebel without a cause."

Thomas, Robert Jay
"An Empirical Study of High School Drop-Outs in Regard to 10 Possibly Related
   Factors"
Journal of Educational Sociology: 28 (September 1954), 11–18

Purpose: To study the relationship of certain factors to dropping out of
school.

Sample: A 70 percent random sample of the 434 students entering a large
four-year high school in the greater Chicago area in 1947, who left or were
graduated by 1951. Students who transferred in or out, who died, or for whom
essential data were not available, were excluded.

Method: Data were taken from school records.

Conclusions: The form of presentation of the results makes it difficult to
judge their reliability. Socioeconomic class, as measured by a set of sixteen
occupational categories, was found to be somewhat related to dropping out,
as was IQ. Involvement in extracurricular activities was the factor most related
to finishing school. What was significant was not the *number* of activities engaged in, but rather whether the student was involved in *any* activities.

Toby, Jackson
"Orientation to Education as a Factor in the School Maladjustment of Lower-
   Class Children"
Social Forces: 35 (March 1957), 259–266

On most indices of school achievement, it is found that middle-class children perform better in school than do lower-class children. Theories advanced
to explain the success of middle-class children, such as the disparate values
system of middle-class teachers and lower-class children resulting in the teacher's rejection of the lower-class child, and the relating of the inferior performance
of the lower-class child directly to economic disabilities of his family, view the
lower-class child in a passive role in his maladjustment to school. The author
proposes the view that some lower-class children view school as a burden, not
as an opportunity, and take an active role in failing the school situation by
choice and are supported in their behavior by their families, friends, and the
surrounding community.

Turner, Ralph H.
The Social Context of Ambition
San Francisco: Chandler Publishing Company, 1964

Purpose: To shed light on the social setting in which ambition (a desire
to abandon one social position and attain another) is nurtured and in which
it is translated into concrete steps in mobility.

Sample: Whole classes in "Social Problems" courses in the twelfth grade of ten schools in Los Angeles and Beverly Hills (1352 boys and 1441 girls) were included. Census tracts were arranged in quartiles on the basis of an index of social rank, and, taking into consideration size, two high schools were selected from each of the top two quartiles and three from each of the bottom two.

Method: A questionnaire was administered in school, in the last semester, containing four types of items: (1) student ambitions, (2) socioeconomic background; (3) class-related values; and (4) sociometric measures.

Conclusions: The level of ambition was found to vary both with family background and with level of neighborhood, with each having about the same effect. IQ was also found to vary by neighborhood to a greater degree than could be attributed to family background alone. In the low-status neighborhoods, ambition was found to be less determined by either family background or IQ than in the higher-level neighborhoods, and IQ was less closely related to family background in the low-level neighborhoods.

Support for the hypothesis that considerable anticipatory socialization occurred was found in the tendency for value discrepancy rather than value contradiction. However, the "reference group-anticipatory socialization theory" likewise is not an adequate explanation "since there are values associated with high ambition which find no counterpart among students from high backgrounds." Further, there was some evidence that anticipatory socialization was not operative in the lower neighborhoods for upwardly mobile men.

There was evidence that social origin did affect ambition, values, and peer-preference patterns, but the impact was "modest." Further, there was no evidence that academic excellence was negatively evaluated in the lower-level neighborhoods. Rather, it seemed that neither academic excellence nor high social origins was particularly relevant in the selection of friends. However, "stratification of destination" was important: "Ambition forms a basis for social cleavage as well as preference, while background does not."

> The peculiarity of social organization among boys in the lower neighborhoods may be stated comprehensively as a pattern of future-orientation without anticipatory socialization. Ambition and academic success are valued, but the distinctive values appropriate to the destination of the highly ambitious are not learned along the way. The failure of anticipatory socialization to accompany future-orientation is probably a consequence of the absence of a high-prestige model from whom to learn the values appropriate to higher strata. [p. 137]

Comparing the emphases within the notion of ambition, Turner found students from higher backgrounds relied on education, while students from lower family origins expected to go further with less education. Their occupational choices were consistent, in that lower-class boys tended to choose those in which it is possible to move up without extensive education. In this context, it may be well to remember Morland's contention (see Appendix for Chapter 3) that the decision about how much education to get is a function of the decision about the level of job that is obtainable.

Udry, J. Richard
"The Importance of Social Class in a Suburban School"
Journal of Educational Sociology: 33 (April 1960), 307–310

Purpose: To test the applicability of conclusions concerning the relationship of social class to intelligence, achievement, and friendship patterns, for a secondary school student body in a rapidly growing suburb.

Sample: From a high school student body of 2500, a random sample of 51 same-sex friendship groups totaling 151 individuals was selected. In addition, a sample of 125 was drawn from grades seven, eight, and nine in a junior high school. Data on achievement and intelligence were taken from school records. Father's occupation was used as a measure of class position, in four categories.

Conclusions: Social class and intelligence were found to be related, the relationship being significant but low. Social class and achievement in school were closely related, but not significantly. Similarly, though same-sex adolescent friendship groups closely followed class lines, the relationship was not significant. The author suggests that where both students and teachers are new to an area, preconceptions about students based on family-class status may not have developed to the point of influencing teacher-student relations.

Wallin, Paul, and Leslie C. Waldo
*Social Class Backgrounds of 8th Grade Pupils, Social Composition of
   Their Schools, Their Academic Aspirations and School Adjustment*
Washington, D.C.: U.S. Office of Education, Cooperative Research Project
   No. 1935, 1964

Purpose: To explain differences in the level of educational aspiration and in the adjustment to the school situation.

Sample: Students in seven junior high schools, chosen for substantial differences in the social-class composition of the student bodies, in the San Francisco Bay Area. Included were 1223 boys and 1202 girls, of whom 135 were Negro boys and 133 were Negro girls. The Negro students were confined to the lowest social classes.

Method: Data were collected early in June 1960 by means of two questionnaires, and from school records. Ratings of the children by teachers were also obtained. The Hollingshead Index of Social Position was used to measure social class and to establish the social-class position of each school.

Conclusions:

1. School and family influences on educational aspirations. The effect of social class was measured on educational goals (how far students wanted to go in school); intensity of desire to go to college; and an index, Level of Aspiration (LOA), based on the first two. Generally, there was a positive relationship between social class and each of these measures. There was little difference between Negro and white boys on the LOA. For the purpose of measuring the effect of school climate, the

schools were ranked on the proportion of students from middle-class families, and dichotomized. There was a positive relationship between high LOA and the ranking of the schools. The influence of school climate was tested against social-class background, occupation of the family head, and father's and mother's education. Climates did exert an influence on the aspirations of boys and girls from similar backgrounds. But the authors conclude that

The relation between LOA and family social class *within* types of schools is much more significant in magnitude than is the association between LOA and type of school for children at the same class level. [p. 88]

Likewise, a climate effect was found using the other variables.

When, however, the effect of school climate was measured against parental educational aspirations for their children, it was found to be considerably reduced. The authors note that the parents of children in middle-class schools tend to have higher aspirations for their children:

. . . the findings can be interpreted as an indication of the greater concern of parents with high aspirations for their children that they be enrolled in what they consider to be the better schools. . . . This greater concern presumably would lead them to try to establish their residence in a school district that would achieve this end. [p. 98]

2. Other factors related to educational aspirations. These factors, IQ level, grade average, general attitude toward school, and certainty of going to college were correlated independently with LOA. But parental influence was found to be of greater importance, although the above factors had an interactive effect on parental aspirations.
3. Quality of parent-child relations. Using four variables, paternal and maternal helpfulness, and paternal and maternal esteem, it was found that respondents with a more favorable perception of their parents' relations to them were more likely to accept the aspirations held for them by their parents.
4. Social-class differences in children's school adjustment. Lower-class children were found to be aware of their poor academic performance and felt less adequate about it. Lower-class children also reported that they had more difficulty in obeying school rules and tended to feel that they were more likely to be unfairly blamed at school for things they did not do. Nevertheless, they were as likely as other children to feel that they enjoyed the favorable regard of teachers.

There were no class nor race differences in such sociometric choices as desired best friend by children of same-sex peers. But higher-status children were more likely to hold elective offices and to participate in extracurricular activities, and to report that they were happy in class.
5. Teacher ratings of children's adjustment. Teachers systematically perceived higher-class children more favorably on a measure of general adjustment, but the findings on two other measures were mixed:

Presumed class-linked cultural differences between teachers and students operated to diminish teachers' sense of understanding only among girls of the lower classes and not among boys. Sex and race differences generally indicate that teachers feel more certain of their judgments and more understanding of the behavior of boys than of girls and of Negroes than of whites. [p. 171]

Warner, William L., Robert J. Havighurst, and Martin B. Loeb
Who Shall Be Educated?
New York: Harper & Row, Publishers, 1944

The major premise of this book is that the teacher, school administrator, school board, and students each play their role to hold people in their place in the social structure.

The first four chapters give a general view of the background of the class system and its relationship to the schools. By describing the typical social patterns in the schools, the authors delineate the pattern of success and dysfunction.

Chapter V discusses the role of school curricula in determining selective pathways to success. It is indicated that social class is a determining factor in curriculum selection, which in turn determines the student's potential for social mobility.

Chapter VI contains a discussion of the relationship of class to the rating of individual ability. Grouping tends to be on a social as well as ability basis. Conformity to middle-class standards of behavior produces favorable responses on the part of peers and school staff. Chapter VII goes on to show how a lower-class person is able to move into a middle-class pattern of life through associations in the school situation.

In Chapter VIII, the authors focus on the teacher and his relationship to the social hierarchy. In Chapter IX they describe the social hierarchy of the school administration, the web, or relationships in which the school administrator is entangled.

Chapter X is an analysis of the American caste system as it operates in the case of Negroes and the disadvantages of Negroes in the educational system. The final chapter offers some propositions for democratizing the educational process and purpose.

Wilson, Alan B.
"Residential Segregation of Social Classes and Aspirations of High School Boys"
American Sociological Review: 24 (December 1959), 836–845

Purpose: To investigate the degree to which the aspirations of the bulk of students in a high school provide a significant normative reference influencing the boys from varying strata.

Sample: Boys in eight of thirteen schools who provided data in a survey of students' interests.

Method: Information is not presented on instruments used in the survey. Schools were categorized as upper white collar, lower white collar, and working class.

Conclusions:

1. It was found, as anticipated, that there was a great divergence between the schools in the proportions of students aspiring to a college education. Nevertheless, within occupational strata, the norms of the school society did modify attitudes. Thus, a larger proportion of working-class children in middle-class schools desired a college education than did their peers in working-class schools.
2. It was demonstrated that this finding was not a result of systematic variations in the attributes of parents by showing that students from relatively homogeneous backgrounds in different kinds of schools reflected the atmosphere of those schools.
3. "The effect of the school society upon aspirations is still found to be operative and strong when holding constant the influence of either parent's education."
4. Educational values and achievement interact and reinforce one another. Those with higher achievement have higher aspirations. The achievement of sons of professionals and white-collar workers is more adversely affected in working-class schools than is their level of aspiration, however.

Wilson, Alan B.
"Social Stratification and Academic Achievement," in
   A. Harry Passow, ed.
   Education in Depressed Areas
New York: Bureau of Publications, Teachers College, Columbia
   University, 1963, pp. 217–235

Purpose: To analyze the effects of social stratification and the homogenizing effect of segregation upon the academic achievement of elementary school children, and to explore some of the social mechanisms within schools mediating these effects.

Sample: High-sixth-grade pupils in fourteen elementary schools in the unified school district of Berkeley, California. The schools fall into three distinct strata following the lines of residential segregation in the community—the Hills, primarily professional and executive; the Flats, primarily Negro working class; and the Foothills, heterogeneous.

Method: In addition to background data, several measures of achievement were gathered: reading and arithmetic scores from tests administered the year of the study by the schools; IQ scores from tests administered the year before; the level of the reader to which they had been assigned by their teachers; and marks assigned by their teachers in several subject areas.

Conclusions: All indices of achievement showed a clear relationship with the stratification of schools by socioeconomic background. Except in the Hills schools, girls show the usual higher level of achievement than boys. Within each school stratum, the socioeconomic background of the child had a substantial impact upon achievement. The discrepancy between boys and girls was sharpest in the schools of the Flats, particularly among children of manual workers, and most particularly, among children of Negro manual workers.

The homogenizing effect of the school milieu is related to two processes: the lateral transmission of values and attitudes among students; and the normalization of differing standards of achievement by teachers.

> In the Flats the boys who are disinterested in extending their education are well-integrated in their classes. . . . In the Foothills, the most heterogeneous schools, college aspirations are irrelevant to social location. . . . Relatively, then, terminal students are the social leaders in the lower economic strata. They gain social support from their peers, and, in turn, set the pace for them, without adopting the standards of success prevalent in the wider community of adults. [p. 228]

It was found that the percentage of high grades assigned followed the rank order of achievement: "however, it is found that while sex, race, and father's occupation have pronounced effects in the same direction as before [as on achievement], that within groups actually fewer high grades are dispensed in the Hills than in either the Foothills or the Flats." In short, students in the Flats are relatively overevaluated by teachers, receiving more high grades than warranted by their achievement, while students in the Hills are underevaluated.

Examining the relationship between IQ scores, reading test scores, and teachers' marks, it was found that teachers' evaluation of Negro and white children was little different. However, oriental children received higher marks than could be accounted for by measured achievement, as did girls and the children from professional or executive home backgrounds.

Wylie, Ruth S.
"Children's Estimates of Their Schoolwork Ability as a Function of
     Sex, Race and Socioeconomic Level"
Journal of Personality: 31 (June 1963), 204–224

Purpose: To test hypotheses that most modest self-estimates of ability occur in girls as compared to boys, Negroes as compared to whites, and children whose fathers are in lower-level occupations as compared with those whose fathers are in higher-level occupations; and to explore tendencies toward a self-favorability bias in self-evaluations of ability.

Sample: 823 boys and girls in grades seven, eight, and nine of the only junior high school in a small, industrial Pennsylvania city.

Method: Children were tested in homerooms. IQ score from SRA Primary Mental Abilities Test was used as a rough estimate of individual difference in ability to do schoolwork. Three kinds of self-estimates of ability were obtained. Father's occupation was taken from school record and was rated on the Hollingshead-Redlich scale.

Conclusions: The hypotheses were supported, while holding constant such factors as age, school attended, and IQ. The results also showed a highly significant self-favorability bias in the group as a whole.

Annotated References for Chapter Three

Bowman, Paul H., and Charles V. Matthews
Motivations of Youth for Leaving School
Chicago: University of Chicago, Quincy Youth Development Project
  Cooperative Reseach Project #200, U.S. Office of Education, 1960

See Appendix, Chapter Two.

Caro, Francis G.
Paths toward Adulthood: A Study of Post-High School Activities
Kansas City, Mo.: Department of Social Problems and Education,
  Community Studies, Inc., 1965

Purpose: To study the activities of young persons in the first two years beyond high school as one aspect of the transition from adolescence to adulthood.

Sample: Based on a follow-up study of 3500 high school seniors who, in the spring of 1961, responded to a questionnaire concerning their posthigh school plans, administered in all public high schools in Jackson County, Missouri. A stratified sample based on sex, race, social class, and aptitude was planned, and information was obtained on 993 of the 1223 selected for inclusion.

Method: Telephone interviews were used for 91 percent of the cases, with questionnaires mailed to those not reached by phone. The contact pattern resulted in a somewhat stronger representation of high-status and high-aptitude persons in the final study group than in the planned sample. Father's occupation and education were used to designate social class. Standardized tests administered in the schools were used as an indication of achievement.

Conclusions:

1. Education. Just over half (57 percent) of the study group attended college on a full-time basis for at least part of the immediate posthigh school period. Social class and academic achievement were strongly related to college attendance. Negroes were twice as likely to go to junior college, as were low-status students. Those with low aptitude were about twice as likely to have left school, but about half survived through the first two years.
2. Work. Male college drop outs were significantly more likely to be holding white-collar jobs than were males who did not attend college, while females were slightly more likely to have that advantage over noncollege girls.

    Two years after graduation, 36 percent of males (61 percent of those not in college) and 40 percent of females (60 percent of those not in college) were working. Those with low social-class backgrounds (difference not significant), with low aptitude ratings (difference significant), and Negroes (difference significant) held white-collar jobs less often than others. There was a sharp discrepancy between the work they hoped to obtain when they were seniors and the work they were actually doing.

Males (difference significant), Negroes (difference significant), and those of low social background (difference significant) and low academic aptitude (difference not significant) were more likely to have had difficulty finding work.

3. Occupational training. Participation in training programs was reported by 22 percent of the study group, 34 percent of those with no college. For the total group, those with low status and low aptitude were more likely to have had training, but when only the noncollege respondents are considered, these differences disappear. For both males and females, those with occupational training were no more likely than those with no additional education to be in white-collar jobs.

4. Military service. Two years after high school, 18 percent of the males (31 percent of the noncollege high school graduates) were in military service. Low academic aptitude was strongly associated with military service, while Negroes and those of low status tended to military service. When only those without college were considered, the relationship of military service to social status disappeared; to aptitude diminished; but the relationship to race increased, with Negroes more likely to be in the service.

Caro, Francis G., and C. Terence Pihlblad
"Aspirations and Expectations: A Reexamination of the Bases for
    Social Class Differences in the Occupational Orientations
    of Male High School Students"
Sociology and Social Research: 49 (July 1965), 465–475

Purpose: To examine possible sources of social-class differences in the occupational orientations of male youths. The general hypothesis is that "the size of the disparity between level of aspiration and level of expectation may be interpreted as a reflection of a person's perception of access limitation." [p. 467]

Sample: Male public high school seniors in Jackson County, Missouri; number not given.

Method: Administration of a structured questionnaire. Aspirations and expectations were categorized on a nine-point scale adapted from the North-Hatt scale. Father's occupation and education were used for social-class designation.

Conclusions: Occupational expectations were found to run somewhat below aspirations and lower-class students did not anticipate coming as close to realizing their desired occupational objectives as did middle- and upper-class students.

The present data show, then, that differential perception of various occupations contributes to social class differences in the occupational orientations of male high school students. . . . The data are consistent with the hypothesis that class differences both in evaluation of the occupational structure and in perception of access to desired occupations contribute to the class differences in occupational orientation. [pp. 468–469]

Caro, Francis G., and C. Terence Pihlblad
"Social Class, Formal Education, and Social Mobility"
Sociology and Social Research: 48 (July 1964), 428–439

Purpose: To determine whether the network of relationships implied from previous research among social-class background, academic aptitude, immediate posthigh school plans, and occupational aspirations can be demonstrated to hold for a single set of respondents.

Sample: 1220 male students in the second semester of their senior year, in Kansas City, Missouri, who fell into one of the three predesignated social-class groups based on father's occupation and formal education: (1) upper level— high prestige occupation and at least high school completed, (2) middle level— father's occupation medium prestige and at least grade school but no more than two years of college, (3) lower level—low-prestige occupation and high school incomplete.

Method: Structured questionnaire used to obtain measure of aspirations. Performance on standardized tests used as a measure of the development of academic abilities.

Conclusions:

1. There was a strong positive relationship between social-class background and academic ability.
2. There was a positive relationship between social status and plans for college, which held at varying levels of academic ability.
3. There was a strong relationship between planning for college and aspiring to high-prestige occupations.
4. There is a positive relationship between social status and the prestige level of occupational aspirations, which holds for varying levels of academic ability.

Cateora, Phillip
An Analysis of the Teenage Market
Austin, Texas: Bureau of Business Research, The University of Texas, 1963

Purpose: To relate social-class background and peer-group influences to teenage consumption patterns.

Sample: 189 students making up the high school junior and senior class population in a city of 200,000.

Method: (1) Standardized index of social characteristics for determining family social status, (2) sociometric analysis to obtain information on peer group structure, and (3) a questionnaire on consumer opinions.

Conclusions: The results indicate that the peer group plays a more important role in influencing expenditures than the family unit. Thus, it is concluded that adolescent attitudes are much less related to social class than to peer-group membership. Other noteworthy conclusions relate to the impatience, brand consciousness, and loyalty of teen-age consumers; their mature and conservative approach to the demands of adult consumer responsibility; their mature awareness of the limitations and pitfalls of credit buying; the lack of class differences in regard to attitudes toward saving; the general think-alike quality of the group.

Coleman, James S.
*The Adolescent Society: The Social Life of the Teenager
   and Its Impact on Education*
New York: The Free Press of Glencoe, 1961

Purpose: An inquiry into the social atmosphere surrounding adolescents and an attempt to learn what factors in school and community generate the different types of adolescent climate.

Sample: 8971 students from ten Illinois high schools of varying sizes, in differing types of communities.

Method: Two questionnaires were administered. Informal interviews were given a number of students in each school and information on all students was obtained from school records. Questionnaires were also distributed to teachers and mailed to parents.

Conclusions: Though still oriented toward their parents, adolescents depend strongly on their peers for approval. The author sees adolescent society as a subculture with a language of its own, its own special symbols and value systems. It affects its members through the rewards and punishments it dispenses. These include popularity, respect, acceptance into a crowd, praise, awe, support, and aid and, conversely, isolation, ridicule, exclusion, disdain, discouragement, disrespect. Rather than attempt to change the patterns of adolescent behavior the author suggests, "take the adolescent society as given and then *use* it to further the ends of adolescent education."

Davis, Allison, and Robert Hess
*Relationships between Achievement in High School, College and
   Occupation: A Follow-Up Study*
Washington, D.C.: U.S. Office of Education, Cooperative Research Project
   No. 542, 1963

Purpose: To determine whether the relative experience and success of teenagers in either the academic or social areas during high school hold a systematic relationship to subsequent performance as young adults.

Sample: Of 351 metropolitan high school seniors studied in 1952, fifty-one males and sixty-nine females were selected who fell into one of four achievement categories, based on dichotomies of achievement in high school and at young adult levels.

Method: From the high school study, data were available for measures of academic talent and achievement, social facility and participation, and attitudes and other internal states. In the follow-up study, data were collected for measures of work achievement and social prestige, measures of social participation and involvement in the community, and measures of psychosocial responses and adaptation to young adulthood.

Conclusions:

1. Relationship of achievement group to adolescent behavior. The absolute level of high school grades was the best indicator of later success, particularly for males. Social participation showed slight association with both high school performance and success in young adulthood. High aspirations on the part of students and parents were related to success in high school, but were not related to future success.

2. Relationship of achievement groups to young adult performance. Those who achieved relatively well as young adults more frequently held memberships in formal organizations. There was no significant relationship between the achievement groupings and personality measures. High school achievers were rated relatively higher, as adults, on willingness to assume responsibility, as did young adult achievers.

3. "The trend that is most clearly supported by our data is that academic achievement in high school is significantly associated with work-related variables in young adulthood. This pattern applies both to occupational level and the tendency to be socially mobile, i.e., to attain a higher social status than one's father. . . . Thus, high school grades, which are generally not highly valued by males, are apparently very important for later successes but are not so indicative of success for girls, who value grades and exert more effort than boys to achieve in the classroom." [pp. vii–10]

Davis, Ethelyn
"Careers as Concerns of Blue-Collar Girls," in
    Arthur B. Shostak and William Gomberg, eds.
    Blue-Collar World
Englewood Cliffs, N.J.: Prentice-Hall, Inc., 1964, pp. 154–164

Purpose: To explore the goals, ambitions, and interests of the adolescent daughter of the blue-collar worker in relation to her probable work experience in later life.

Sample: 2549 girls, 925 of whom were daughters of blue-collar workers, in seventh through twelfth grades in seventy communities in Texas and near-by states.

Method: Questionnaire completed during December 1961 and early 1962.

Conclusions: A higher proportion of blue-collar girls than girls whose fathers were in occupations other than blue-collar believe most women would like a job in addition to a home and children. Proportionately, more blue-collar girls wish to be secretaries and fewer of them express an interest in teaching or other professions. Only one quarter of the blue-collar girls really expect to obtain the jobs they prefer. While 44 percent of them would like to go to college, almost twice as many (86 percent) of the daughters of professionals and managers would like to do so. A little more than one quarter of the blue-collar girls work after school or on Saturday, about the same proportion as the daughters of other fathers.

Dyer, William
"Parental Influence on the Job Attitude of Children from Two Occupational Strata"
Sociology and Social Research: 42 (January/February 1957), 203–206

Purpose: To relate children's attitudes toward jobs to father's occupational status, hypothesizing that the children of white-collar workers will have a more favorable attitude toward the father's occupation than will the children of blue-collar workers.

Sample: 97 blue-collar and lower white-collar families in Ames, Iowa, randomly selected from the city directory.

Method: Questionnaire administered individually to each member of the family pertaining to the father's job.

Conclusions: The results support the hypothesis postulated. Although neither group wished the child to follow in the father's footsteps, the children were aware of prestige factors and considered blue-collar jobs less prestigeful.

Empey, Lamar
"Social Class and Occupational Aspirations: A Comparison of Absolute and
    Relative Measurement"
American Sociological Review: 21 (December 1956), 703–709

Purpose: To study the absolute and relative occupational status aspirations of lower,- middle,- and upper-class youth, and to relate these aspirational levels to preferred and anticipated occupations.

Sample: Probability sample of one tenth of all male seniors in public high schools in the state of Washington during the spring semester of 1954.

Method: Occupation measured by a combination of Hatt-North and Smith occupational prestige scales.

Conclusions: The data indicate that upper- and middle-class students tend to have higher absolute aspirations than lower-class students. However, lower-class students prefer or anticipate attainment at a higher level than their fathers, thus supporting the view of relative aspiration level.

Galler, Enid Harris
"Influence of Social Class on Children's Choices of
    Occupations"
Elementary School Journal: 51 (April 1951), 439–445

Purpose: To determine to what extent social-class culture influences a child's choice of occupation and the reasons behind this choice.

Sample: 207 boys and girls of lower-class background, students at a lower-class school, and 285 boys and girls of upper-middle- and middle-class background, students at the University of Chicago laboratory school. The age range was nine through fifteen.

Method: Class was determined in terms of the school of attendance and occupation of father. Data was obtained via essay responses to a question relating to future job aspirations and ideas concerning qualities desired in an occupation.

Conclusions: The results indicated that social class does influence children's choice of occupations and the reasons for the choices. Major differences between groups were in terms of middle-class children's choice of occupation on the basis of intrinsic value of the job and altruistic motives, and lower-class children's emphasis on extrinsic factors. More middle- and upper-middle-class children chose their father's occupation as a vocational goal.

Gist, Noel P., and William S. Bennett, Jr.
"Aspirations of Negro and White Students"
Social Forces: 42 (October 1963), 40–48

See Appendix, Chapter Two.

Goetz, Wilma Marie
"Occupational Aspirations of the Male Students in a Selected High
    School"
American Catholic Sociological Review: 4 (Winter 1962), 338–349

Purpose: To investigate the occupational aspirations and actual occupational expectations of high school boys with high and low socioeconomic background in relation to their attitudes toward monetary success as a life goal and toward work as a value, their acceptance of illegitimate means, and their perceptions of the opportunities accessible in the social structure for the realization of their goal.

Sample: 141 students, the entire male enrollment of a coeducational parochial high school.

Method: Administration of a questionnaire.

Conclusions:

1. Occupational aspirations varied positively with social status.
2. The value put on work varied positively with social status. Low-status

students desire money as much as do those with high status, but perceive less opportunity to gain it. There is no difference, based on status, in willingness to accept illegitimate means.

3. The author suggested that the low acceptance of illegitimate means may have been a function of the value system of the parochial school.

Goodman, Paul
Growing Up Absurd: Problems of Youth in the Organized System
New York: Random House, Inc., 1956

Purpose: To describe the problems facing the lower-class adolescent in his attempts to find a meaningful existence in a world that tends to deny his value.

Method: The sources of data are not specified although a good deal of it is based on the author's observations and insights. This is not in any way a rigorous analysis and the conclusions must be evaluated in this light.

Conclusions: Goodman's major point is that the underprivileged and deprived adolescent develops a syndrome of conceit and hostility as a reaction to these conditions. Disaffected from ordinary society, he finds meaning in life by breaking its laws. The essential property of juvenile delinquency is personality and behavior of a kind that guarantees getting caught, punished, and tabulated. For children and adolescents, it is essential to have a coherent, fairly simple and viable society to grow up into; otherwise they are confused and some are squeezed out. Our present culture does not offer the traditions and standards that provide the necessary developmental experiences for youth.

Haire, Mason, and Florence Morrison
"School Children's Perception of Labor and Management"
Journal of Social Psychology: 46 (November 1957), 179–197

Purpose: To study the way in which schoolchildren see problems of labor-management relations utilizing a phenomenological approach.

Sample: 755 subjects ranging in age from twelve to sixteen, in grades seven to eleven, all attending schools in the San Francisco area of California. The groups were divided equally between low- and high-income students.

Method: The subjects were given four short semiprojective tests pertaining to attitudes toward labor and management and a twenty-three-item socioeconomic questionnaire.

Conclusions: The findings are considered in terms of the children's perception of labor and management relations as well as the way in which these attitudes originate. In the first case, even at the youngest ages children of lower social-class background were more prolabor, showed undifferentiated approval of workers, agreed on issues with them, and identified with them. Prolabor sentiment increases with age in both groups but at a faster rate for lower-class children. In the second case, children of lower social-class background tended to show less differentiation in perception of labor-management relations and had different ways of organizing perceptions.

Hall, Oswald, and Bruce McFarlane
Transition from School to Work
Ottawa, Canada: Department of Labour, The Interdepartmental
    Skilled Manpower Training Reseach Committee
    Report No. 10, December 1962

The study was undertaken in 1961 in a typical Ontario community to trace the experiences of young people as they moved from the school system into the labor force. Within the community, an effort was made to find all those who had been born in 1940 and who attended the community's schools. The sample studied included 274 girls and 253 boys of 816 who constituted the original universe. Information was obtained from 408 by means of personal interviews, and 119 through questionnaires, as well as from school and employment records.

The authors found that intelligence was somewhat correlated with survival in school, but a significant minority of bright students dropped out of and poor students completed high school. Children from white-collar homes were more than twice as likely to complete senior matriculation as those from manual workers homes. Social class may be as important in determining who goes to college as intelligence: of the top 10 percent entering high school, only one in five went on to higher education. For those who took a vocational orientation in high school, or who left high school without completing it, there appeared to be far more training facilities for girls than for boys, all of which facilitated the entry of young girls into white-collar jobs at a relatively early age.

> The specific guidance services of the schools have left only a vague imprint on the vast majority of students passing through the high schools. . . . By and large, the formal facilities for bridging the transition from school to work are ignored; students use their own initiative and/or flounder in moving from school to work. [p. 77]

Haller, Archibald O., and C. E. Butterworth
"Peer Influences on Levels of Occupational and Educational
    Aspiration"
Social Forces: 38 (May 1960), 289–295

See Appendix, Chapter Two.

Havighurst, Robert J., Paul H. Bowman, Gordon P. Liddle,
    Charles V. Matthews, and James V. Pierce
Growing Up in River City
New York: John Wiley & Sons, Inc., 1962

The aim of this study is to determine the chief formative influences involved in the growing-up process. The investigators sought to relate major institutions—family, school, church, and youth-serving organizations—to the main tasks of growing up; namely, going to school, being graduated or dropping out, getting jobs, going to college, and getting married.

River City is a Midwestern community of 45,000. The sample studied consisted of 400 students, the entire sixth grade at the time the study began, in 1951. They were followed until most of them were twenty years old. In addition to the administration of tests of intelligence and personal and social adjustment, the members of the sample were observed in their normal routines.

The study explores the question of the conditions under which talent, defined as promise of superior performance, is actually developed. The authors note a strong tendency for students from higher-status families to appear on the talent list (talent being conceived of as covering three areas: intellectual, leadership, and artistic) more frequently than those of lower-status families.

Aggressiveness and personal maladjustment were found to be closely related to dropping out of school and to underachievement in school, as well as to maladjustment in work, marriage, and college. There was some tendency for maladjustment to be related to lower IQ and lower status. Personal and social adjustment was positively related to church and organizational participation and, as might be expected, lower-class youth are not active in these organizations.

College, marriage, and work are conceived of as three possible routes to adulthood. Each of these routes has special difficulties for working-class youth. Those with ability are less likely to have the appropriate expectations from peers and family and/or achievement motivation. Marriage has its shortcomings because those who marry early are likely to be characterized by lower intelligence, poor social adjustment, little contact with church, and withdrawal from school. Similarly, success on the job seems to be related to success in school, and the lower one goes in class rank, the less likely one is that jobs will pay adequately and hold promise for future upward mobility.

Heath, Robert W.
What Does Youth Want from Education and Jobs
Purdue Opinion Panel Poll Report: No. 48, 1958

Purpose: To determine the vocational and educational aspirations, expected financial needs, projected earnings, and attitudes toward jobs of high school students from various sectors of society.

Sample: 2000 subjects selected from a total sample of 10,000 high school students, grades ten, eleven, and twelve.

Method: A questionnaire covering areas mentioned above as well as attitudes toward future wars, economic conditions, and control of money.

Conclusions: The results can be summarized by saying that socioeconomic class and mother's education were most discriminating in measuring the plans of students. Results showed that the lower income groups have significantly lower aspirations than the higher group. Most of the low income group expect to remain in this group after high school. They expect to earn less per week than do their fellow students, have adjusted their economic standards accordingly, and believe they can support a family on less. They think a smaller amount of savings is necessary before marriage. These students are less optimistic about the future of the country. They foresee a greater likelihood of wars and depression than those whose parents have higher incomes and are better educated.

Himes, Joseph S.
"Some Work-Related Cultural Deprivations of Lower-Class
   Negro Youth"
Journal of Marriage and The Family: 26 (November 1964),
   447–449

Purpose: To explore how race and class affect the socialization to work of lower-class Negro youth.

Conclusions: "Exclusion of lower-class Negroes from important sectors of the work force . . . eventuates in a series of work-related cultural deprivations." These include (1) socialization to irrelevant job models, that is, models that are not in the mainstream of the industrial economy; (2) exclusion from the prevailing work ethos—so many Negroes are in dead-end type jobs that young people cannot see the link between effort and advancement; the work they do, further, has no intrinsic goodness or importance; and (3) alienation from the culture of the modern factory and office: lower-class Negro youth cannot become familiar, through peers, parents, or friends, with the tools, jargon, and customs associated with regular factory and office jobs.

Holloway, Robert G., and Joel V. Berreman
"The Educational and Occupational Aspirations and Plans of
   Negro and White Male Elementary School Students"
Pacific Sociological Review: 2 (Fall 1959), 56–60

See Appendix, Chapter Two.

Kahl, Joseph
"Educational and Occupational Aspirations of Common Man's Boys"
Harvard Educational Review: 23 (Summer 1953), 186–203

See Appendix, Chapter One.

Krippner, Stanley
"Junior High School Students' Vocational Preference and
   Their Parents' Occupational Levels"
Personnel and Guidance Journal: 41 (March 1963), 590–595

Purpose: To explore the relation between father's occupational level and his son's career choice, and mother's occupational level and her daughter's career choice.

Sample: 351 seventh- and eighth-grade pupils (189 boys and 162 girls) in an upper-middle-class Chicago suburban community.

Method: During 1960 and 1961, a vocational interest questionnaire was administered, which included questions about parents' occupation and the occupational preference of the respondent. All vocations selected were categorized by means of Roe's occupational classification scale. No fathers were found in the lowest category.

Conclusions: There was a significant relationship between the occupational level of children's preference and the suggestions of parents of either sex. Father's suggestions for sons compared significantly with their own vocation, but that of father for daughter or of mother for son or daughter did not. At all occupational levels, fathers appeared to suggest careers for their sons that would raise them slightly above their own job level.

Liversidge, William
"Life Chances"
The Sociological Review: 10 (March 1962), 17–34

Purpose: To compare occupational aspirations and expectations of children from different social origins in British grammar and modern schools.

Sample: 616 respondents from two grammar schools, three modern schools, and four primary schools that feed into these schools; 232 categorized as upper class and 384 as lower class.

Method: Administration of a questionnaire.

Conclusions: Grammar school boys had higher aspirations and expectations than modern school boys, and grammar school girls had higher expectations than modern school girls. Within the modern schools, there was no difference in aspirations based on social origins. There was, however, a significant difference in expectations for both boys and girls, with higher-status youth expecting higher-status positions. Girls within the modern school tended to have higher expectations than boys, but this may have been a consequence of their orientation to white-collar office work. The relatively higher aspirations and expectations of lower-class boys and girls in grammar schools and the relatively lower aspirations and expectations of higher status boys in modern schools is taken as evidence of the impact of school climate.

Lott, Albert J., and Bernice E. Lott
Negro and White Youth: A Psychological Study in a Border-State Community
New York: Holt, Rinehart and Winston, Inc., 1963

See Appendix, Chapter Two.

Miller, S. M.
"The Outlook of Working Class Youth," in
    Arthur B. Shostak and William Gomberg, eds.
    Blue-Collar World
Englewod Cliffs, N.J.: Prentice-Hall, Inc., 1964, pp. 122–133

Purpose: This paper presents another view of the advantages of dropping out of school and its relationship to the general question of job opportunities and outlook for working-class youth.

Method: The sources of data and sample are not specified although a good deal of the material appears to derive from secondary sources. The author also uses unsystematic observations of the behavior, attitudes, and problems of working-class youth in the Syracuse, New York, area.

Conclusions: A major point of the paper is that dislike of school does not adequately explain the 30 percent drop-out ratio of working-class youth, since many do not leave school until their senior year and most do not express an antipathy towards school. An alternative line of explanation is that many prospective drop outs never really expect to graduate and have a job level in mind that does not require more education. This assumption appears to be realistic on the basis of material that indicates that finishing high school does not pay off to the extent that is assumed for the working-class boy, particularly for the Negro youth. The author concludes that the job world for the young and unmarried working-class youth is a shadowy phenomenon, and he is more concerned with his peer activities until marriage makes earning a living a more meaningful part of his life. With the continuing need for semiskilled and manual workers it may be unrealistic to underrate the value of these occupations and give the school dropout a complete sense of worthlessness in the occupational world.

Miller, S. M., and Frank Riessman
"The Working Class Subculture: A New View"
Social Problems: 9 (Summer 1961), 86–97

Purpose: To present a more realistic picture of workers, stressing the cognitive and structural aspects of working-class life.

Method: The sources of data are not specified.

Conclusions: The analysis is aimed at developing themes in working-class life. Thus the author is involved in interpreting the meanings of findings rather than reporting new findings. A picture of the essential characteristics of the stable American worker is presented, emphasizing his traditional religious and patriarchal orientation, his liking for discipline, his anti-intellectualism, his family centeredness, and his sense of estrangement from some of the institutions such as the school and the political system.

In discussing themes in working-class life, the author discusses the workers' striving for security. Chief among the external factors promoting instability are unemployment and lay off. Chief among the internal factors is family discord. Another theme is that of intensity. It is found in the areas in which workers have belief and emotional involvement. The person-centered theme is also threaded through working-class life. This involves an emphasis on personal qualities in relationships. Two final themes are the pragmatic orientation of workers and the appreciation of excitement. The importance of understanding these underlying themes is in the development of the stable working-class style among lower-class and working-class youth as a goal of educational and other socializing and remedial forces rather than instilling the middle-class value structure.

Morland, J. Kenneth
"Kent Revisited: Blue-Collar Aspirations and Achievements," in
    Arthur B. Shostak and William Gomberg, eds.
    Blue-Collar World
Englewood Cliffs, N.J.: Prentice-Hall, Inc., 1964, pp. 134–143

Purpose: To find out what happened to an "enclave" of mill families in the ten years since the original study.

Sample: Over 100 "Kentians," including most of the heads of ninety-six mill families studied in detail in 1948, were chosen at random to represent the 290 families in the village sections.

Method: Interviews, and a questionnaire on educational and occupational aspirations administered to pupils in junior and senior high schools.

Conclusions: Of the 132 children who either dropped out of school or graduated during the ten-year period, 51.5 percent had become blue-collar textile workers, though in 1948 only 3.5 percent of the schoolchildren said they wanted to become millworkers. Education beyond high school was necessary for mill children to break into white-collar jobs. There was no significant difference in the levels of occupational aspiration between mill and town boys, although a higher proportion of town children (75.0 percent) expected to enter the occupation of their choice than of mill children (63.3 percent).

> . . . the great majority of mill children expressed belief that getting ahead in Kent was a matter of individual desire and effort. They demonstrated through their own aspirations that they shared the American dream of moving upward. . . . But in view of the discrepancy between the aspirations of the mill children in 1948 and their outcome ten years later, we must assume that *there is little relation between aspiration and fulfillment among children of the enclave.* [p. 142]

Sewell, William H., Archie O. Haller, and Murray A. Strauss
"Social Status and Educational and Occupational Aspiration"
American Sociological Review: 22 (February 1957), 67–73

See Appendix, Chapter Two.

Simpson, Richard L.
"Parental Influence, Anticipatory Socialization, and
   Social Mobility"
American Sociological Review: 27 (August 1962), 517–522

Purpose: To explore the effects on career aspirations of parental and peer-group influences, considered separately, and to see whether the relationships found are independent of each other.

Sample: 743 boys out of a total of 917 in the white high school of two Southern cities.

Method: Questionnaires administered in 1960. From information on the occupations of the boys' fathers and the occupations they themselves expected to enter, they were classified into four groups: (1) ambitious middle class, (2) unambitious middle-class, (3) mobile working class, and (4) nonmobile working class.

Conclusions:

> A working-class boy was most likely to aspire to a high-ranking occupation if he had been influenced in this direction by both parents and peers, and least likely to be a high-aspirer if he had been subjected to neither of these influences. Among the middle-class boys, only those low in both influences differed significantly from the rest. . . . Of the two types of influence, that of parents appeared to have the stronger effect. Working-class boys influenced toward upward mobility by either parents or peers tended to have higher aspirations than middle-class boys not influenced toward high aspirations by either parents or peers. [pp. 521–522]

Smelser, William T.
"Adolescent and Adult Occupational Choice as a Function of
   Family Socioeconomic History"
Sociometry: 26 (December 1963), 383–409

Purpose: To study the relationship of family economic and occupational achievement to son's personality structure and occupational choice.

Sample: 93 families each with a son in a longitudinal study.

Method: Families were divided into five groups on the basis of ratings on the Warner scale made in 1928 and 1946: high and low status upwardly mobile, high and low status stationary and downwardly mobile. The sons, born in 1928–1929, were compared on intellectual development, occupational choices, adult occupation, and adult perception of self and parents.

Conclusions: The two upwardly mobile groups of sons and the high stationary group chose higher-status occupations at age fifteen and one-half. Sons from downwardly mobile families ranked highest in their mean IQ at age six, but last at age eighteen. They also ranked lowest in the mean status of their adolescent occupational choices. They

. . . perceived themselves as relatively weak, emphasized affection more than strength in their perceptions of their fathers, and were the only group to perceive the mother as stronger (on the average) than the father. [p. 409]

The influence of mobility on adolescent choice was observed in two comparisons: (1) the mean status of occupational choices of sons from high-status upwardly mobile families and high-status stationary families; and (2) the choices of sons from low-status upwardly mobile and low-status stationary families. The means of the Warner ratings for the former in 1946 were not significantly different, yet sons from high-status upwardly mobile families chose higher-status occupations than did the other group of sons. The means of the 1928 Warner ratings for the latter were not significantly different, yet sons from upwardly mobile low-status families chose higher-status occupations than did sons from low-stationary families.

Smith, Benjamin F.
"Wishes of Negro High School Seniors and Social Class"
Journal of Educational Sociology: 25 (April 1952), 466–475

Purpose: To discover the relationship between written wishes and social-class status of urban Negro high school seniors.
Sample: 265 students in the senior English classes in five high schools in Durham and Charlotte, North Carolina, and Richmond, Virginia, in 1950–1951.
Method: The Washburne Social Adjustment Inventory was administered. Social status was determined by an adaptation of Warner's ISC, based on data obtained directly from the heads of the family of each student.
Conclusions:

The written wishes concerning vocations were positively related with class. There was a larger percentage of upper middle and lower middle seniors aspiring to professional jobs than was true for the two lower classes. The lower classes were indefinite about their vocations. [p. 472]

Sprey, Jetse
"Occupational Choice among New Haven Negro High School Students"
Ph.D. Dissertation, Yale University, 1960

Purpose: To compare occupational choice patterns of Negro and white adolescents and to analyze the choices of different groups within the Negro portion of the total sample.
Sample: All ninth-grade pupils in the New Haven public schools in the spring of 1958.
Method: Students filled in a brief questionnaire in school. In addition, all Negro boys in the total sample were interviewed at home.

Conclusions: Significant aspirational and expectational choice differences were found between Negro and white pupils. The educational plans of the pupils in the total sample were related to parental occupational level—the higher the level, the larger the proportion of children enrolled in college-preparatory courses. Negro girls did not differ from white girls in their occupational-choice patterns. Negro boys of Southern background deviated from Negro boys of Northern background as did the latter from white boys. The author sees great significance in the fact that Negro boys showed a markedly different choice pattern from that of Negro girls. He concludes that the discrepancy between the social-prestige positions within the Negro group may tend to increase and lead to difficulty in the areas of mate selection and marital adjustment.

Sprey, Jetse
"Sex Differences in Occupational Choice Patterns among
   Negro Adolescents"
Social Problems: 10 (Summer 1962), 11–23

Purpose: To compare patterns of occupational and educational choice of Negro and white public high school pupils, paying special attention to differences between the sex categories within the Negro group, and to attempt to explain the findings within the framework of the theory of anomie.

Sample: 1154 ninth graders in New Haven, Connecticut, of which 183 were Negro, and 1442 ninth graders in Harrisburg, Pennsylvania, of which 350 were Negro.

Method: A questionnaire covering occupational choice, distinguishing between aspirations and expectations; curriculum choice as an indication of actual preparation for the future; mobility aspirations and expectations measured relative to the father's occupational position.

Conclusions: Negro boys have aspirational levels significantly below those of white pupils and Negro girls. Further, Negro boys show a higher rate of indecision than do students in any other category. While boys have lower expectations than girls, the difference between Negro boys and girls is far greater than that between white boys and girls. Finally, Negro boys show a significantly lower enrollment in the college-preparatory curriculum than white pupils and Negro girls. Sprey considers that the findings concerning the Negro males reflects a "retreatist" adjustment to the social structure.

Stefflre, Buford
"What Do High School Students Really Want from a Job?"
The School Counselor: 4 (November 1956), 16–18

Purpose: To determine what students from rural and metropolitan areas are looking for in jobs.

Sample: 145 students of the junior class of a high school in a town of 8500 compared with 783 students of the classes in a metropolitan area.

Method: The study utilizes the center's check-list of job values that the individual feels is most important to him.

Conclusions: The results indicate that both male and female adolescents differ from the adult population in what they are looking for in jobs. Boys are more oriented toward jobs that offer an interesting experience, profit, and fame while girls are also interested in an interesting experience as well as in social service. Adults were mainly concerned with independence in jobs. The only statistically significant difference between the rural and urban groups were the rural girls' greater interest in social service.

Stephenson, Richard
"Mobility Orientation and Stratification of 1,000 Ninth Graders"
American Sociological Review: 22 (April 1957), 204–212

Purpose: To determine if students distinguish between plans and aspirations, and to study the extent to which students' stratification position affects their plans and aspirations.

Sample: 1000 ninth graders in four semi-industrial, medium-sized communities in New Jersey.

Method: A questionnaire consisting of items related to occupational plans and aspirations, educational plans, and father's occupation. The Edwards scale of occupational categories was used as the basis for determining social class as well as categorizing occupational plans and aspirations.

Conclusions: The data indicate that students distinguish plans from aspirations and that social position affects aspirations and plans. Although there is a descending level of aspirations and plans in terms of descending social status, the students' aspirations for professional and managerial occupations never fall below 54 percent in any group, while their plans for these occupations fall to 18 percent in the lower-class group. Both curricular choices and educational plans conform to occupational plans.

Stewart, Lawrence H.
"Relationship of Socio-Economic Status to Children's
    Occupational Attitudes and Interests"
Journal of Genetic Psychology: 59 (September 1959), 111–136

Purpose: To investigate the relationship between certain aspects of socio-economic status and children's attitudes toward occupations, and the relationship between these occupational attitudes and certain types of children's behavior.

Sample: 243 fifth grade boys from five elementary schools in one school district near San Francisco, and from one school affiliated with the University of California at Berkeley. Nonwhites and recent immigrants were excluded.

Method: In the spring of 1947, the Dreese-Mooney Interest Inventory was administered verbally. Then a fifty-minute interview was held with each student, during which the student was asked to associate various symbols of socioeconomic status with a set of nine pictures showing men working at various occupations. A Guess-Who test was then given twice to each boy who was asked to respond (1) with reference to the occupational pictures, and (2) with reference to his peers.

Conclusions: The boys were aware of social class symbols but their perceptions were not biased significantly by their own status. Children from various classes held similar ideas of children's social class behavior. The reputation of peers was relatively independent of the socioeconomic status of the raters and of the persons being rated. The occupational level interest scores were independent of perceptions of class symbols and of ideas about social-class behavior.

Stinchcombe, Arthur L.
Rebellion in a High School
Chicago: Quadrangle Books, 1964

See Appendix, Chapter Two.

Uzell, O.
"Occupational Aspirations of Negro Male High School Students"
Sociology and Social Research: 45 (January 1961), 202–204

Purpose: To investigate the occupational aspirations of a selected sample of urban senior high schools in eastern North Carolina as they relate to social background characteristics.

Sample: A proportionate random sample of 301 respondents in fourteen schools.

Method: Questionnaires and interviews.

Conclusions:

1. There was a significant relationship between level of aspiration and parents' educational status, but not between level of aspiration and parents' occupations.
2. There was a significant relationship between level of aspiration and success in school.
3. Role models were important in the choice of occupations.
4. Lack of money and inadequate academic performance were mentioned most often as difficulties the respondents expected to encounter in entering preferred occupations.

Youmans, E. Grant
"Occupational Expectations of Twelfth Grade Michigan Boys"
Journal of Experimental Education: 24 (June 1956), 259–271

Purpose: To test the hypothesis "Position in the social structure, that is, social origin, is more important in formulating the occupational expectations of youth than are such factors as the home, the school, work experience and type of community."

Sample: A representative sample of 6789 tenth- and twelfth-grade youths from fifty-six public and private high schools in Michigan, from which a sub-sample of 1279 was used for this study.

Method: A self-administered questionnaire of eighty items.

Conclusions: There is a "substantial and statistically significant" relationship between social stratification and occupational expectation of boys. Among factors measuring influence of home situation, there was no significant relationship between occupational expectations and amount of work done at home, amount of spending money, or whether an allowance was received. There was a significant positive relationship between the size of the family and the father's education and expectations. In regard to school influence, those who entered academic curriculum had higher expectations than those who entered vocational curriculum, with class controlled. The influence of work experience was the less the work experience, the higher the occupational expectations. Boys with only white-collar work experience had slightly higher occupational expectations than boys with only manual experience, with class controlled.

While the author argues that his findings support the significance of social stratification, for many of the measures it could well be argued that the results demonstrate that those with higher aspirations behave differently—they engage in white-collar work and select academic curricula, for example.

Young, Marechal, and Merl Ellison
"Some Sociological Aspects of Vocational Guidance for Negro Children"
Journal of Negro Education: 15 (Winter 1946), 21–30

Purpose: To study the discrepancy between the vocational aspirations of Negro children and the opportunities realistically available to them.

Sample: 202 Negro girls were studied via questionnaire; 100 girls were selected from this sample for more intensive study.

Method: All subjects were given a questionnaire concerned with information related to interests, vocational choices, expectations, and influences contributing to choices. For the more intensive study group, cumulative records were analyzed and home visits and community study were conducted.

Conclusions: The data indicate that while 75 percent of the children expressed interest in professional and clerical choices, only 55 percent indicated that first choices would be achieved. Parental background played a role in determining attitudes toward high school education with those from the South viewing high school from a more glorified perspective. Home atmosphere also was a determinant in the kinds of educational planning engaged in, with the small percentage of stable families being involved in realistic educational planning. College was considered an objective by 50 percent of the students and parents with little thought given to the relationship of higher education to specific training requirements for a particular occupation. Most students and parents knew little or nothing about trade school, and those who did consider it saw it as primarily a supplement to high school or academic education.

Annotated References for Chapter Four

Blum, Alan F.
"Social Structure, Social Class, and Participation in Primary Relationships," in
  Arthur B. Shostak and William Gomberg, eds.
  Blue-Collar World
Englewood Cliffs, N.J.: Prentice-Hall, Inc., 1964, pp. 195–207

Purpose: (1) To review relevant contemporary research on social-class differences in primary relationships; (2) to do this from the perspective of a coherent and systematic theoretical framework; and (3) to facilitate an examination of some sociological conceptions concerning the involvement of the working classes in primary relationships.

Conclusions: It is the author's contention that social-structural determinants are the key in explaining the nature of primary relationships in the working class. The working-class male is subjected to greater social restraints than the middle-class male by the social network within which he is located, and this in turn mitigates against involvement in other groups and voluntary associations. For both marriage partners, commitment to a close-knit social network tends to free them from mutual dependence and to create greater distance between them. The author cites evidence contrary to the usual finding concerning familism in the lower class, arguing that "although primordial attachments delineate the boundaries of the relationship and implicitly define the field of eligibles, personal criteria ultimately set the standards for the inclusion of new members."

Bott, Elizabeth
Family and Social Network
London: Tavistock Publications Ltd., 1957

Purpose: To develop hypotheses concerning psychological and sociological dimensions of conjugal relations by intensive study of a small number of families.

Sample: Twenty families from "various districts" of London, with children under ten years of age. Partners had been married from four to eleven years. Husbands' incomes ranged from 330 to 1800 pounds a year.

Method: An average of thirteen two-hour-plus interviews per family (range: eight to nineteen) conducted by the author (a social anthropologist) and a social psychologist.

Conclusions: There are many degrees of variation between the extremes of considerable differentiation and segregation of husband and wife roles, and considerable fusion. One set of factors affecting such variations is the pattern of relationships maintained by each with external networks of persons. It is only the beginning of an analysis to observe that differences in conjugal segregation may be attributed to class differences; what is needed is to discover what factors in social class operate to produce the differences. The suggestion of this study is that families with close-knit extrafamilial networks are likely to be of the working class, but not all working-class families have close-knit networks.

Bradburn, Norman M.
In Pursuit of Happiness
Chicago: National Opinion Research Center, 1963

Purpose: To explore the assumption that there is a dimension called, variously, mental health, subjective adjustment, happiness, or psychological well-being; and that individuals can be described as being relatively high or low on such a dimension.

Sample: Samples were drawn in each of four Illinois communities which differed along a dimension of economic prosperity: two were chronically depressed, one was improving from chronic depression, and one was experiencing a boom. Sample consisted of 393 males, age twenty-five to forty-nine, plus 1613 others, either the head of the household or a relative.

Method: Interviews were conducted with the males age twenty-five to forty-nine; self-administered short forms were left with the head of the household and the nearest relative of the opposite sex, or, where the head was interviewed, with his wife and one other adult relative. Two status levels were utilized: (1) at least two of the following attributes—family income of 5000 dollars or more, high school graduate or more, and white-collar occupation; (2) none or only one of these.

Conclusions: There is a strong positive correlation between happiness (as measured by response to the question "Taking all things together, how would you say things are these days—would you say you are very happy, pretty happy, or not too happy?") and both education and income. At every level of education, making more money is associated with being happier, but having more education is not always related to being happier. Among the relatively wealthy, the well-educated most often say they are "not too happy."

There is a negative relationship between age and happiness. While this appears to be strongest among lower-status males, poorly educated higher-income people show a positive relationship between age and happiness.

Marital unhappiness is reported more frequently among men of lower status, but marital tension is more frequently reported by men of higher status. An important characteristic of higher status men seems to be an increased emotional sensitivity and psychological responsiveness to their environment. At the same time, they have more compensatory positive feelings to balance any increase in negative feelings. At every level of marital tension, lower-status men report more dissatisfaction with their marriage.

Lower-status and older men are more likely to worry about "uncontrollable" areas such as growing old, their health, or the atomic bomb. Higher-status men and younger men are more likely to worry about "controllable" areas of life.

Caro, Francis G.
Paths toward Adulthood: A Study of Post-High School Activities
Kansas City, Mo.: Department of Social Problems and Education,
   Community Studies, Inc., 1965

See Appendix, Chapter Three.

Cohen, Albert K., and Harold M. Hodges, Jr.
"Characteristics of the Lower-Blue-Collar-Class"
Social Problems: 10 (Spring 1963), 303–334

Purpose: In part, to contribute to a descriptive knowledge of the lower-lower class, but primarily to suggest theory to account for some of the characteristics of that class. The concern was only with those findings that showed the lower-blue-collar stratum to be significantly different from all others.

Sample: Approximately 2600 male heads of families residing in three tiers of California counties, divided into subsamples resident in contiguous subareas.

Method: Six sets of self-administered questionnaires, three open-ended questionnaires, and one Rorschach schedule were used. The questionnaires were designed to elicit information relating to some thirty basic variables such as infant training and child rearing, religious values, self-concepts, status concern, career orientations, familistic loyalties, sex norms, leisure-time activities, and so on. The project involved six waves of interviewing, and each respondent filled out one of the nine schedules.

Conclusions: Findings are organized around the following themes:

1. Family and kinship. The lower blue collar (lower-lower class, LL) interact much more with relatives who typically live nearby. This may represent a tenacity of individual (husband and wife) kinship systems in contrast to the middle-class pattern, which may represent "reorganization of the networks of both spouses in the interest of the solidarity and primacy of the conjugal unit." [p. 309]
2. Neighboring. "The responses . . . suggest a class of people who, even with neighbors, are slow to establish even superficial relationships, as measured by getting through their doors, but who, insofar as they sustain a social life with anybody other than kin, are heavily dependent upon neighbors." [p. 315]
3. Participation in voluntary associations. The LL respondent participated least in voluntary associations.
4. Preference for the familiar. "One of the clearest outcomes of this study is an image of the LL as one who is reluctant to meet new people and new situations, to form new social relationships, and above all to initiate actions with strangers." [p. 316]
4. Anti-intellectuality. LL respondents expressed the least admiration for intellectuals; most disliked symphonic, ballet, and operatic music; and reacted most negatively to TV programs they defined as high brow.

"It would seem natural that people should be distrustful of what they do not understand, disdainful of skills they do not possess, and threatened by modes of reasoning and interaction in which they cannot participate creditably. . . . people tend to disvalue standards of evaluation which result in the disparagement of the self." [p. 318]

5. Authoritarianism. LL subjects agreed most strongly with Adorno F-Scale items.
6. Intolerance. Lower-middle stratum was least forgiving of violations of conventional morality—heterosexual misconduct, drunkenness, and swearing. The LL "was most harsh in condemnation of other sorts of deviants: the atheist, the homosexual, the 'un-American,' the radical, the artist-intellectual. But it was above all toward the ethnic minority that he directed his animosity." [p. 321]
7. Pessimism-insecurity. In the view of the LL, nothing is certain; in all probability, however, things will turn out badly as they have in the past.
8. Misanthropy. LL's, more than the members of any other stratum, are cynical and distrustful, as reflected in the Rosenberg Misanthropy scale.
9. Extrapunitiveness. Findings with regard to "pessimism" and "misanthropy" may be viewed from the perspective of extrapunitiveness— people high on extrapunitive characteristics usually handle their aggression by directing it outwards.
10. Patriarchy. LL men agree that men should make the important decisions in the family, but also report that LL women take the major share of responsibility for budgeting, bill paying, and child care, to a greater extent than in other classes. It may be that the LL male feels he should be the boss in a general and not in a particular sense.
11. Toughness. LL subjects were more "tough-minded" on selected items from Eysenck's T-Scale. "Much of the 'toughness' of the LL and his insistence on autonomy is undoubtedly 'tough talk' that is very different from his performance and makes it possible for him to enjoy some of the gratifications of more than one pattern of adaptation to authority." [p. 330]
12. Consumption patterns. The LL's show a higher investment in cars and basic appliances than do upper-blue-collar respondents. Authors propose several alternative explanations for this phenomenon.

Freedman, Ronald, Pascal K. Whelpton, and Arthur A. Campbell
Family Planning, Sterility, and Population Growth
New York: McGraw-Hill, Inc., 1959

Purpose: To ascertain the beliefs, attitudes, expectations, and practices of young married women with respect to births and miscarriages, sterility, methods of avoiding pregnancy, and number of children.

Sample: A national area-probability sample of 2713 white married women between eighteen and thirty-nine years of age, living with husbands or temporarily separated by armed services. By education, the percentage composition of the sample was as follows: college, 15 percent; high school, four years, 44 percent; high school, one to three years, 25 percent; grade school, 16 percent.

Method: From one- to three-hour interviews by 150 women on the national field staff of the Survey Research Center of the University of Michigan.

Conclusions: Elaborate breakdowns by social and economic characteristics are presented in the 500-page publication, most of them not specifically related to lower-class life.

Freedman, Ronald, Pascal K. Whelpton, and John W. Smit
"Socio-Economic Factors in Religious Differentials in Fertility"
American Sociological Review: 26 (August 1961), 608–614

Purpose: To determine whether the fertility complex for Protestants and Catholics is different from that of Jews when they have similar social and economic characteristics, or whether there is a residual difference associated with religion even when these social and economic characteristics are taken into account.

Sample: 66 Jewish couples from a national probability sample were matched with equal numbers of Catholic and Protestant couples on the following variables: occupation of husband; education of wife; income of husband; duration of marriage; metropolitan character of present residence, and farm background.

Method: Comparison of the three groups of matched couples against results for all couples, from data of national survey. Design and major findings of the basic study are reported in Freeman, Whelpton, and Campbell; see preceding entry.

Conclusions:

> Comparisons between the matched groups can be summarized as indicating that the fertility complex for Protestants is very much like that for Jews when they have similar social and economic characteristics, but this is not true for Catholics. On almost all of the comparisons, the differences between Jews and Catholics is as great or greater when the social and economic characteristics are controlled as when they are not. Apparently, the distinctiveness of Catholic fertility behavior as compared with that of Jews and Protestants cannot be explained by differences in the background characteristics considered here. [p. 610]

Glick, Paul C., and Hugh Carter
"Marriage Patterns and Educational Level"
American Sociological Review: 23 (June 1958), 294–300

Purpose: To examine the relationship between educational level and such marriage patterns as trends in the number of marriages, age at marriage, stability of marriage, resident and nonresident marriages, number of times married, broken marriages, and bachelorhood and spinsterhood.

Sample: Some of the source material comes from decennial censuses, but most comes from a special study of about 9000 persons who married between 1947 and 1954.

Method: Data for the special study were collected in the Census Bureau's Current Population Survey for June 1954.

Conclusions:

1. Upward trend in marriage and in education. The positive relationship found between educational level and increase in marriage, among both whites and nonwhites, implies "that more of the better-education persons were forming families and that family formation was taking place at a younger age than before." [p. 295]
2. Age at marriage. College graduates are the oldest, on the average, at first marriage, and high school drop outs the youngest. Differences between the ages of spouses tends to decrease as the amount of education increases.
3. Education of husband and wife. There is a general tendency for the education of husband and wife to be of a similar level.
4. Stability of marriage. Higher educational attainment is positively related to greater marriage stability.
5. Resident and nonresident marriages. Among couples with nonresident first marriages—both parties were residents of different states from the one in which they were married—the husband tended to be younger and less educated than average.
6. Employment of recently married women. The better-educated women probably continue to work longer after marriage and to postpone childbearing longer than women with less education.
7. Number of times married. There is a strong negative relationship between the frequency of marriage and the amount of education among recently married persons not classified by age.
8. Broken marriages. "Among both men and women with broken marriages who are still in the age range when most remarriages occur, divorced persons have more education and income, on the average, than widowed and separated persons." [p. 298]
9. Bachelor and spinsterhood. "Men who marry and continue to live with their wives have more education and income, on the average, than men with broken marriages or men who remain bachelors. On the other hand, women who remain spinsters have more education and income, on the average, than women who marry." [p. 229]

Men in the middle and upper economic strata tend to have not only a high amount of education but also a high marriage rate, an above-average age at marriage, and a low divorce rate. These facts suggest that circumstances which encourage persons to continue successfully through high school or college and to postpone marriage past teen age also discourages them from dissolving their marriages by divorce. [p. 300]

Havighurst, Robert J., Paul H. Bowman, Gordon P. Liddle,
Charles V. Matthews, and James V. Pierce
Growing Up in River City
New York: John Wiley & Sons, Inc., 1962

See Appendix, Chapter Three.

Hill, Thomas J.
"Dating Patterns and Family Position"
Clearing House: 29 (May 1955), 552-554

Purpose: To explore the effect of socioeconomic position of the adolescent's family on dating patterns and habits within the school.

Sample: 229 pupils in grades nine through twelve in the laboratory school of the University of Florida.

Method: Pupils were rated on the basis of Warner's ISC. Data were collected from school records, home visits, and interviews with teachers and students.

Conclusions:

1. The number of dating partners increases with social-class level, and with grade level until grade eleven, and declines in grade twelve.
2. Lower-class students tend to go outside the school for dating partners.
3. Most of a pupil's dating is done within his social class and within his school class.
4. When a student goes outside his social class to date, he usually goes outside his school class also.

Hollingshead, August B.
Elmtown's Youth: The Impact of Social Classes on Adolescents
New York: John Wiley & Sons, Inc. (Science Editions), 1961

See Appendix, Chapter Two.

Hurvitz, Nathan
"Marital Strain in the Blue-Collar Family," in
    Arthur B. Shostak and William Gomberg, eds.
    Blue-Collar World
Englewood Cliffs, N.J.: Prentice-Hall, Inc., 1964, pp. 92–109

Purpose: To analyze sources of marital strain in the blue-collar family.

Sample: 24 blue-collar couples whose names were supplied by blue-collar couples in counseling, but without known marital problems.

Method: Use of a marital-roles inventory from which is derived an index of strain.

Conclusions: Described as an artificially created model family, this group is neither lower class as measured by objective criteria, nor middle class as seen subjectively. It is in the process of leaving the working class. There is some conflict associated with class self-definition, with the wife leading the way to change, influenced by the mass media, and the husband holding, influenced more by family, fellow workers, and friends. The blue-collar worker feels he is the most exploited, the least secure, and the least significant person in the productive process, and these feelings of self-depreciation and lack of worth are shared by husband and wife.

Rankings of the role sets on the marital-roles inventory suggest the following:

1. Both husband and wife give first rank to his livelihood-earning role. "It is because he maintains his role as a breadwinner on his own job, in his own plant, and, through this, in the economy as a whole that he creates the wherewithal upon which his family functions and from which he gains his authority and status in the family." [p. 98]
2. The husband gives second rank to his companionship role, which is an indication of his dependence on his wife. However, there are few companionship activities in which the spouses participate together.
3. "The wife's companionship role is less important to her, and she gives a higher rank to her roles relating to the children, because they need her more and also they offer more gratification."
4. Differences in values are reflected in the couple's ideas of how to help the children grow.

The husband believes that he helps his children to grow by teaching them how to fight back, by training them for physical stamina and endurance, and by teaching them to get ahead because they fear him. . . . The mother rejects such training. . . . She is more likely to reason with children, to comfort them, to teach them to fulfill her expectations for them because they love her, and to allow gratification of their wishes while the father inhibits them. [p. 100]

5. Managing the family income is a significant source of strain.
6. "The husband ranks his sex-partner role comparatively high, whereas the wife ranks this role comparatively low; and it may therefore be expected that the spouses' interaction about this role may be a source of strain." [p. 102]

7. It is only after his roles as breadwinner, manager of the family income, companion, and sex partner to his wife, that the blue-collar husband ranks his two roles related to the children. To a considerable extent, the children appear to be a consequence of marriage and do not seem to play a significant part in his everyday activities and attitudes. [p. 102]
8. The wife ranks practicing the family religion or philosophy sixth, whereas the husband ranks it last (twelfth).
9. Both the husband and wife rank last the wife's role to help earn the living.

Jaffe, Frederick S.
"Family Planning and Poverty"
Journal of Marriage and The Family: 26 (November 1964), 467–470

Purpose: To explore the factors responsible for the fact that many low-income families, and a disproportionate number of nonwhite families, remain outside the area of effective fertility control.

Method: A review of data from the 1960 Growth of American Families study, and other sources.

Conclusions: There is widespread evidence that low-income families would prefer smaller families, but tend to have larger families with more children than they desire. Likewise, it is known that "lower-class couples do not use contraceptives as regularly as higher-class couples, nor do they employ methods which are as effective." Jaffe believes that the motivational analyses of Rainwater (see *And the Poor Get Children* below) have obscured more important considerations; namely, "the concrete conditions under which impoverished Americans receive their medical care, and the bearing that these conditions and other institutional factors may have on the availability of contraception to these families." He notes for example, that the most effective methods of birth control are usually prescribed by private physicians for their private patients, and low-income families are unlikely to have private physicians.

Komarovsky, Mira
Blue Collar Marriage
New York: Random House, Inc., 1964

Purpose: To fill a descriptive gap in our knowledge of the nature of working-class marriage relationships.

Sample: 58 couples, white, native-born, predominantly Protestant (101 of the respondents), husbands with semiskilled occupations. Twenty-five of the wives and eighteen of the husbands had completed high school. Thirty-eight of the wives and thirty-eight of the husbands were under thirty years of age.

Method: A minimum of six hours of interviewing with both husbands and wives.

Conclusions: Although all are stable, as many as one third of the families "fail to rate our assessment of 'moderately happy.'" [p. 331] Families are characterized by a sharp separation of masculine and feminine tasks and interests; husbands and wives are not generally expected to be close friends or companions; life in general is impoverished. These families displayed more physical "togetherness" than Bott's East Londoners; but given their "incapacity to share," the togetherness may produce shallower rather than deeper relationships.

Nye, F. Ivan
"Adolescent-Parent Adjustment—Socio-Economic Level as a Variable"
American Sociological Review: 16 (June 1951), 341-349

Purpose: To explore the general hypothesis that socioeconomic level is one of the variables in the differential adjustment of adolescents to parents.

Sample: 1472 adolescents from grades eight and eleven from fifteen of the public schools in Michigan.

Method: An instrument for measuring adolescent-parent adjustment was administered to students taking required subjects. Socioeconomic level was measured by a scale weighting equally the occupation of the head of the family, estimated income, church attendance of each of the parents, education of each of the parents, number of memberships in organizations, and working status of the mother.

Conclusions:

> Socio-economic level of the family is a significant variable in the adjustment of adolescents to parents. It is not, however, the only significant sociological variable. Residence, size of family, broken homes, employment status of mother, and age and sex of adolescents are also significant factors. Moreover, socio-economic level is not equally significant in all sub-groups considered in this study. Very small families, families with employed mothers, and broken families fail to show significant differences between socio-economic levels. [p. 349]

Pavenstedt, Eleanor
A Comparison of the Child-Rearing Environment of Upper
 Lower and Very Low Lower Class Families
American Journal of Orthopsychiatry: 35 (January 1965), 89–98

See Appendix, Chapter One.

Rainwater, Lee
And the Poor Get Children
Chicago: Quadrangle Books, 1960

Purpose: To explore the social and psychological variables affecting the use and nonuse of contraceptives among married couples in the working class.

Sample: A quota sample of 100 respondents selected by interviews from designated blocks in Chicago and Cincinnati working-class areas. The final report was based on responses of forty-six men and fifty women; twenty-seven of the men and twenty-nine of the women were classified as lower-lower class; the rest, upper lower.

Method: "Intensive conversational depth interviews" averaging two hours. In addition, two of the original Murray Thematic Apperception Test cards were used, and two cards especially designed for this study.

Conclusions: Working-class couples are resistant to the use of contraceptives for several interrelated reasons: their inability to discuss sexual matters frankly with one another, their ignorance of physiological processes, their pessimism concerning their ability to control fate, their distaste for things "unnatural."

Rainwater, Lee, Richard P. Coleman, and Gerald Handel
Workingman's Wife
New York: Oceana Publications, Inc., 1959

See Appendix, Chapter One.

Rainwater, Lee, and Gerald Handel
"Changing Family Roles in the Working Class," in
    Arthur B. Shostak and William Gomberg, eds.
    Blue-Collar World
Englewood Cliffs, N.J.: Prentice-Hall, Inc., 1964, pp. 70–76

Purpose: To describe changes observable in the family roles of men and women of the upper portion of the working class.

Sample: Data are drawn from three studies: (1) a study of changes in the life styles of upper-lower-class families based on interviews with about 300 working-class couples and 100 middle-class couples in five cities; (2) a study of middle- and lower-class family-size norms and family-planning behavior based on interviews with 150 couples, most of them in Chicago; (3) a study of day-to-day life problems drawn from interviews with 1000 men and women.

Conclusions: Two changes are of crucial importance: (1) the increased prosperity and security experienced by this group, and (2) the increased residential mobility, which has the effect of breaking up the close-knit social networks found by most researchers. These have the following effects:

1. The upper-lower-class couple seems to focus more sharply on the nuclear family, with husband and wife falling back on each other and on their children for a sense of involvement and social worth. "The focus on the nuclear family rather than on the close-knit networks of relatives, and long-time friends who become almost like kin, can be taken as the defining characteristic of a modern rather than traditional working-class life style." [p. 72]
2. In terms of the husband-wife relationship, there is a shift to more mutual involvement. They tend to relate as a couple. In the face of prosperity, working-class men and their wives focus on the home as the locus of all good things.
3. ". . . shifts in the direction of greater cooperation and solidarity based on interpenetration of role activities in marriage carry with them an increased intimacy in the sexual sphere." [p. 74]
4. Lower-class beliefs concerning appropriate family size and those of the middle class are converging at about three or four children. "For the working-class parents, within this ideal, there seems to be a growth of interest in the individual child and in the desire to do well by him." [p. 74]

Smith, Ernest A.
American Youth Culture
New York: The Free Press of Glencoe, 1962

A descriptive analysis, derived from a wide range of literature, of American youth culture as it is distinguished from adult culture. Areas examined include youth-adult conflict, family orientation, the structure and functions of cliques, gangs and crowds, and patterns of dating, courtship and marriage. Distinguishing characteristics of the culture ". . . were shown as youth norms, largely concerned with sex behavior, differentiating appearance, dress, and language, all resulting in a strict conformity of behavior." Evidence points to ". . . a marked degree of lack of integration with adult culture, but also a relatively high degree of unity and organization in itself." Conflict between youth and adult cultures results in the "withdrawal of youth from adult supervision and control" and a ". . . consequent conspiracy of silence applied to adults."

Stone, Robert C. and F. T. Schlamp
"Characteristics Associated with Receipt or Nonreceipt
   of Financial Aid from Welfare Agencies"
Welfare in Review: 3 (July 1965), 1–11

See Appendix, Chapter One.

Annotated References for Chapter Five

Babchuk, Nicholas, and Ralph V. Thompson
"The Voluntary Associations of Negroes"
American Sociological Review: 27 (October 1962), 647–655

Purpose: This report focuses on the extent to which Negroes affiliate with formal voluntary associations and on selected situational determinants and personal attributes.

Sample: 120 adult Negroes, twenty years of age and older, selected on a prorated basis in Lincoln, Nebraska, (population 130,000) during February and March 1960.

Method: A structured questionnaire was employed. The three measures of social background used were occupation (classified into nonmanual, skilled, and unskilled), education, and family income. Married women were classified according to the occupations of their husbands.

Conclusions: Data did not support the hypothesis that Negroes would be less likely to be affiliated with voluntary associations than whites. "Three out of every four persons interviewed were affiliated with one or more formal voluntary associations and were, in addition, members of a church." While the "direct but slight relationship between occupational rank and multiple memberships" was expected, "the extent of affiliation of persons in the blue-collar occupations was much higher than we would have predicted." The relationship between membership and educational achievement and family income was essentially the same as that established for occupation and membership.

Berger, Bennett M.
Working-Class Suburb: A Study of Auto Workers in Suburbia
Berkeley, Calif.: University of California Press, 1960

Purpose: To test the effect of a move to a new suburb on a working-class population.

Sample: 100 Ford automobile workers living in a San Jose, California, suburban tract.

Method: Approximately one-hour interviews in the homes of the respondents, during August and September of 1957. In most interviews there was direct participation of the wives.

Conclusion: The move to the suburbs brought no discernible changes in the style of life of the sample studied. Working-class suburbanites did not, to any great extent, take on the behavior or beliefs associated with white-collar suburbs. Berger concludes that the myth of suburbia as a "major phenomenon" is fostered by "the media, mass and otherwise," and suburbia's large supply of visible symbols.

Cox, Christine
"A Study of the Religious Practices, Values and Attitudes
in a Selected Group of Families"
Dissertation Abstracts: 17 (1957), 2,703–2,704

Purpose: To describe formal religious practices and patterns of participation in a group of families of high educational and socioeconomic status, to determine the religious values and attitudes of the parents, to investigate the relationships between the religious values and attitudes of parents and the formal practices and patterns of participation in their homes, and to compare religious practices and patterns of participation in families of orientation and procreation.

Sample: 41 families of high educational and socioeconomic status.

Method: A questionnaire interview was used to obtain information about religious practices. The Allport-Vernon scale of values was used to measure religious values, and the religious scales from the Gardiner Attitude Questionnaire was used to measure religious attitudes.

Conclusions: Data indicate that there is a high degree of religious identification with and participation in church activities, formal religious activity in the home, satisfaction in religious denomination, and high religious values in families in which the parents are highly educated and the fathers are professional men. Religious participation and religious values are higher in Catholic families. There is a positive relationship between the frequency of church at-tendance and other formal religious activity in the home, higher religious values and degree of satisfaction with religious denomination. There is also a positive relationship in the extent of religious activity in families of orientation and pro-creation and between religious values and attitudes and the extent of formal activity.

Dotson, Floyd
"Patterns of Voluntary Association among Urban Working Class Families"
American Sociological Review: 16 (October 1961), 687–693

See Appendix, Chapter Seven.

Frazier, E. Franklin
Negro Youth at the Crossways
Washington, D.C.: The American Council on Education, 1940

Purpose: To analyze the effects of minority status on the personality of Negro youth living in the border states (Missouri, Maryland, Kentucky, Dela-ware, West Virginia) and in the District of Columbia.

Sample: Subjects, from Louisville, Kentucky, and Washington, D.C., were not selected according to statistical methods of sampling.

> Groups of youth were chosen in such numbers and residence in the city as to correspond roughly to the distribution of the Negro population accord-ing to socio-economic groupings and according to residence in the five zones of settlement.

Method: Multiple interviews with the youth and their parents.

Conclusions: Negro youth in lower-class families were influenced in their self-conceptions by their parents' acceptance of the belief of Negro inferiority and the inevitability of Negro subordination to whites. Middle-class children showed the same accommodation to their subordinate racial status but differed in their degree of sophistication toward this status, and did not accept the view of the inherent superiority of whites. Upper-class children were more worldly and were influenced both by their parents' cultural identification with upper-class whites and a tradition of family achievement. They, however, faced the prob-lems of ambivalent attitudes toward their own Negro identity and Negroes in general.

The border-state schools stimulated in Negro pupils ambitions and aims similar to those stimulated in white students. "But the vast majority . . . must seek employment in a world which bars them because of color." It is in con-nection with seeking employment that Negro youth have their important con-tacts with the larger world.

The Negro church, though created, controlled, and supported by Negroes, "does little to give Negroes a sense of personal worth and dignity in a world where everything tends to disparage the Negro."

Frazier, E. Franklin
"Problems and Needs of Negro Children and Youth Resulting
   from Family Disorganization"
Journal of Negro Education: 19 (Spring 1950), 269–277

A theoretical analysis of the resultant problems of family disorganization. Economic difficulties stem from the family dependency on the mother's earnings. Serious social problems arise from the absence of family traditions, the emphasis on day-to-day existence, the lack of figures with whom the child can identify (especially serious for the male child), inadequacy of discipline, and the unsatisfied emotional needs of the children because of the overburdened mother. The author concludes that family disorganization among Negroes, resulting from the failure of the father to take his necessary place in family life, awaits those changes in our society that will enable the Negro father to play the role required of him.

Havighurst, Robert J., Paul H. Bowman, Gordon P. Liddle,
   Charles V. Matthews, and James V. Pierce
Growing Up in River City
New York: John Wiley & Sons, Inc., 1962

See Appendix, Chapter Three.

Hollingshead, August B.
Elmtown's Youth: The Impact of Social Classes on Adolescents
New York: John Wiley & Sons, Inc. (Science Editions), 1961

See Appendix, Chapter Two.

Kvaraceus, William C.
"Delinquent Behavior and Church Attendance"
Sociology and Social Research: 28 (January 1944), 283–289

Purpose: To explore the relationship between church attendance and delinquent behavior.

Sample: 761 delinquents, 563 boys and 198 girls, referred to the Passaic (New Jersey) Children's Bureau during a five-year period.

Method: Information was collected concerning stated religious affiliation and regularity of church attendance. Findings were compared with New Jersey figures on church membership.

Conclusions: Of the 594 youths for whom information was available, 54 percent claimed to attend church regularly (including Sunday School); 25 percent seldom or never; and 20 percent claimed to attend on an irregular basis. No significant difference was found between the proportion of delinquents who were active church members and the proportion of the general population reported as having church membership.

Lenski, Gerhard
The Religious Factor
New York: Doubleday & Company, Inc., 1961

Purpose: This study is concerned with the influence of religion on secular institutions.

Sample: 656 completed interviews from a cross-section of 750 Detroit residents, in early 1958. Also interviewed was a cross section of the clergymen serving the 656 respondents. The groups studied were white Protestants, Catholics, Negro Protestants, and Jews.

Method: Home interviews were conducted by The Detroit Area Study, a facility of the University of Michigan. The questions covered a wide range of material including types and degrees of religious commitment (communal and associational), economic behavior, political behavior, and family life.

Conclusions: It seems clear to the author that religious organizations have retained their vigor and are influential in contemporary American society with most signs pointed to further gains in the foreseeable future.

> . . . through its impact on individuals, religion makes an impact on all the other institutional systems of the community in which these individuals participate. Hence, the influence of religion operates at the social level as well as at the personal level.

Lewis, Hylan
"The Changing Negro Family," in
   Eli Ginzberg, ed.
   The Nation's Children
New York: Columbia University Press, 1960, Vol. I, pp. 108–135

The Nation's Children was published in three volumes for the Golden Anniversary White House Conference for Children and Youth to provide delegates to the conference "with materials that would help to outline the major developments in the field of children and youth since the 1950 Conference and would provide a basis for charting directions for the next decade." The first volume contains essays on "The Family and Social Change"; the second, "Development and Education"; and the third, "Problems and Prospects."

Lewis examines and interprets

. . . family structure, functions, roles and values among Negroes, mainly in the context of changes that have occurred, matured, or become salient in American society during the last ten years. There is a concern for what these mean or might mean for the larger community, as well as for the Negro family. [pp. 108–109]

Lynd, Robert S. and Helen Merrell Lynd
Middletown
New York: Harcourt, Brace & World, Inc., 1929

The culture of an American city, described in terms of how it gets its living, makes its homes, trains its young, uses its leisure, observes religion, and engages in community activities. Comparisons are made throughout between what is called the business and the working classes. These distinctions are made on the basis of the nature of an individual's work. The business class is defined as those who address their activities primarily to people, while the working class is defined as those who address their activities primarily to things. A major conclusion and a theme that runs throughout the work is that being born into one of these two groups is the most significant single cultural factor tending to influence what one does throughout one's life.

The city selected for study is in the East-North Central group of states with a population of over 35,000. It is an industrial city with a largely native-born population interspersed with 2 per cent foreign born and 6 percent Negro. The method of data collection was diverse, although in the main observational techniques were used. The study concentrates on the institutional life of the city.

Moberg, David O.
The Church as a Social Institution
Englewood Cliffs, N.J.: Prentice-Hall, Inc., 1962

This study of the church as a major American social institution analyzes "all organizations which directly seek to kindle, renew, and guide the religious life of people." It examines "the roles and statuses of the persons in such groups, their ideological values, goals, and group-related activities, and all the social structures and processes related to religious worship, prayer, association, and other activities in ecclesiastical organizations."

Peil, Margaret
"The Use of Child-Rearing Literature by Low-Income Families"
Ph.D. Dissertation, Department of Sociology,
    University of Chicago, 1963

See Appendix, Chapter One.

Remmers, H. H., and D. H. Radler
The American Teenager
Indianapolis: The Bobbs-Merrill Company, Inc., 1957

See Appendix, Chapter Two.

Rosen, Bernard Carl
*Adolescence and Religion: The Jewish Teenager in
American Society*
Cambridge, Mass.: Schenkman Publishing Co. Inc., 1965

Purpose: To determine the attitudes of Jewish adolescents toward certain traditional religious beliefs and practices, and to show how their religious attitudes and conduct are related to their membership in certain groups.

Sample: Five separate samples from four cities, two in Philadelphia, one in Yorktown, Pennsylvania, and two in Nebraska—during 1948–1949, 513 respondents; during summer 1950, 49 respondents in Philadelphia; during 1950–1952, every Jewish adolescent in Yorktown of high school age, a total of 50; in 1962–1963, 247 adolescents in Omaha and Lincoln. Most were secured by visiting Jewish youth groups, predominantly high school fraternities and sororities. The sample was essentially middle class, among whom about three quarters belonged to Orthodox or Conservative Congregations.

Method: Three research tools, two personal-interview schedules and a questionnaire were used in various combinations.

Conclusions: The author found that about two thirds of the respondents believed in a personal God and that about half accepted the idea of heaven and hell. The respondents reported going to services far less often than they considered adequate for Jews in general.

The attitudes were related to membership in four groups: the family, the peer group, the minority group, and the national society. Social class was not used as a variable for analysis.

Rosen, Bernard Carl
"Race, Ethnicity, and the Achievement Syndrome"
American Sociological Review: 24 (February 1959), 47–60

Purpose: To determine the degree to which the disparity between the vertical-mobility rates of some racial and ethnic groups can, in part, be explained as a function of different psychological and cultural orientations toward achievement.

Sample: 954 mothers and sons residing in sixty-two communities in four Northwestern states, representing six "ethnic" groups: French-Canadian, Italian, Greek, Jewish, Negro, and white Protestant.

Method: Two research instruments were used, a projective test developed by McClelland to measure achievement motivation and a personal interview to obtain information on achievement-value orientations. Social class was measured by the Hollingshead Index of Social Position.

Conclusions: The different groups studied placed different emphases on independence training and the development of achievement motivation in their children. Greeks, Jews, and white Protestants showed higher achievement motivation than Italians, French-Canadians and Negroes. Jews, Greeks, and Protestants were more likely to hold achievement values and higher educational and vocational aspirations than Catholics. Negroes had the lowest vocational aspirations of any group.

> Social class and ethnicity interact in influencing motivation, values, and aspirations; neither can predict an individual's score. Ethnic differences persist when social class is controlled, but some of the differences between ethnic groups in motivations, values, and aspirations are probably also a function of their class composition. [p. 60]

Smith, Ernest A.
American Youth Culture
New York: The Free Press of Glencoe, 1962

See Appendix, Chapter Four.

Stark, Rodney
"Class, Radicalism, and Religious Involment in Great Britain"
American Sociological Review: 29 (October 1964), 698–706

Purpose: To explore the relationship between social class, radical politics, and religious participation in England.

Sample: A national sample of approximately 1600 adults.

Method: Reanalysis of data collected in 1957 by a survey organization.

Conclusions: The author begins by attacking Lenski's position that the lower rate of lower-class religious participation simply reflects their general participation. He shows, from a national-sample survey conducted by Gallup in 1960, that blue-collar workers are less likely than white-collar workers to attend church, without regard to the extent of their participation in other voluntary associations.

From the British data, Stark shows that regardless of class, "those who cast their lot with political change are consistently less likely to participate in church." [p. 704] Further, "radicals" were more likely than conservatives to say that politics had more influence than religion on the way people live, and less likely to believe in the hereafter. The author concludes,

> These data provide considerable support for the thesis that radical solutions for status deprivation imply a lessening of religious involvement and that

the strength of lower class radicalism in Great Britain partly accounts for lower class religious apathy. Thus, the failure of long-held deprivation theories to account for the religious alienation of the working classes may well be laid to failure to consider alternative outlets for status dissatisfaction. [p. 706]

Wright, Charles R., and Herbert R. Hyman
"Voluntary Association Memberships of American Adults:
  Evidence from National Sample Surveys"
American Sociological Review: 23 (June 1958), 284–294

See Appendix, Chapter Seven.

Annotated References for Chapter Six

Bloch, Herbert A., and Arthur Niederhoffer
The Gang: A Study in Adolescent Behavior
New York: Philosophical Library, Inc., 1958

This study of adolescent groups includes the results of a cross-cultural survey and analysis of adolescent behavior in varied societies and cultures; a review of recent data from the behavioral science; and direct observations made by the authors, one a sociologist, the other a sociologically trained police officer. They suggest the following for further serious consideration:

> When a society does not make adequate preparation, formal or otherwise, for the induction of its adolescents to the adult status, equivalent forms of behavior arise spontaneously among adolescents themselves, reinforced by their own group structure, which seemingly provides the same psychological content and function as the more formalized rituals found in other societies. This the gang structure appears to do in American society, apparently satisfying deep-seated needs experienced by adolescents in all cultures. [p. 17]

Chapman, Ames W.
"Attitudes toward Legal Authorities by Juveniles"
Sociology and Social Research: 40 (January/February 1956), 170–175

Purpose: To investigate the attitudes of delinquent and nondelinquent boys toward legal agencies of authority for juveniles and to determine the extent or degree of difference.

Sample: 160 boys, ages thirteen to seventeen, forty of whom had official contact with the juvenile court. The boys were from low-rent areas of the city and were matched for age, number of school years completed, race, intelligence, occupation of father, and residence.

Method: Ninety-eight items, from a possible 250, were used as the basis for Likert-type scales in the various areas of concern. The scales were (1) police, (2) juvenile court, (3) probation, (4) detention, and (5) boys' industrial school.

Conclusions: Delinquent boys, compared to nondelinquents, are generally more hostile toward legal agencies of authority for juveniles. Hostility is greater toward police than toward any other agency. There was no statistically significant difference in the attitudes toward the other agencies mentioned, indicating more friendly methods of treatment employed by these agencies.

Cohen, Albert K., and Harold M. Hodges, Jr.
"Characteristics of the Lower-Blue-Collar Class"
Social Problems: 10 (Spring 1963), 303–334

See Appendix, Chapter Four.

Easton, David, and Robert D. Hess
"Youth and the Political System," in
    S. M. Lipset and L. Lowenthal, eds.
    Culture and Social Character
New York: The Free Press of Glencoe, 1961, pp. 226–251

This theoretical paper seeks to focus attention on the importance of research on youth by developing a framework for analysis that stresses the cruciality of political socialization in the maintenance of political systems. The authors suggest that political stability requires, among other things, "the development of shared knowledge about political matters as well as a set of shared political values and attitudes."

These common expectations concerning knowledge, values, and attitudes are acquired through the process of political socialization. They relate to three major objects or levels: government—the day-to-date authorities of the system; regime—the basic forms and norms of the system; and community—the unit encompassing the system. Thus, political socialization may be viewed as the process of acquiring knowledge, values, and attitudes directed to these major objects. Accepting the evidence that the preadult stage is crucial in the socialization process, the authors suggest a developmental approach as the most useful way of undertaking research, and propose the following as worthwhile questions, using research findings, and the lack of them, as support for the need for such research:

1. When does political socialization have its start?
2. Are there any well-defined stages of political socialization?
3. To what extent is the path along which political socialization moves continuous or discontinuous?
4. Is there any special order in the transmission to youth of the different kinds of orientations linked to each level of a political system?

5. To what extent are political orientations less subject to challenge by youth themselves compared to orientations in other areas?

Finestone, Harold
"Cats, Kicks, and Color"
Social Problems: 5 (July 1957), 3–13

Purpose: To describe the "social type of the young colored drug user."

Sample: "50 male colored users of heroin in their late teens and early twenties selected from several of the areas of highest incidence of drug use in Chicago."

Method: Intensive interviews conducted during 1951–1953.

Conclusions: The cat rejects "the obligation of the adult male to work." He "seeks through a harmonious combination of charm, ingratiating speech, dress, music, the proper dedication to his 'kicks' and unrestrained generosity to make of his day to day life itself a gracious work of art. . . . As a form of expressive behavior, . . . the social type of the cat represents an indirect rather than a direct attack against central conventional values."

Gans, Herbert J.
The Urban Villagers
New York: The Free Press of Glencoe, 1962

Purpose: To study slum life, and the characteristics that differentiate working- and lower-class from middle-class people. To test the validity of the approach currently used by city planners and associated professions: the use of "middle-class values to help low-income population solve their problems and improve their living conditions."

Sample: 100 to 150 residents of a Boston neighborhood known as the West End. Intensive contact with about twenty, with a concentration on native-born Americans of Italian parentage. The study was made during parts of 1957–1958 and was part of a research project entitled "Relocation and Mental Health: Adaptation Under Stress," conducted jointly by Harvard Medical School and Massachusetts General Hospital at the Center for Community Studies. The neighborhood studied was subsequently torn down under an urban-renewal program.

Method: Participant-observer. The author used neighborhood facilities; attended neighborhood meetings and gatherings, both public and private; interviewed community functionaries; used informants and personal observation.

Conclusions:

> . . . the West Enders were not frustrated seekers of middle-class values. Their way of life constituted a distinct and independent working-class subculture that bore little resemblance to the middle-class . . . the behavior

patterns and values of working-class subculture ought to be understood and taken into account by planners and caretakers.

Goodman, Paul
Growing Up Absurd: Problems of Youth in the Organized System
New York: Random House, Inc., 1956

See Appendix, Chapter Three.

Gottlieb, David
"Goal Aspirations and Goal Fulfillments: Differences between
   Deprived and Affluent American Adolescents"
American Journal of Orthopsychiatry: 34 (October 1964), 934–941

See Appendix, Chapter Two.

Gottlieb, David, and Charles Ramsey
The American Adolescent
Homewood, Ill.: The Dorsey Press Inc., 1964

A general study of contemporary American adolescent society and its relationship to the adult world. The study includes a discussion of youth culture, age and sex roles, occupational choice, courtship, marriage, education, and "social areas in which young people have participated in some significant manner." The authors note, "Our goal was to move beyond a theoretical formulation of youth behavior and to note areas where the gap between the generalizations might be lessened."

Greenstein, Fred I.
Children and Politics
New Haven, Conn.: Yale University Press, Inc., 1965

Purpose: To study the political development of children between the ages of nine and thirteen, in the last five years of elementary school—the nature of political awareness and involvement, what is learned and the sequence of political learning, and the relevance of political development during this period for later political participation.

Sample: 659 children, grades four through eight, from three public schools and one private school in New Haven, Connecticut. Of the respondents, 433 were lower SES, 266 upper SES, with neighborhood used as a measure of social status. Fifteen percent of the "lower school" cases were Negro, while none of the 182 upper school or 102 private school cases were. Eight percent of the lower SES respondents were Negro, less than 1 percent of the upper SES were.

Method: A paper-and-pencil questionnaire administered in classrooms in January through March of 1958. Twenty loosely structured interviews were also conducted.

Conclusions:

1. Orientation toward issues and parties. A significantly higher proportion of upper SES seventh and eighth graders refer to issues in their attempts to distinguish between political parties. In addition, at every age level, the upper SES children are more likely to respond in political terms when asked how they would "change the world."

   There is no class difference in tendency to possess a party identification, but upper SES respondents are better informed about party differences and better able to name party leaders.
2. There is no class difference in information about formal governmental institutions. Nor is there any class difference in propensity to vote or in belief that "elections are important." However, upper SES respondents are significantly more likely to mention public figures both as famous persons they would want to be like, and would not want to be like.
3. Evidence in support of the impression of the lower level of politicalization among lower-status children is found in the data that they are more likely to say that the president, governor, and mayor are doing "a very good job." In addition, lower SES respondents were more likely to rate both Eisenhower and Stevenson favorably than were upper SES respondents.

The New Haven data certainly indicate that differences in educational accomplishment and the related differences in intellectual skill make up part of the childhood heritage of the different classes and in this way contribute to political participation differences. . . . It is especially notable that lower socioeconomic status children do not share the explicit unwillingness to participate in politics found among adults of the same background. But they *do* show a greater deference toward polittical leadership; unlike upper-status children they do not bring to display in sixth, seventh, and eighth grades a sense that political choices are theirs to make—that *their* judgments are worth acting upon. [p. 106]

Hess, Robert D., and David Easton
"The Child's Changing Image of the President"
Public Opinion Quarterly: 24 (Winter 1960), 632–644

Purpose: This study is essentially concerned with developmental aspects of political socialization—the examination of the image of the President as it appears at successive grade levels in an elementary school.

Sample: 350 children, grades two through eight, in a middle-class, largely Republican suburb of Chicago.

Method: A multiple-choice questionnaire that explored the following areas: (1) personal and moral qualities of the President, (2) role competence, (3) information about him. The children were asked the same information about their own fathers and a hypothetical figure called the President of China.

Conclusions: In general, the children held a highly positive image of the President, even in terms of the hypothetical figure. In the early grades this image is close to that of the father. The data suggest that the socialization takes place early and the image is difficult to dislodge.

Hess, Robert D., and David Easton
"The Role of the Elementary School in Political Socialization"
The School Review: 70 (Autumn 1962), 257–265

Purpose: To study political socialization at the elementary school level.
Sample: Children, grades two to eight.
Method: A questionnaire devised to obtain the child's image of the president; a short essay describing the cartoon figure, Uncle Sam; an essay response to the question, "How can I help make our government better?"
Conclusions: The child's first attitudes toward political authority are formed by his family experiences. He transfers his images of parental authority to political figures. By identifying with his family, he becomes attached to a particular political party and ascribes virtues only to the candidates of this party. Eventually the child differentiates between role performance and personal merit and he "begins to see the difference between the office of the presidency and the characteristics of the incumbent."

Hess, Robert D., and Judith V. Torney
The Development of Basic Attitudes and Values toward Government
and Citizenship during the Elementary School Years. Part I
Washington, D.C.: U.S. Office of Education, Cooperative Research
Project No. 1078, 1965

Purpose: To study the conceptions of figures in the world of government and politics as they emerge in the child during his elementary school years; to study the child's emerging conception of the symbols, terms, and labels of government; to study the school and family as agents of political socialization; and to study the change and development of attitudes and involvement, with age.
Sample: Grades two through eight in eight cities, one large (over a million) and one medium-sized (under 40,000) within each of four regions. Within each city, four schools were selected, two from a middle-class and two from a working-class area. Within each school, two classrooms were selected at each grade level.
Method: Data collected on family status (occupation of father), intelligence, social participation, religious affiliation and church attendance, family structure, and political-party preference by means of a questionnaire. Questionnaires were also used to measure educational practices and attitudes of teachers in the schools and to get at the role of the school in political socialization.
Conclusions: The authors explore the development of attitudes in five areas: (1) attachment to the nation, (2) attachment to political figures and institutions,

(3) compliance and response to the law, (4) influencing government policy, and (5) participation in the process of elections. They trace the evolution of attitudes and then explore the role of such agents as family, status, religion, peers, and school in the process of political socialization.

Religion appears to be important only in the development of political affiliation, with Catholic children tending to become Democrats. The effect of social status is seen through the family, where class differences in the perceived strength and effectiveness of the father, and family concern with politics and current events affect the developing orientation of children. Intelligence turns out to be a significant factor both in the rate of development of political attitudes, in interest in political affairs, and in a critical appraisal of government. By and large, the authors find the effect of social status to be less significant than that of intelligence, when both are significantly related to some aspect of political socialization.

Horton, Roy E., Jr.
"American Freedom and the Values of Youth," in
    H. H. Remmers, ed.
    Anti-Democratic Attitudes in American Schools
Evanston, Ill.: Northwestern University Press, 1963, pp. 18–60

Purpose: To study attitudes toward freedom as defined by the Bill of Rights, and the values of freedom and fascism.

Sample: From a sample of 18,052 pupils in 103 schools in thirty-four states, a subsample of 3000 twelfth graders was drawn.

Method: Data was collected in 1951–1952 by means of questionnaire. Areas included for study were freedom as defined by the Bill of Rights, general fascistic tendencies, patriotism, the economic ideology of Marx, and anticommunist attitudes.

Conclusions: Correlation analysis showed belief in the Bill of Rights to be negatively related to acceptance of fascist ideology, to chauvinistic expressions of super patriotism, to acceptance of Marxian ideology, and to extreme feelings of anticommunism. Acceptance of the Bill of Rights is partially related to knowledge score. Most liberal responses are most significantly related (positively) to mother's education, and the knowledge score of the pupil.

Lane, Robert E.
"Fathers and Sons: Foundations of Political Belief"
American Sociological Review: 24 (August 1959), 502–511

Purpose: To study the extent of political rebellion in the father-son relationship.

Sample: 15 native-born employed males, ages twenty-five to fifty-four mostly in their thirties. They were white, married fathers, urban and Eastern, of middle income, working- and middle-class occupations. They were drawn from a total of 220 male tenants in a moderate-income housing development in an Eastern industrial city.

Method: Loosely structured taped interviews conducted in conversational style. Content covered (1) current social questions; (2) political parties; (3) political leadership and leaders; (4) social groups and group membership; (5) ideological orientation toward democracy, freedom, equality, and government; (6) personal values and philosophy of life; (7) personality dimensions; (8) life histories including attitudes towards parents, brothers, sisters, school, and so forth. In addition, tests were administered on anxiety, authoritarianism, information, and certain social attitudes.

Conclusions: There seems to be very little political rebellion in the relationships of sons with fathers. This differs markedly from the findings of European studies, particularly in Germany. The reasons offered for the lack of rebellion are (1) low salience of politics for the parents; (2) choice of other routes of rebellion closer to the core of American values, for example, quitting school; (3) low salience of father in American family structure—not one choice as the focus of rebellion; (4) general permissiveness in home which lessens need to rebel.

Levin, Murray B.
The Alienated Voter: Politics in Boston
New York: Holt, Rinehart and Winston, Inc., 1960

Purpose: A study of the pattern of voting among constituents in a Boston mayoralty election.

Sample: 500 Boston voters.

Method: Home interview on a variety of questions pertaining to personal background and voting choices. The socioeconomic status of the respondent is based on his subjective identification rather than on any objective criteria of the authors.

Conclusions: In the author's view the most significant finding is that feelings of desperation, hopelessness, and cynicism about politics and politicians are strongest among those who have lived in Boston for many years. Social-class position is related to the form taken by political alienation. The upper- and middle-income groups tend to withdraw and identify with a charismatic leader as a result of their sense of powerlessness.

Litt, Edgar
"Civic Education, Community Norms and Political Indoctrination"
American Sociological Review: 28 (February 1963), 69–75

Purpose: To determine whether communities differing in socioeconomic characteristics differ in the materials used for civics education and in political attitudes and norms that are reflected in that educational process.

Sample: A major secondary school in each of three communities in the Boston metropolitan area, one upper class, one lower middle class, and one working class.

Method: Content analysis was made of a random sample of paragraphs of all textbooks used in civic-education programs over previous five years. Interviews were conducted with civic and educational influentials, educational administrators, teachers, and current and past officers of PTA and major civic groups in each community.

Conclusions: Differences were found among political themes in civic education texts, the attitudes of community leaders, and the effects of courses on student political attitudes. Basic beliefs are not taught in all the communities. But the effect of the content and approach in the working-class community is not to encourage a belief "in the citizen's ability to influence government action through political participation." In the lower-middle-class community there is an emphasis on political responsibility but little concern with the dynamics of political decision making.

> Only in the affluent and politically vibrant community are insights into political processes and functions of politics passed on to those who, judging from their socio-economic and political environment, will likely man those positions that involve them in influencing or making political decisions. [p. 74]

Logan, R.F.L., and E. M. Goldberg
"Rising Eighteen in a London Suburb"
British Journal of Sociology: 4 (December 1953), 323–345

Purpose: To study various aspects of the physical, psychological, and social lives of young men.

Sample: 74 youths born between April 1 and June 1, 1931, who resided in a local London borough and had to register for National Service on May 21, 1949.

Method: Questionnaires, interviews, and clinical examination.

Conclusions: Physical health was generally satisfactory; there were few major but many minor physical disorders. Mental health was not so satisfactory. Much emotional disturbance was observed, which seemed to have roots in family background. Ill-health was concentrated among youth in semi-skilled and unskilled work, who were also less mature than others. Both physical and psychological disorders were generally neglected.

> A changing pattern of sexual behavior in the community may be indicated by the attitudes of the young men to pre-marital relationships, which were remarkably free of guilt and by their belief in the role of women as full partners in both pre-marital and marital relationships. Nevertheless, the ethics of a double standard of morality seemed to linger on as they expected their sisters and future wives to be chaste. [p. 343]

The lack of involvement in their job of most semiskilled and unskilled workers raises the problem of the sources of satisfaction while at work. Juvenile labor turnover was not a problem of any magnitude. The majority did much the same with their leisure time; a "class" difference was apparent only in reading. Most were not interested in life of the community around them. Reading rarely extended beyond the daily newspaper, except for students.

Maccoby, Eleanor E., Richard E. Matthews, and Anton S. Merton
"Youth and Political Change"
Public Opinion Quarterly: 18 (Spring 1954), 23–39

Purpose: To investigate the extent to which young people follow their parents' lead politically, the direction taken when there is a political difference, and to explore the psychological and sociological variables associated with this change.

Sample: 339 subjects, aged twenty-one to twenty-four, in Cambridge, Massachusetts. The sample was suitable for the study, but not considered representative of the city.

Method: Interviews were used to obtain information on party preferences, and voting behavior; parental party preferences, and voting behavior; political and social values; degree of strictness in home; educational level; occupation; amount of political discussion with spouse, peers, and fellow-workers; degree of disparity in political views with these groups; and social mobility.

Conclusions: Agreement on candidate and party choice is highest between the young person and his family (parents and spouse), next highest with friends, and least high with fellow workers.

Among lower socioeconomic groups, rejection of parental political values is associated with strict discipline in the home. The highest conformity exists in homes where moderate control is exerted.

Upwardly mobile youth tend to adopt the political behavior of the group into which they have moved. Downwardly mobile young people remain as Republican, or more so, than the class from which they came.

Middleton, Russel and Snell Putney
"Student Rebellion against Parental Political Beliefs"
Social Forces: 41 (May 1963), 377–383

Purpose: Two questions are examined: (1) Do college students today rebel politically in the directions of conservatism? and (2) Are campus conservatives predominantly rebelling against parental liberalism?

Sample: 1440 male and female students from sixteen colleges and universities representing a variety of regions and types of institutions.

Method: Questionnaires presented the students with a "simple left-to-right continuum" from which they were asked to compare this view to the political position held by their parents.

Conclusions: Two fifths of the students rebelled from their parents' political views, overwhelmingly in the direction to the left of their parents. Student conservatives reflected conservative family beliefs, whereas socialists and liberals were rebels from this same conservative tradition. The students were less likely to rebel from parents holding conventional views. Those who did rebel, did so in the direction of unconventionality.

Miller, S. M., and Frank Riessman
" 'Working-Class Authoritarianism': A Critique of Lipset"
The British Journal of Sociology: 12 (September 1961, 263–273

This paper presents a criticism of Lipset's concept of working-class authoritarianism in terms of the questionability of certain of Lipset's underlying assumptions concerning democracy, the limited applicability of the F scale as a measure of authoritarianism, and a questionable use of psychodynamic variables in interpreting adult attitudes.

Nye, F. Ivan, James F. Short, Jr., and Virgil J. Olson
"Socioeconomic Status and Delinquent Behavior"
American Journal of Sociology: 62 (January 1958), 381–389

Purpose: This study tests the null hypothesis that there is no significant difference in the delinquent behavior of children from different socioeconomic strata.

Sample: Western sample of 2350 boys and girls, grades 9–12 in the high schools of three cities with populations of 10,000 to 25,000. A Midwestern sample of 250 boys and 265 girls, from high schools in a suburban residential town, a rural community, and a consolidated high school in a rural township. No samples from large cities or from large non-Caucasion groups.

Method: Data gathered by questionnaire. Delinquent behavior was measured by means of a delinquency check list and a delinquent-behavior scale. Socioeconomic status was determined by the father's occupation using a combination of the North-Hatt and Mapheus Smith occupational prestige scales.

> The data were put to five tests: (1) The chi-square test was applied to the data in four-by-four tables for boys and girls separately and combined; (2) Delinquent behavior categories were dichotomized, and the chi-square test was applied to the data in two-by-four tables; (3) a test of significance of difference between proportions was applied to subgroups showing marked differences for the two-by-four tables; (4) A test was made of the distribution of delinquency scale types by socioeconomic status, and; (5) A separate test was made with adolescents of fourteen and fifteen years of age to minimize the effect of school "dropouts." [p. 388]

Conclusions: "The tests employed failed to uncover enough significant differences to reject the null hypothesis." Independent measure of the father's status-educational level uncovered no significant differences.

Padilla, Elena
Up from Puerto Rico
New York: Columbia University Press, 1958

An examination of the way of life and changing culture of Puerto Ricans living in a New York City slum. The social pattern of neighborhood life is described in detail, as are the problems faced by both adults and children. For two and a half years the author and her assistants visited and formed friendships with over 500 persons within the community she calls "Eastville." In addition to informal participant-observer interviews, open-end type questionnaires were administered to forty-eight Puerto Rican family heads living in every third apartment of each fifth building.

Polk, Kenneth
"Juvenile Delinquency and Social Areas"
Social Problems: 5 (Winter 1957–1958), 214–17

Purpose: An ecological study of juvenile delinquency "using the framework of social area analysis."

Sample: All juvenile delinquents reported to juvenile authorities by police in 1952 in San Diego, California.

Method: Census-tract data was obtained from San Diego census bulletins for the year 1950. Ninety-four tracts were studied. Reports on juvenile delinquents "were tabulated and distributed into census tracts according to the place of residence of the offender." Indexes of status were computed as follows:

> *Economic Status* is based on education and occupation; *Family Status* on fertility, percentage of mothers working and percentage of single-family dwelling units; and *Ethnic Status* on the percentage of persons belonging to ethnic groups living in the census tracts.

Conclusions: Delinquency was found to be "highest in areas of low economic status, . . . low family status . . . and high ethnic status." With the use of partial correlation analysis the relationship between juvenile delinquency and each of the specified variables was reduced.

Reckless, W. C., S. Dinitz, and E. Murray
"Self-Concept as an Insulator against Delinquency"
American Sociological Review: 21 (December 1956), 744–746

Purpose: To determine whether it is "possible to identify certain components that enable young adolescent boys to develop or maintain non-delinquent habits and patterns of behavior in the growing up process."

Sample: 125 sixth-grade boys from schools in the highest white delinquency areas in Columbus, Ohio. They were selected "by their teachers as being 'insulated' against delinquency." The boys had no record of involvement with law enforcement agencies.

Method: The boys

were given a series of four self-administered scales to complete. These included, in somewhat modified form: 1) the delinquency proneness and, 2) social responsibility scales of the Gough Personality Inventory, 3) an occupational preference instrument, 4) and one measuring the boy's conception of self, his family, and other interpersonal relations.

In a seperate interview "the mother or mother-surrogate was interviewed with an open-ended schedule to determine the boy's developmental history, his patterns of association, and the family situation."

Conclusions: "While this pilot study points to the presence of a socially acceptable concept of self as the insulator against delinquency, the research does not indicate how the boy in the high delinquency area acquired his self image." A possible way in which this self-image was acquired was as "an outgrowth of discovery in social experience that playing the part of a good boy and remaining a good boy bring maximum satisfactions (of acceptance) to the boy himself."

Remmers, H. H., and Richard D. Franklin
"Sweet Land of Liberty," in
　　H. H. Remmers, ed.
　　Anti-Democratic Attitudes in American Schools
Evanston, Ill.: Northwestern University Press, 1963, pp. 61-72

Purpose: To compare the responses of students polled between 1951 and 1960 regarding their attitudes toward relevant current applications of the Bill of Rights.

Sample: Subsample of those who responded (about 12,000) to the Purdue Opinion Panel polls, stratified to be representative.

Method: Self-administered questionnaires.

Conclusions: A strong minority supported press censorship and a majority of respondents supported censorship of books and movies and a bar against the printing and sale of communist literature. Barely half were opposed to government interference with free speech, although a majority supported freedom of assembly, and there was strong support for freedom of religion.

Somewhat more than a majority supported the right to trial by jury, protection against arrest without formal charge, and protection against search without a warrant. There was some increase in support of the right to protection again self-incrimination, but by 1960 only about half the respondents were in favor. On the other hand, there was an increase (to over half) in the proportion that would not extend basic American rights to foreigners. Finally, less than half the student sample agreed with a statement on "integrated schools," though a larger proportion would have extended equal rights in jobs to minorities.

Remmers, H. H., and D. H. Radler
The American Teenager
Indianapolis: The Bobbs-Merrill Company, 1957

> *See Appendix, Chapter Two.*

Smith, Ernest A.
American Youth Culture
New York: The Free Press of Glencoe, 1962

> *See Appendix, Chapter Four.*

Whyte, William F.
Street Corner Society: The Social Structure of an Italian Slum
Chicago: University of Chicago Press, 1943

> *See Appendix, Chapter One.*

Annotated References for Chapter Seven

Berger, Bennett M.
Working-Class Suburb: A Study of Auto Workers in Suburbia
Berkeley, Cal.: University of California Press, 1960

> *See Appendix, Chapter Five.*

Bernard, Jessie
"The Neighborhood Behavior of School Children in
    Relation to Age and Socio-economic Status"
American Sociological Review: 4 (October 1939), 652–662

Purpose: An exploration of the degree to which children rely on the neighborhood for associational relationships, and an attempt to determine at what point in the child's development he becomes emancipated from the neighborhood in which he lives, moving to a functional basis.

Sample: 420 boys and girls.

Method: A questionnaire pertaining to neighborhood attitudes and activities.

Conclusions: Age is a major factor in neighborhood behavior. The higher the social status, however, the earlier the neighborhood pattern is displaced, occurring at fifteen in the highest status group and seventeen in the middle status group. The neighborhood pattern is most pronounced in the lowest status group and tends to endure into adulthood.

Clarke, Alfred C.
"The Use of Leisure and Its Relation to Levels of
 Occupational Prestige"
American Sociological Review: 21 (June 1956), 301–307

Purpose: An examination of the role of leisure as a part of the life style of individuals occupying different prestige levels.

Sample: Approximately 500 persons, about 100 from each of five levels of occupational prestige, using the North-Hatt scale.

Method: A mail questionnaire.

Conclusions: Significant differences were found to exist between occupational prestige and leisure use. Craft interest varied inversely with prestige level. The highest status group reported they would use extra leisure time for reading and study, the lowest status group for relaxation and rest. Respondents at each level devoted most of their leisure time to nonspectator activities.

Coleman, James C.
The Adolescent Society: The Social Life of the Teenager and Its Impact on Education
New York: The Free Press of Glencoe, 1961

See Appendix, Chapter Three.

Cramer, M. Ward
"Leisure Time Activities of Economically Privileged Children"
Sociology and Social Research: 34 (July/August 1950), 444–450

Purpose: To explore leisure-time activities of upper-status children.

Sample: 68 students in a private day school in Pennsylvania, aged six to fourteen, from an economically privileged community.

Method: Data apparently collected by means of interviews.

Conclusions: About one third of the group spent at least five hours per week in music lessons and practice. The modal group, consisting of about a third of the students, listened an average of eleven hours per week to the radio. Almost all the students attended movies, with over two thirds going at least once a week. Almost half the students belonged to organized groups and participated in them. About four fifths took outside trips during the school year.

Dotson, Floyd
"Patterns of Voluntary Association among Urban Working-Class Families"
American Sociological Review: 16 (October 1951), 687–693

Purpose: A study of the social organization of urban working-class families.

Sample: 50 families from a working-class district in New Haven, Connecticut, chosen at random from a street index of the city directory. Attention was focused on unskilled and semiskilled workers and only families in which parents were either native stock or American-born were included.

Method: Each family was interviewed at least twice concerning people with whom they maintained face-to-face relationships. The interviews were semi-structured.

Conclusion: The majority of the families studied do not participate in organized voluntary associations. Family and kinship play a major role in providing companionship and social life.

Globetti, Gerald, and Margaret McReynolds
"A Comparative Study of the White and Negro High School
    Students' Use of Alcohol in Two Mississippi Communities"
State College, Miss.: Mississippi State University, Social Science
    Research Center, 1964

Purpose: To understand the sociocultural factors associated with the use of beverage alcohol by teen-agers in the white culture and Negro subculture of two Mississippi communities.

Sample: From a universe of 2495 high school students in one hill and one delta community, a sample of 581 was drawn, from which 519 usable schedules were obtained.

Method: Administration of questionnaires to groups of about twenty-five. Father's occupation was used as a measure of socioeconomic status, creating three levels—high, middle, and low. No indication that fieldworkers were matched with respondents on race.

Conclusions:

1. There was little difference in frequency of use. Among white students, 12.9 percent were frequent users and 63.2 percent were abstainers. Among Negro students, the comparable proportions were 9.6 percent and 60.1 percent.
2. There was less use in the hill community, where there was strong prohibitionist sentiment.
3. There was a tendency for use to increase with grade in school.
4. There was a positive relation between use and status for both groups.
5. There was a negative relation between use and church attendance for both groups.

Hausknecht, Murray
*The Joiners: A Sociological Description of Voluntary
    Association Membership in the United States*
New York: The Bedminster Press, 1962

Purpose: A study of the extent of voluntary association membership in the United States and the relationship between membership and socioeconomic status.

Sample: Two surveys using national samples of population were used. Two thousand individuals were represented in a 1954 study made by the American Institute of Public Opinion; 2379 in a 1955 study by the National Opinion Research Center. The primary purpose of both surveys was to collect information relevant to problems of health and sickness.

Method: Questionnaires. The AIPO consisted of thirty-three questions; the NORC schedule contained 136.

Conclusions: Declining participation in associational life is attributed to the achievement of many of the goals formerly pursued by voluntary associations. Recognition of "salient moral problems" (such as civil rights) "provide a stimulus for organization and a focus for action." As these and other "moral issues emerge as salient we may expect to see a concommitant rise in the importance of associational life."

Havighurst, Robert J., Paul H. Bowman, Gordon P. Liddle,
   Charles V. Matthews, and James V. Pierce
Growing Up in River City
New York: John Wiley & Sons, Inc., 1962

See Appendix, Chapter Three.

The Hofstra Research Bureau, Psychology Division
Use of Alcoholic Beverages among High School Students
Hempstead, New York: Hofstra College, 1953

Purpose: To understand the conditions surrounding the use of alcohol by high school students.

Sample: 1000 students, not all chosen randomly, from twenty-nine of the thirty-one public and private high schools in Nassau County, New York, primarily in grades ten, eleven, and twelve, drawn in proportion to the size of the school.

Method: Group administration of questionnaires.

Conclusions:

1. Little or no relation between the use of alcohol and the number of organizations in which the students participate.
2. No relation between use and the number of offices held in organizations.
3. Positive relation between grades and nonuse, particularly with nonuse of beer.
4. Positive relation between numbers of rooms in student's residence and presence of beer in the home.

Hollingshead, August B.
Elmtown's Youth: The Impact of Social Classes on Adolescents
New York: John Wiley & Sons, Inc. (Science Editions), 1961

See Appendix, Chapter Two.

Kansas, University of; Department of Sociology and Anthropology
Attitudes towards Use of Alcoholic Beverages
Lawrence, Kan.: University of Kansas, 1956

Purpose: To discover the drinking experience of high school students, to compare the behavior of metropolitan and nonmetropolitan students in the Kansas region, and to assess the effects of urbanization on drinking behavior.

Sample: Sample stratified for location: (1) 1207 students from a metropolitan county; and (2) 1119 students from twenty-three counties outside of standard metropolitan areas. Sample designed to be representative of public high school enrollees in the two areas of Kansas.

Method: Administration of questionnaires to groups of about twenty-five. Number of rooms in home and father's highest grade completed used as indicator of socioeconomic status.

Conclusions:

1. In nonmetropolitan areas, farm children and those in places of less than 1000 are less likely to be users; students in schools of less than 100 drink less, but there is no difference in users in larger schools.
2. There is a positive relationship between use and status, but it is significant only in metropolitan areas.
3. There is some tendency for boys with high grades to drink less than those with average or low grades.
4. There is no relationship between use and participation in organizations, but there is a negative relationship with number of offices held.
5. There is no relationship between use and the number of scholastic activities engaged in.
6. There is a positive relationship between use and participation in interscholastic athletics for girls.
7. Use is inversely related to attedance at church. Catholic students report more often that they have permission to drink at home, and that they use alcoholic beverages.

MacDonald, Margherita, Carson McGuire, and R. J. Havighurst
"Leisure Activities and the Socioeconomic Status of Children"
American Journal of Sociology: 54 (May 1949), 505–519

Purpose: To test the hypotheses that there is a systematic relation between children's social status and leisure activities, and that there are exceptions, representing a form of cross-cultural learning.

Sample: 241 children in fifth, sixth, and seventh grades (age ten to twelve) of a public school in Chicago.

Method: Children were asked to record daily activities for one week in April and one week in May 1947. The children were arranged into four social groupings on the basis of housing and occupations of their parents.

Conclusions: There were systematic class differences in participation in organized recreational groups, with the middle-class child taking part mainly in Scouts and YMCA activities and the lower-class child participating mainly in two centers or clubs for "underprivileged children." Social class was also positively related to such individual activities as taking music lessons, reading books, and, somewhat, to listening to the radio, and, negatively, to going to the movies.

Maddox, George L., and Bevode McCall
Drinking among Teen-Agers
New Brunswick, N.J.: Center for Alcohol Studies, Rutgers, The State
    University, 1964

Purpose: To explore the hypothesis that drinking is part of the American culture and that teen-agers learn to drink as part of the process of becoming adults.

Sample: Teenagers in the eleventh and twelfth grade of three public high schools in a middle-sized Midwestern city. From the 1962 usable questionnaires (95 percent of the sample), were chosen 177 "drinkers" (used beverage alcohol and identified themselves as drinkers), 279 "users" (indicated use but did not identify themselves as drinkers), and 17.3 percent random sample of 1506 nondrinkers.

Method: Questionnaires administered to all students present on a particular day.

Conclusions: With reference to the relationship between social class and use, authors found that the measure of social class employed affected the result. When the census classification of the father's occupation was the measure, the users were found in the lower occupational classification. When Warner's ISC was used, users were more likely to be found at the upper and lower extremes of the class structure with nonusers in the middle range. Among boys, use of alcohol seemed related to the expectation of upward social mobility, while among girls, the relationship was less certain but tended in the opposite direction.

Social class was not used as a variable for any additional analyses.

Michigan, Univeristy of; Institute for Social Research, Survey
    Research Center
*Adolescent Girls: A Nation-wide Study of Girls between Eleven
    and Eighteen Years of Age*
Ann Arbor, Mich.: Univeristy of Michigan, 1956

Purpose: To study the needs and interests of adolescent girls and to determine the role to be played by youth agencies in serving this age group.

Sample: 1925 girls, a representative national crosssection of the approximately 7.3 million girls in the United States in grades six through twelve.

Method: Personal interviews with questions of the open-end type, lasting from thirty minutes to two hours.

Conclusions: In noting the diversity of interests found among adolescent girls, it is suggested that no single program could be formulated to appeal to the entire group. Agencies seeking broad membership are advised "to permit local units relative freedom to select content and organizational designs best suited to the particular community and youth they serve."

Michigan, University of; Institute for Social Research, Survey
   Research Center
A Study of Boys Becoming Adolescents
Ann Arbor, Mich.: University of Michigan, 1960

Purpose: To find out as much as possible about boys eleven to thirteen in order to help a national organization trying to meet the needs and interests of preadolescent boys.

Sample: 1435 boys chosen by probability-selection methods, representative of boys eleven through thirteen years of age, in grades four through eight. An additional 514 boys outside of the eleven to thirteen year-age span completed the cross section sample of boys in grades five through eight. Boys were contacted in March and April of 1959.

Method: An hour-long face-to-face interview with open questions, which were later categorized.

Conclusions: Parents of higher-status boys are more supportive of boys joining a club. Leisure activities highly rated by this age group are passive entertainment (movies, TV), indoor activities, hobbies, and individual sports.

Scott, John C.
"Membership and Participation in Voluntary Associations"
American Sociological Review: 22 (June 1957), 315–326 .

Purpose: To determine the relation between variations in sex, age, education, religion, occupation, marital status, family status, friends, nativity, residence, home tenure, and social status to variations in the degree to which persons participate in voluntary associations.

Sample: A 5 percent random sample of 232 people from Bennington, Vermont, with 387 memberships was secured by selecting persons, ten years of age and older, living in every twentieth dwelling unit. Work was done in September 1947.

Method: An interview consisting of twenty-two basic questions.

Conclusions: Membership in voluntary associations occurs more frequently for those with increased education, nonmanual jobs, Protestant religious affiliation, and higher social status.

Smith, Henry P.
"A Study in the Selective Character of American Secondary
   Education: Participation in School Activities as
   Conditioned by Socio-Economic Status and Other Factors"
Journal of Educational Psychology: 36 (April 1945), 229–246

See Appendix, Chapter Two.

White, R. Clyde
"Social Class Differences in the Uses of Leisure"
American Journal of Sociology: 61 (September 1955), 145–150

Purpose: An examination of the thesis that the use of leisure is a function of class position and that the differentiation increases with age up to maturity.

Sample: 1741 persons over six years of age in Cuyahoga County, Ohio, selected at random from fourteen census tracts, representative as to income, education, distribution of occupations, conditions of housing, and the age distribution of the population.

Method: Respondents were asked to give information on how their leisure was spent during the week preceding the interview.

Conclusions: The uses of leisure are conditioned by social class and to some extent by age and sex. The upper-middle class selects libraries, home diversions, and lecture-study groups more often than do other classes, whereas the two lowest classes use parks and playgrounds, community chest agencies, churches, museums, and commercial entertainment relatively more often.

Wisconsin, University of; University Extension Division, Bureau of Economics,
    Sociology and Anthropology
"Attitudes of High School Students toward Alcoholic Beverages"
Madison, Wis.: The University of Wisconsin, 1956

Purpose: To discover, with reference to Racine County (Wisconsin) high school students (1) how much they drink, (2) whether state laws hinder their drinking, and (3) whether there is a real relationship between home or school conditions and their drinking.

Sample: Systematic sample of 1000 students from nine high and three junior high schools (ninth grade only) in Racine County, drawn in February 1955.

Method: Administration of questionnaires to groups of thirty to fifty students.

Conclusions:

1. The proportion of nondrinkers of beer has a slight but not significant positive correlation with the number of organizations to which respondents belong.
2. There is no relation between use and number of offices held in organizations.
3. There is a positive relation with grades for nonbeer users; positive but not as strong relation for nonusers of hard liquor; and no relation for nonwine users.

4. Having hard liquor in the house is positively correlated with the number of rooms in a respondent's residence.

Wright, Charles R., and Herbert H. Hyman
"Voluntary Association Memberships of American Adults:
   Evidence from National Sample Surveys"
American Sociological Review: 23 (June 1958), 284–294

Purpose: Evidence is presented bearing on the pattern of membership in voluntary associations of adult Americans in general, and of specific subgroups, such as racial and religious minorities.

Sample: Two national probability samples of the adult, noninstitutionalized population of the U.S. over twenty-one years of age. First sample (1953) contained 2809; the second (1955), 2379 men and women. In addition, findings from NORC studies of localities were used.

Method: Secondary analysis of survey data.

Conclusions: Voluntary association membership is not a major characteristic of Americans. Nearly half of the families and almost two thirds of the respondents belong to no voluntary association. Membership is somewhat more characteristic of whites than Negroes. The highest rate of membership is found among Jews. Data support the positive correlation between social status and membership.

Name Index

Abrahamson, Stephen, 33, 41, 46, 160
Adams, Walter, 52, 186
Alexander, C. Norman, Jr., 52, 160
American Institute of Public Opinion, 266
Antonovsky, Aaron, 50, 161

Babchuk, Nicholas, 102, 242–243
Baeumler, Walter L., 46, 161
Bardach, J. L., 11, 159–160
Becker, Howard S., 40, 162
Bennett, William S., Jr., 50, 69, 180–181, 217
Bell, Robert R., 22, 136
Berelson, Bernard, 17n, 19, 20, 107n
Berger, Bennett M., 102, 122, 243, 263
Bernard, Jessie, 127, 263
Berreman, Joel V., 50, 69, 185, 221
Bertrand, Alvin L., 39, 163
Bell, Gerald D., 52, 163
Bell, Robert R., 22, 136
Block, Herbert A., 109, 111, 250
Blood, Robert O., 23, 88n, 136–137
Bloom, Benjamin, 5
Blum, Alan F., 88, 89, 231
Boek, Walter E., 8, 137
Bordua, David J., 54, 164
Bott, Elizabeth, 89, 231–232
Bowman, Paul H., 39, 74, 84–85, 164, 211, 219–220, 236, 245, 266
Boyd, George F., 50, 165
Bradburn, Norman M., 87, 232
Brazer, Harvey E., 39n, 172
Bronfenbrenner, Urie, 7n, 8, 10, 16, 22, 23
Brookover, Wilbur B., 47, 165
Brooks, Deton J., 25, 138
Brooks, Edna E., 22, 26, 138–139
Brown, Bert, 32, 176
Burchinal, Lee, 24, 139
Buri, J., 22, 26, 138–139
Buswell, Margaret M., 45, 46, 166
Butterworth, D. C., 52, 66, 182, 219

Byrne, E. A., 22, 26, 138–139

Campbell, Arthur A., 94, 234–235
Campbell, Ernest Q., 52, 160–161
Caro, Francis G., 51, 57, 62, 63, 65, 66, 76, 80, 85, 167–168, 211–212, 213, 233
Carroll, Eleanor E., 23, 147
Carroll, Rebecca Evans, 29, 139
Cateora, Phillip, 213–214
Carter, Hugh, 39, 235–236
Chapman, Ames W., 109, 110, 250–251
Charters, W. W., 184
Chicago, University of, 217
Chinoy, Eli, 65n, 77
Clarke, Alfred C., 120, 264
Cloward, Richard A., 39, 168
Cohen, Albert K., 85, 88, 91, 115, 233–234, 251
Cohen, Elizabeth G., 53, 168
Cohen, Wilber J., 39n, 172
Coleman, Hubert A., 32, 46, 170–171
Coleman, James S., 53, 55, 55n, 56, 58, 123, 124, 125, 130, 192, 193, 214, 264
Coleman, Richard P., 10, 22, 26, 87, 88, 153, 241
Cook, Edward S., Jr., 45, 170
Coster, John K., 48, 171
Cox, Christine, 103, 243–244
Cramer, M. Ward, 126, 127, 264
Curry, Robert L., 33, 171–172
Cutler, R., 159–160

Davie, James S., 39, 46n, 174
David, M. H., 39n, 172
Davidson, Helen H., 41, 59, 172
Davis, Allison, 18, 35, 36, 62, 71, 80, 140, 174–175, 214, 215
Davis, Ethelyn, 68, 73, 215–216
DeGroat, Albert F., 41, 175
Demke, H. R., 146

Deutsch, Martin, 10, 32, 34, 35, 60, 140–141, 175, 176
Dillon, Harold J., 39, 177
Dintz, S., 109, 261–262
Dotson, Floyd, 101, 122, 244, 264
Douvan, Elizabeth, 25, 141
Downing, Gertrude L., 19, 20, 142
Dreger, Ralph Mason, 31, 33, 177
Dyer, William, 64, 216

Easton, David, 113, 115, 251–252, 254–255
Eckert, Ruth E., 39, 178
Edgar, R. W., 19, 20, 142–143
Educational Testing Service, 193–194
Eells, Kenneth, 175
Elder, Glenn H., Jr., 51, 54, 178
Ellison, Merl, 230
Empey, Lamar, 65, 66, 216
Erikson, Erik, H., 4, 6, 8, 9, 13, 14, 20, 21, 22, 24, 25, 27, 28, 29

Finestone, Harold, 111, 112, 242
Folger, John K., 40, 195–196
Fox, Robert S., 42, 179–180
Franklin, Richard D., 117, 262
Frazier, E. Franklin, 101, 244
Freedman, A., 11, 159–160
Freedman, Ronald, 94, 234–235

Gage, N. C., 184
Galler, Enid Harris, 65, 217
Gans, Herbert J. 112, 127n, 252
Gardner, Bruce, 24, 139
Gerver, Joan M., 59, 172–173
Gildes, M. L., 27, 146
Ginzberg, Eli, 64n, 246–247
Gist, Noel P., 50, 69, 181, 217
Glick, Paul C., 39, 235–236
Glidwell, J. C., 27, 146

Globetti, Gerald, 128, 265
Goodman, Paul, 28n, 111, 112, 218, 253
Goetz, Wilma Marie, 66, 217
Goldberg, E. M., 127, 258–259
Goldberg, Miriam L., 31, 33, 36, 181
Gomberg, William, 90, 91, 215–216, 223, 224, 231, 237–238, 241
Gottlieb, David, 50, 60, 110, 181, 253
Greenberg, Judith W., 59, 172–173
Greenstein, Fred I., 115, 253–254

Haire, Mason, 78, 218
Hall, Oswald, 76, 81, 219
Haller, Archibald O., 18, 23, 30, 51, 52, 55, 66, 67n, 143, 155, 182, 199–200, 219, 224
Handel, Gerald, 10, 22, 26, 87, 88, 91, 92, 94, 153, 241
Harris, A. J., 19, 20, 142–143
Hausknecht, Murray, 122, 265
Havighurst, Robert J., 29, 31n, 38, 74, 84, 104, 106, 130, 143, 157, 175, 208, 219, 236, 245, 266, 267–268
Hawkes, Glenn R., 24, 139
Health and Welfare Association of Allegheny County, 39, 183
Heath, Robert W., 220–221
Heimann, Robert A., 33, 183–184
Hess, Robert D., 14, 15, 26, 62, 71, 80, 113, 115, 116, 144, 214–215, 251–252, 254–256
Hill, Thomas J., 83, 237
Himes, Joseph S., 78, 221
Himmelweit, Hilde L., 19, 144–145
Hodges, Harold M., Jr., 85, 88, 91, 115, 233–234, 251
Hoehn, Arthur J., 41, 184
Hofstra Research Bureau, Psychology Division, 128, 266
Hollingshead, August B., 31n, 38, 83, 84, 105, 130, 184–185, 200, 206, 237, 245, 249, 266
Holloway, Robert G., 50, 69, 185, 221

Horton, Roy E., Jr., 116, 118, 256
Hudson, M. C., 22, 26, 138–139
Hunt, J. McV., 4, 6, 8, 9, 13, 14, 20, 21, 28
Hurvitz, Nathan, 90, 91, 237–238
Hyman, Herbert, 101, 121, 122, 250, 271

Jackson, Brian, 55n, 60
Jackson, David, 14, 15, 26, 144
Jaffe, A. J., 52, 186
Jaffe, Frederick S., 95, 238–239
Jones, James A., 39, 168
Jones, Mary Cover, 46, 186

Kahl, Joseph, 22, 55, 145, 187, 221
Kansas, University of, 128, 267
Kantor, Mildred B., 27, 146
Karpinos, Bernard D., 39, 187, 188
Kennedy, Wallace A., 32, 188–189
Kernberg, L., 142–143
Kluckhohn, Florence, 24, 146
Kohn, Melvin L., 23, 146–147
Komarovsky, Mira, 86, 87, 239
Krauss, Irving, 52, 54, 60, 189
Krippner, Stanley, 52, 66, 68, 190, 221–222
Kvaraceus, William C., 106, 245

Lane, Robert E., 115, 256–257
Lang, Gerhard, 41, 173
Lenski, Gerhard, 100, 101, 102, 103, 246, 249
Lerner, Melvin, J., 50, 161
Leshan, Lawrence L., 19, 148
Levin, Murray B., 115, 257
Lewis, Hylan, 101, 246–247
Liddle, Gordon P., 74, 84–85, 219–236, 245, 266
Lippitt, Ronald O., 42, 179–180
Lipset, Seymour M., 18, 64n, 119, 148, 251, 260
Litt, Edgar, 116, 257–258
Liversidge, William, 71, 222
Livingstone, A. Hugh, 39, 190
Loeb, Martin B., 38, 208

Logan, R. F. L., 127, 258–259
Lorwin, Lewis L., 50, 161
Lott, Albert J., 51, 70, 191, 222
Lott, Bernice E., 51, 70, 191, 222
Lowenthal, L., 251
Lynd, Helen Merrell, 92n, 101, 103, 247
Lynd, Robert S., 92n, 101, 103, 247

Maas, Henry S., 15, 148–149
McCall, Bevode, 128, 268
McClelland, D. C., 24, 25, 141, 154, 249
Maccoby, Eleanor E., 7n, 115, 259
McDill, Edward L., 53, 55, 56, 58, 192, 193
MacDonald, Margherita, 125, 267
McFarlane, Bruce, 76, 81, 219
McGuire, Carson, 267–268
McKinley, Donald S., 16, 17, 149
McReynolds, Margaret, 128, 265
Maddox, George L., 129, 268
Marden, Dennis, 55n, 60
Marshall, Thomas O., 39, 178
Matthews, Charles V., 39, 74, 84, 85, 164, 211, 219–220, 236, 245, 266
Matthews, Richard E., 115, 259
Mensh, I., 27, 146
Merton, Anton S., 115, 259
Michael, John A., 57, 193–194
Michigan, University of, 235, 268, 269
Middleton, Russel, 115, 259–260
Miller, Arthur, 27
Miller, Kent S., 31, 33, 177–178
Miller, S. M., 62, 75, 109, 119, 223–224, 260
Miller, Walter B., 17n, 86
Milner, Esther, 35
Mitchell, James V., Jr., 28, 149
Moberg, David O., 101, 102, 247
Moles, Oliver C., Jr., 24, 26, 150
Morgan, James N., 25n, 39n, 172
Morland, J. Kenneth, 68, 76, 77, 205, 224

Morrison, Florence, 78, 218
Mugge, Robert H., 31, 195
Murray, E., 109, 261–262

Nam, Charles B., 40, 195–196
National Committee on Employment of Youth, 81
National Opinion Research Center, 87, 122, 182, 232, 266
Neugarten, Bernice, 45, 196
Niederhoffer, Arthur, 109, 111, 250
Nye, F. Ivan, 82, 109, 110n, 239, 260

Olson, Virgil J., 109, 110n, 260
Opinion Research Corporation, 72n, 79n, 80
Oppenheim, A. N., 45, 196–197

Padilla, Elena, 112, 261
Palmore, Erdman, 39, 197
Parsons, Talcott, 4, 5, 9
Passow, A. Harry, 10, 34, 35, 39, 60, 140–141, 168, 175, 176, 181, 209
Paterson, Ann, 47, 165
Pavenstedt, Eleanor, 11, 16, 26, 84, 86–87, 151, 240
Peil, Margaret, 16, 102, 151, 247
Pierce, James V., 74, 84–85, 219–220, 236, 245, 266
Pihlblad, C. Terence, 65, 66, 212, 213
Pohlman, Vernon C., 51, 198
Polk, Kenneth, 113, 261
Putney, Snell, 115, 259–260

Radler, D. H., 47, 48, 49, 104, 105, 198–199, 248, 263
Rainwater, Lee, 10, 19, 22, 26, 84, 87, 88, 91, 92, 94, 95, 96, 152, 153, 239, 240, 241
Ramsey, Charles, 110, 253
Reckless, W. C., 109, 261–262
Remmers, H. H., 47, 48, 49, 104, 105, 117, 198–199, 248, 256, 262, 263
Riessman, Frank, 22, 40n, 109, 119, 153, 223–224, 260

Robinson, Myra, 29, 143–144
Roper Public Opinion Research Center, 186
Rosen, Bernard C., 24, 105, 106, 153–154, 248
Rosenberg, Morris, 24, 29, 154
Rue, R., 159–160

Schenk, Quentin F., 33, 183–184
Schlamp, F. T., 86, 156, 242
Schmuck, Richard A., 42, 44n, 179
Schultz, Raymond E., 33, 199
Scott, John C., 121, 269
Scott, R. B., 8, 150
Sewell, William H., 23, 30, 51, 66, 67n, 155, 199–200, 244
Sexton, Patricia Cayo, 31n, 39, 200
Shailer, Thomas, 18, 30, 143
Shipman, Virginia, 14, 15, 26, 144
Short, James F., Jr., 109, 110n, 260
Shostak, Arthur B., 90, 91, 215–216, 223, 224, 237–238, 241
Siemans, Leonard B., 53, 200–201
Simpson, Richard L., 66–67, 225
Smelser, William T., 68–69, 225
Smit, John W., 235
Smith, Benjamin F., 69, 226
Smith, Ernest A., 83, 109, 111, 112, 116, 242, 249
Smith, Henry P., 46, 130, 201, 269
Sprey, Jetse, 69, 226–227
Stark, Rodney, 101, 249–250
Sommers, Herbert J., 39, 188
Stefflre, Buford, 227–228
Steiner, Gary A., 17n, 19, 20, 107n
Stendler, Celia Burns, 25, 44, 155, 202–203
Stephenson, Richard, 66, 228
Steren, H. F., 19, 20, 142–143

Stewart, Lawrence H., 67, 228–229
Stinchcombe, Arthur L., 56, 77, 203, 229
Stone, Robert C., 86, 156, 242
Strauss, Murray A., 19, 51, 66, 67n, 156–157, 199–200
Sussman, Marvin, 8, 137

Thomas, Robert Jay, 204
Thomas, Shailer, 18, 30, 47, 143, 165
Thompson, George D., 41, 175
Thompson, Ralph V., 102, 242–243
Toby, Jackson, 35, 36, 204
Torney, Judith V., 113, 115, 116, 255
Turner, Ralph H., 25, 56, 157, 204

Udry, J. Richard, 46, 206
U.S. Bureau of the Census, 73, 195, 198, 236
Uzell, O., 69, 229

Van De Riet, Vernon, 32, 188–189

Waldo, Leslie C., 41, 58, 206–208
Wallin, Paul, 41, 58, 206–208
Warner, William L., 38, 137, 145, 208
Whelpton, Pascal K., 94, 234–235
White, James C., Jr., 32, 188–189
White, Martha S., 12, 157–158
White, R. Clyde, 121, 270
Whyte, William F., 84n, 112, 117, 127n, 158, 263
Williams, J. R., 8, 158
Wilson, Alan B., 32, 57, 208–210
Wisconsin, University of, 128, 270
Wolf, Richard M., 15, 159
Wortis, H., 11, 159–160
Wright, Charles R., 101, 121, 122, 250, 271
Wylie, Ruth S., 47, 210

Yankauer, Alfred, 8, 137
Youmans, E. Grant, 65, 229–230
Young, Marechal, 230

AFDC recipients, characteristics, 156; intellectual achievements, 31–32, 195
Achievement, and aspiration, 47, 57, 165–166; by income class, 188–189; picture of good achiever, 59, 173; picture of poor achiever, 59–60, 173; related to class, race, and intelligence, 32, 33, 248–249; and self-concept of ability, 47, 165–166; and socioeconomic status, 32–33, 171–172, 183–184; and teacher behavior, 41–42
Achievement motivation, McClelland test of, 25, 141, 153–154; and social status, 24, 25, 141; and religious affiliation, 106–107; of youth, 24, 178
Achievement syndrome, 153, 156–157, 248–249
Activities, out-of-school, 123–130; school-related, 130–131; See also Extracurricular activities
Adams F-Scale, 234
Adjustment, problems of, 28, 149–150
Adolescence, as stage of child development, 27–30; end of, 84; transition to adulthood, 211–212; See also Adolescents; Youth
Adolescents, adjustment to parents, 82, 239–240; lower-class, image of women, 84; needs of, 156–157; organizations, 161–162 (see also Gangs); problems of, 198–199; protective organization, 82; religious life, 104–107; use of leisure time, 120–131; working- and middle-class contrasted, 112
Adults, religious life of, 100–104
Aggression, expression of, 18, 36
Alcohol use, by youth, 127–130, 265–270; and church attendance, 106
Alienation theme, of working-class culture, 111, 118
Allport-Vernon Scale, 243
Ambition, 25, 56, 157, 204–205; See also Aspirations
Anderson-Clifton Simplification of Anderson-Brewer scheme, 184
Anxiety, in middle-class children, 19, 144–145
Aptitude, academic, and college attendance 63 (table); of high-status seniors, 57–58
Aspirations, occupational, 63–69, 136, 161, 167–168, 178–179, 185–186, 199, 212, 213, 217–218, 220–221; of youth, 22, 29, 47–58, 139–140, 145, 160–161, 163, 164, 178, 189–190, 206, 228
Associational activity, and status, 101–102, 121, 123, 231, 242–243, 246, 264–265, 269, 271
Australia, study of boys, 13, 14, 65n
Authoritarianism, 119; of parents, 12, 15, 18, 88, 148

Authority, adolescent's anarchic relation to, 111
Autonomy, in development of child, 8–9, 10

BPC Personality Inventory, 170
Balance, interpersonal, 160–161
Behavior, standards of, 23
Bell Adjustment Inventory, 201
Bill of Rights, acceptance of, 116, 117, 256, 262
Binet I.Q. Test, 189
Blue-collar class (see Workers, blue-collar)
Boys, "corner boys" and "college boys," 158; study of, 269
British youth, working class attitudes to school, 49n; See also Great Britain

California Achievement Test, 171, 189
California Test of Mental Ability, 171
California Test of Mental Maturity, 175, 194
California Test of Personality, 24, 28, 30, 143, 149, 175
Child, culturally deprived, 22, 153, 172; See also Disadvantaged child
Child-centeredness of middle-class homes, 19, 145
Child development, 4–30; nursery school through 2nd grade, 13–20; elementary school, 20–27
Child-rearing practices, 3, 7–30, 36, 137, 150, 151, 157–158, 159–160
Childhood, early, 8–12
Children, effects on tendency of women to work 98 (table); working-class, socialization experiences, 4
Church attendance, 104–105; and alcohol use, 128; and delinquent behavior, 245–246; and school activities, 106
Church membership, and other activities, 108; and poor, 101
Classroom learning atmospheres, 42, 179–180
Cognitive development, 5, 6, 8, 10, 14–15, 21, 140–141, 144
College orientation, and status, 52, 63, 136, 169, 186, 189–190, 192–193
College pressure, 53–58, 164, 192–193
Communication, importance in child-rearing, 15; in sexual matters, 96
Conscience, 13–14, 17–18
Conservatism, as student rebellion, 259–260
Contraception, attitudes toward, 94, 95, 234–235, 238–239, 240
Control, skills of, 36
Cornerville study, 84, 112
Correlation coefficients, in quality of education, 43–44

Counseling, and early school leaving, 177
Cultural orientation, 24

Davis hypothesis, 144–145
Decision making, in marriage, 88; parental, 147
Delinquency (*see* Juvenile delinquency)
"Denial," surfeit of, 14
Dependency need, 145
Desertion, as poor Negro's divorce, 89
Detroit Beginning First-Grade Intelligence Test, 166
Devotionalism, defined and distinguished from orthodoxy, 102
Disadvantaged child, 10, 140–142; *See also* Child, culturally deprived
Discipline techniques, 23, 47; and social status, 16, 18; *See also* Controlling devices; Punishment
Divorce, index of proneness, 89
Draw-a-Person Test, 153
Dreese-Mooney Interest Inventory, 228
Drop outs, 39, 62, 164–165, 170–171, 177, 178, 183, 187–188, 190–191, 223; and delinquency, 197–198; employment and training, 81; and low-income status, 39–40; political socialization of, 116; work experience of, 74–75
Drug users, Negro, 252

Economic behavior, and religion, 103
Economic Opportunity Act, 81
Education, and divorce proneness, 89, 235; parental attitudes toward, 22, 26, 138–139, 145; as preparation for work, 62–63; quantity and quality of, 38–46, 200; related to occupation, 74–78; and the state, 38; and tendency of married women to work, 97
Ego (*see* Self)
Employers, barriers raised by, 81
Employment, of school-age youth, 72–78
Environment, family, 11, 15, 16, 148–149, 151, 159; importance in early development, 5; supportive, in infancy, 5
Expenditures, per-pupil, and income levels, 43
Extracurricular activities, and college orientation, 55; and status, 46, 55, 130, 201
Extrafamilial networks, 89, 91, 231
Eysenck's T-Scale, 234

Families, disorganized, 17, 151; growth of, 95; kinship solidarities, 85
Family, educational level, and labor-management attitudes, 80 (table); effect on occupational choice, 68, 225–226, 230; lower-class, power structure, 88; of orientation, 3–30, 148–149; of procreation, 82–99; role in educational aspirations, 25, 53–58, 157, 192, 200–201; as source of class differences, 115; *See also* Environment

Family relationships of adolescents, 15, 148–149; lack of research on, 29–30
Family size, conceptions of, 94–95
Family structures, working-class, 91, 149, 231
Family ties, effect of church associations, 103–104
Father, and child-rearing responsibilities, 23, 147; education of, and college plans, 56, 58, 172; status and aspirations of, and college pressures, 55
Father's occupation, and aspirations of children, 201; and child-rearing practices, 16, 149; and children's occupational choice, 64, 66, 199, 216, 221–223; and children's personality adjustment, 24, 139; and status, 128–129
Father-son relationships, and adolescent self-esteem, 30
Fathers, absence of, 17; hostility to sons, 16, 17, 149; and political attitudes, 115, 256–257
Fertility complex, and religious and social differences, 235
Free Drawing Tests, 172
Freedom of speech, attitudes toward, 117; and teachers, 47
Friends, choice of, 44–45, 56, 196–197

Games, of boys, and sex-role identification, 17
Gang, adolescent, 83, 84, 111, 250
Gardiner Attitude Questionnaire, 243
Gates Reading Readiness Test, 166
Gesell Development Schedules, 158
Girls, alcohol use, 128; aspirations of, 47, 58; classification by lower-class boys, 84; development of, 17; and early marriage, 85; early work experience, 73; leisure-time activities, 124, 125; occupational choices of, 66, 68, 70, 73 (table), 215–216; and premarital sex, 84; study of, 268; values of, 25; in white-collar work, 76
Goal Preference Inventory, 191
Goals (*see* Aspirations)
God, belief in, 105
Golden Anniversary White House Conference for Children and Youth, 246–247
Grades, high, and social status, 33; high school, and later success, 63
Graduation, high school, and occupation, 74–78
Gratification, deferred, and socioeconomic status, 19, 156–157
Great Britain, college-oriented youth in, 55n; religious participation, 101, 249–250; study of middle-class children, 19, 144–145; study of occupational aspirations, 71, 222; youth study, 258–259
Growth of American Families Study (1960), 95
Guess-Who Test, 196, 202, 229
Guilt feelings, of children, 18, 19
Guttman Scale, 154

Henman-Nelson Intelligence Test, 159, 184
High school graduates, 81
High school seniors, survey of occupational choices, 72, 73 (table)
High school social structures, and college intentions, 55, 192–193
High school students, tests of, 37, 38 (table)
High schools, aspirational climates of, 57–58, 192–194
"Higher Horizons," 61, 153
Hollingshead's Index of Social Position, 24, 154, 183, 206
Hostilities, of lower-class individual, 148

I.Q., 5; correlated with environments, 15, 176–177, 205; correlated with socioeconomic level, 15, 32, 159, 170, 176–177; of Negro children, 189
Identity, search for, 27
Incest taboo, 17
Income, and leisure activities, 125, 126 (table)
Independence training, and achievement, 54
Industry, sense of, 21, 22, 24, 25, 27
Infancy, 5–8, 158
Inferiority, sense of, 21, 24
Initiative, testing of limits of, 13–14, 16
Inputs, and adolescent intellectual growth, 29; environmental, to developing child, 7, 23n
Intellectual growth, 10–11, 28–29, 140–141
Intelligence, development of, 5, 6; and family environment, 15, 159; and political attitudes, 113–114; utilization of and satisfaction with teacher, 42
"Intrusive mode," 13
Iowa Every Pupil Test of Basic Skills, 166, 190
Iowa School Ability Test, 199
Iowa Test of Educational Development, 199, 201
Italian-Americans, 112, 252

Jewish youth, study of, 105, 248
Junior high schools, "special service," 142
Justice, attitudes toward, 110–112
Juvenile delinquency, among low-income youth, 109–110, 250–251, 260, 261–262; and religion, 106, 245–246

Kinsey data, 83, 84, 92, 93

Labor force, participation of wives, 96–99; survey, 73
Labor-management relations, attitudes toward, 78–79, 218
Law enforcement agencies, and youth, 109–112, 250–251
Learning process, 142
Learning styles, related to teaching styles of mothers, 14–15, 144
Leisure-time activities, 120–131, 258–259, 264, 267

Levels of aspiration, 206–207
Life styles, differences, 121, 156, 264
Likert-type scales, 251
Lorge-Thorndike Test, 176

Mapheus Smith prestige scale, 260
Marital relationship, working-class, 86–94, 231, 232, 237
Marriage, and concern with advancement, 78; early, 85; and gangs, 84; goals, 151; and premarital pregnancy, 84
Maturation, physical versus social, 28; disadvantaged child, 10, 140–141
Middle class, "submerged," 55n
Mobility, and adolescent choice, 226; and church involvement, 103; and parental pressure for college, 53–54, 168–169; and white-collar work, 76–77
Mobility aspirations, 178–179; and class, 50, 154; parental influence in, 67
"Models," in child development, 9, 29, 143–144; of sex-role identification, 14
Moral development, 20
Moral ideology, of Negro boys and girls, 29, 139–140
Moreno Sociometric Test, 196
Motherhood, and lower-class wives, 93
Mother figures, 6
Mothers, emotional support from, 17; occupation, and children's occupational choice, 66, 68, 221–222; educational aspirations for children, 22, 136; strong emotional bond with sons, 17; teaching styles of, 14–15, 144
Motor tasks, performance affected by child-rearing practices, 8, 158
Murray Needs Test, 187
Murray Thematic Apperception Test, 240

Negroes, aspirations of youth, 29, 49–51, 60, 139–140, 165, 180–182, 185–186, 229, 230; associational activity, 242–243; child-rearing practices of, 8, 11, 14, 16, 144, 151–152, 158; and college attendance, 62; and divorce, 89; education of children, 22; educational achievements, 199; and family disorganization, 182, 245; graduation and place in labor force, 75; intellectual tests of, 31–32, 33, 176, 188–189; and juvenile delinquency, 110; minority status and personality development, 244; mothers' aspirations for children, 136; occupational choice, 66, 69–72, 161, 226–227, 230; religious participation, 101–102; socialization to world of work, 78, 221; "stimulus deprivation," 140
Neighborhood, and associational relationships, 262; effect on ambition, 56
New Stanford Arithmetic Test, 138
New Stanford Reading Test, 138
Nonreading, and low income, 123
North-Hatt occupational prestige values, 199, 212, 260, 264

Obedience, parental concern with, 26–27
Occupational choice, 63–72, 167–168, 199, 216, 217
Occupational drift, concept, 64
Occupational plans, expectation versus aspiration, 66, 67n, 70, 71 (table), 217–218, 229–230
Oedipal crisis, 13, 17
"Omnipotence," sense of, 21
Organizations, membership in, 46, 127, 161–162
Orthodoxy, doctrinal, defined, 102; and status, 105, 106, 107 (table); among youth, 107 (table)

Pairing-off processes, 82
Parent-child relationships, and reading readiness, 194–195; and socioeconomic status, 27, 146
Parental concern, in lower class, 22, 145
Parental education, and children's ambition, 25
Parental responsibilities, 23, 147
Parents, adolescents' adjustment to, 82, 239–240; and adolescent aspirations, 163, 168–169; education, and children's education, 172; identification with, 19; motivation in college pressures, 54, 55, 164, 186–187; and occupational choice, 64–65, 66–67, 225; support of school, 25, 155; values and attitudes, 26, 52, 146–147, 155
Parsons-Hunt-Erikson distinctions, 5
Peer-pair relations, 52
Peers, effect on achievement, 44, 45, 46, 160–161, 166–167; influence on educational and occupational aspirations, 54–56, 66–67, 160–161, 225
Permissiveness, in child-rearing, 8, 11, 157
Personality adjustment, and socioeconomic status, 18–20, 23–24, 28, 30, 139, 143, 144–145, 155, 170
Personality development, and socioeconomic status, 24, 28, 139, 225–226
Piaget's notation, 21
Political development of children, 114, 115, 117, 253–259
Political system, attitudes concerning, 113–118, 148, 251
Politics as substitute for religion, 101, 249–250
Possession index, as measure of status, 124
Poverty, as psychological problem, 153
Pregnancy, lower-class attitudes to, 94, 234–235; premarital, 84
Preschool attendance, parental attitudes, 155
Preschool experience, and achievement in school, 34–38, 177
Prestige, and occupational choice, 65, 199; occupational, and leisure time, 120–121
Progressive Achievement Test, 175
"Project Talent," 37, 38, 42, 43, 59

Prosperity, and working-class family, 90
Psychic-emotional development, 14, 20
Psychological health of children, and child-rearing practices, 12
Puerto Ricans in New York City, 112, 261
Punishment, physical, 23, 147; related to social status, 41, 160–161
Purdue Opinion Poll, 47, 198, 262

Race, and alcohol use by teenagers, 265; and educational aspirations, 50–51, 165, 180–181, 185–186, 191–192; influence of, and social-class level, 32; and motor acceleration, 158; and need for recognition, 51; and occupational choice, 69–72, 227, 229; and place in labor force, 75 (table); psychological comparisons, 177–178; and reading habits, 152; and religion, 108; See also Negroes
Reading, as leisure activity, 122, 123
Reading habits, and child-rearing, 151–152
Reading readiness, and parent-child interaction, 35, 194–195
Rebellion, expression of, 112, 115, 116n, 259–260
"Rebellion," high school, 56, 77, 203
"Reciprocity," denial of, 7, 9
Recognition, social and academic, 51
Relationships, primary, in working class, 88, 89, 231
Religion, role in American society, 100–108, 246
Religious beliefs, of adolescents, 105; impact of, 103–104, 243–244
Religious participation, and socioeconomic status, 101–102, 108
Reproduction, and socioeconomic status, 94–96
Restrictions on children, 23; excessive, 9
Revised Beta Examination, 138
Revised Stanford Binet, 166
Rewards, and achievement motivation, 25, 33; expectation for performance, 16
Rivalry, 13
Rogers Test of Personality Adjustment, 139
Role segregation, conjugal, 88–89, 90, 91, 92, 231, 237–238, 239, 241
Rorschach schedule, 233
Rosenzweig Misanthropy Scale, 234
Rosenzweig Picture-Frustration Test, 20, 142
Roxbury Youth Project, 84

SRA Primary Mental Abilities Test, 210
School attendance, problems of, 26, 39, 138, 163–164; socioeconomic factors, 187–188; See also Drop outs
School buildings, and income levels, 43
School retention, 195–196
School system, compensating for lack of family orientation, 25; as grooming for labor force, 62–63
Schooling, importance of, attitudes to, 35–

Schooling (*continued*)
36, 39, 48 (table), 168, 171, 174–175; low-income versus high-income attitudes, 48 (table)
School(s), and discrimination against less privileged, 40; and family, as social systems, 163–164; motivation toward, class differences, 36; pattern of, 130; and political socialization, 115, 116; secondary, choice of, 51, 198; schedules, and income levels, 43; seen as necessary evil, 22; socializing role of, 155, 186–187; types of, and income level, 42–43
Segregation, effects on achievement, 32, 209–210
Self, ideal, development of, 29, 143–144; *See also* Self-image
Self-concept of ability, 47, 165
Self-control, development of, 18–19
Self-image, adolescent, 25, 29–30, 154; negative, 45; programs in support of, 61
Semantic Differential Test, 172
Sewell Socioeconomic Status Scale, 143
Sex, American infatuation with, 82; ignorance of lower-class women, 93; and working-class couples, 94
Sex differences, and achievement, 183–184; in occupational choice, 69–70, 227–228
Sex-role identification, 13, 14, 17
Sexual intercourse, and "going steady," 84; in marriage, 92
Sexual role of wife, 91
Sims Score Card for Determining Socio-Economic Status, 166, 201
Sixteen Personality Factor Test, 30, 143
Skill handicaps, 34–35
Social acceptability, and achievement, 46, 160
Social factors, and alcohol use, 129 (table)
Socialization, political, 113, 115, 116, 118, 251, 253–259
Socialization process, 4, 149, 169, 174, 186–187
Socioreligious groups, attitudes of, 103
Status, in adolescent social systems, and educational aspirations, 53, 192–193
Status symbols, 44, 202–203; and occupational choice, 67
"Stimulus deprivation," 140
Stratification, social, destination versus origin, 56; power of, 45, 230
Student government, attitudes on, and income status, 49 (table)
Students, employed, 73; high- and low-income, achievement of, 43–44; labor-management attitudes, 79, 80 (table); and responsibility, 47
Study of Values Test, 191
Suburban life, effect on working class, 243
Superego development, 19
Support, by mother, "undersupport" versus "oversupport," 6–7; middle-class and lower-class, 8

System Personality Factor Test, 18
Szondi Test, 152

Teacher Approval-Disapproval Scales, 175
Teachers, amount of experience and income level of school, 43; authority problems of, 162–163; career of, 162; education of, 142; middle-class orientation of, 40–41, 184; pay related to performance, 47, 48; and political socialization, 115; relations to pupils, 40–41, 45, 173, 175, 179–180, 184
Television viewing, 122; control of, 23, 136–137
Tension, marital, 87, 90, 232–237
Thematic Apperception Test, 153, 154
Toilet training, 7, 8, 160
Trial by jury, support of, 117–118
Trust, basic sense of, in child development, 6, 7, 8

Unemployment rate of drop outs, 74
Unit Scale of Attainment Battery, 170

Value orientations, 154
Values, class, and college pressure, 54; home-given, 58; of lower-class adolescents, 111, 112; middle-class, attitudes toward, 111, 112; parental, and educational motivation, 52; and socioeconomic status, 23, 25, 146–147; and television viewing, 136–137
Vineland Social Maturity Scale, 159
Voting, pattern of, 257

Warner's Index of Status Characteristics, 28, 128, 149, 184, 194, 237, 268
Warner's Occupational Scale, 159
Weaning, 7, 8
Welfare families, relationships in, 86; and school drop outs, 138
Weltanschauungen, diverse, and school behavior, 36
Wife, working-class, 10, 22, 153; attitude to school, 22; autonomy in household management, 88; and husband's social life, 86–87; labor-force participation, 96–99
Work, 62–81, 221
Work experience, early, 72–78
Workers, blue-collar, 85, 88, 91, 233–234; white-collar, and high-school graduation, 75
Working-class youth, drop outs and jobs, 223; and completion of college, 72, 189–190

Youth, church attendance of, 104 (table); and political and legal agencies, 109–119, 250–251; and political movements, 115; *See also* Adolescence; Adolescents
Youth culture, adolescent, 27, 82–83, 242